T0284849

The Ultimate Guide to Responsible Franchising

JOE MATHEWS

The Ultimate Guide to Responsible Franchising

IDENTIFYING AND INVESTIGATING
THE RIGHT FRANCHISE TO
MAXIMIZE YOUR REWARDS
AND MINIMIZE RISK

WILEY

Published by John Wiley & Sons, Inc., Hoboken, New Jersey.
Published simultaneously in Canada.

For general information on our other products and services or for technical support, please contact our Customer Care Department within the United States at (800) 762-2974, outside the United States at (317) 572-3993 or fax (317) 572-4002.

Wiley also publishes its books in a variety of electronic formats. Some content that appears in print may not be available in electronic formats. For more information about Wiley products, visit our web site at www.wiley.com.

Library of Congress Cataloging-in-Publication Data

Names: Mathews, Joe, author.
Title: The ultimate guide to franchising : identifying and investigating the right franchise to maximize rewards and minimize risk / by Joe Mathews.
Description: Hoboken, New Jersey : Wiley, [2024] | Includes index.
Identifiers: LCCN 2024021305 (print) | LCCN 2024021306 (ebook) | ISBN 9781394243266 (hardback) | ISBN 9781394243280 (adobe pdf) | ISBN 9781394243273 (epub)
Subjects: LCSH: Franchises (Retail trade) | Sale of business enterprises.
Classification: LCC HF5429.23 .M39 2024 (print) | LCC HF5429.23 (ebook) | DDC 658.8/708—dc23/eng/20240613
LC record available at https://lccn.loc.gov/2024021305
LC ebook record available at https://lccn.loc.gov/2024021306

Cover Design: Wiley
Cover Image: © Designer's Circle/Adobe Stock
Author Photo: Courtesy of the Author

I would like to dedicate this book to my family and friends:

My wife, Tara (Merchant) Mathews, whom I met through franchising.

My sons, Michael and Casey Mathews, and my daughter, Taylor (Mathews) Hernandez, and her husband, Obed Hernandez, who are both career franchising professionals. A franchise candidate whom my daughter was recruiting for a franchisor once asked her if she knew a certain franchising book. Grimacing, she said, "The author is my dad." I got to be "the cool dad" for one day. By publishing this work, I hope to have a few more "cool dad" experiences.

My grandchild, Margaret, whom I hope will be the third generation of Mathewses who found franchising and entrepreneurship to be their calling.

My brothers, Paul, Ken, Jamie, and Danny, who all rose above their circumstances and made a difference with their lives and careers.

My best friends, Paul Rawlinitis, Paul Moore, Ki Chon, Mark McGuire, Charlie Rogoff, and Kwok Wong, who befriended me in college and stayed loyal friends my entire life.

And finally, my parents, Jim and Carol Mathews. My mom always thought I should have worked for the phone company because they have great benefits. But they let me be me and figure it out on my own. This book is the latest chapter in my never-ending process of figuring it out.

Most importantly, I dedicate this book to you all. I had you in mind every time I sat at my computer. Helping people like you find a satisfying and profitable business has brought me joy and a sense of purpose. Entrepreneurs are a different breed of animal. You are job creators. You are difference makers in your community. As a Christian, I believe that when Jesus decided to transform his world, he recruited, trained, and developed 12 entrepreneurs and then set them loose on the world.

Contents

Preface

I have spent an entire lifetime in franchising. My first job out of college was a rank-and-file, low-man-on-the-totem-pole franchisee recruitment manager in 1985 for a small Regional sandwich chain we now all know as Subway. Over the next few years, I witnessed Subway grow from a Regional brand to a National brand sporting a household name. For the next 17 years I moved up through the ranks, working for different brands and eventually making it into the franchisor C-suite. In 2002 I left the corporate world to start a consultancy I still manage called Franchise Performance Group (FPG), specializing in franchising best practices, particularly helping franchisors build their brand by recruiting top franchisee talent.

Prior to my starting a business, there was little entrepreneurship in my family. I grew up in the lower-middle-class town of West Haven, Connecticut, in a highly ethnic Irish and Italian, largely blue-collar neighborhood. My dad was one of the few college-educated men in our neighborhood, and the first college-educated man in the Mathews family. I am the second oldest of five boys, raised in a close-knit tribe consisting of my immediate family and my grandparents, who lived only two miles away. This certainly would go on to influence my future, because when properly executed, franchising is more than a business relationship – it's also a close-knit tribe.

My mom and dad have been married almost 65 years. My mom was a stay-at-home mom, managing the seven of us in our small three-bedroom, one-bath home. I shared a tiny bedroom with two other brothers, where I learned how to share and get along, and to pick and choose my battles. In franchising you need these skills because you share a brand and limited resources with a larger community, requiring constant collaboration and compromise.

When I was eight, my mom took me aside and said, "Joey, I want you to know we have enough. You will always have food and clothes and a roof over your head. But if you want more than that, you have to go out and earn it." Two weeks later, I secured an early-morning daily paper route. I made about $8 a week; I spent $3 and banked $5. I learned hard work and the value of a dollar, and lived with no entitlement. This taught me the way of the entrepreneur, meaning you have to learn how to make your way in this world with cunning, hustle, and skillful allocation of scarce resources.

My dad is a staunch Catholic who taught my brothers and me transcendent moral guiding principles, which I still believe to be true and have adopted as my own code of business conduct. For instance, I believe it is wrong to steal, not because society norms or laws of the land declare it so, but because those truths existed before society existed. This is important because I hold franchisors to a higher standard of conduct than what is stated in the franchise agreement. My experience tells me that franchising, when done right, takes the form of an immaterial social contract, not a material legal contract. When a franchisor takes the hard-earned money and custodianship of an entrepreneur's goals and dreams, they assume the responsibility of the high calling to do what it takes and within reason to transform those goals and dreams into actuality. This responsibility cannot be housed or articulated in a franchise agreement any more than a soldier can articulate in a contract his responsibility to guard the life of the soldier next to him in the foxhole. I've come to the conclusion that for the brand and franchisees to thrive and fulfill the promise and potential of the brand, the franchisor and franchisees have to think and act outside a command-and-control or legal compliance mentality and adopt a "we are in this together" viewpoint. (I describe this in more detail throughout this book.) For a franchisor that means checking your ego at the door. The franchisor exists to serve the franchisee, not the other way around. And for the franchisee it means losing your entitlement. Like any entrepreneur, if you want success and freedom, you earn it on the street.

Fast-forwarding now to my dysfunctional and failed social experiment described as "my high school experience," I developed a skill and passion for fine art. In the few pictures of me taken for my high school yearbook, I'm found with long, shaggy '80s hair and a sketch pad. In 1981 I enrolled in the University of Connecticut fine arts program, hoping to pursue a career in graphic arts. Long story short, while I was a good high school artist, I wouldn't have cut it on Madison Avenue. In my junior year, I changed my major to marketing and learned business.

But I stuck with art long enough to learn that artists know art is more than a pursuit. It's a particular way of looking at the world, distinctly different from the paradigms of business. Regarding branding, I think the artists have it right. While my learned business paradigms helped me relate to entrepreneurs and executives, my artist mind helps me see things in business that other people miss. I will briefly describe it here. You will experience unique vantage points in my writing.

In my experience, businesspeople are almost always reductionists, meaning they try to reduce things down to individual and simpler components, such as processes, systems, and even business silos such as accounts receivable and social marketing.

Conversely, artists know that "the whole" is bigger and different than the total sum of the parts. In other words, you can't accurately describe the ceiling of the Sistine Chapel as the sum total of Michaelangelo's individual brushstrokes. The final artwork itself is bigger, grander, and more majestic than the added sum of the brushstrokes strokes and bigger than the artist himself. The Sistine Chapel lives on as its own entity, as its own brand. When franchising is done right, It is the same with a franchise brand. The brand is bigger than the founder, the franchisor, and the franchisees combined. The brand lives on as its own entity, like Harley-Davidson and Apple Computers, for customers to build unique experiences on their own terms. Franchisors who build meaningful, valuable brands possess a certain artistry and release the brand into the public domain to possess its own identity.

When artists begin the creative process, they start with a blank paper or canvas and an idea about what they want to see in the end. Artists are supposed to create something unique and different that they release into the world for others to experience and enjoy. Franchise brands operate seemingly differently, consciously or unconsciously. Franchisors are almost always replicators, not originators. For instance, franchisors didn't invent hamburgers, ice cream, pool cleaning, maid service, or the way to unclog drains. Franchisors get products and services to market better, faster, cheaper, and more conveniently than the competition. Franchisor founders almost always start with what already exists and seek to improve it, but they don't generally invent it. Why is that important? The net result is that the franchisor brand landscape has become littered with commoditized, copycat brands. They often lack personality, creativity, identity, and flair, and they struggle to add unique value and find their place in the market, which often ultimately translates into a bad investment for franchisees. We will show you how to spot them.

I lived 12 years in Nashville and befriended many career musicians and songwriters. When composing music, many said, "The music seemed to always exist. I heard it and recorded it, but I didn't create it." Musicians often have the experience of stewardship, not authorship. While they may own the legal rights to a particular song, the successful recording artist would often say the ownership model doesn't accurately describe their relationship to the song. Successful franchise brands operate the same way. The brand lives as its own thing or being, as a separate and distinct entity from the franchisor, founders, franchisees, customers, and suppliers.

Let's return to Harley-Davidson for a moment. What started as a motorcycle brand took on a life of its own with the help of its brand fan customers, creating a whole lifestyle category beyond what the founders originally intended. Along the same lines, I find it intriguing that corporate entities are legal persons. You'll also find that franchisors' brands are like people. But just what kind of people are they? Are they heroic? Dependable? Loyal? Or are they boring copycats, frauds, phonies, or thieves? Franchising has all of these, which we will help the reader distinguish throughout this work.

I'm proud that you've invested time, money, and energy in this body of work. I am committed to showing that the value you receive is worth the price of admission.

So let's begin.

Introduction

If you are reading this, presumably you are looking to achieve your definition of getting ahead. You may be looking for additional income streams as you approach retirement. Maybe you're looking for a highly profitable and scalable business in order to build your empire. Or your goals may be more modest and a simple family business might do. Regardless of your definition of success, I know what you need to know and do, and you will find it here.

If you are a first-time business owner, you will soon find that intense emotions often accompany thoughts about starting a business. Some people become pumped up, excited about the prospect of taking action and making positive changes. Others are simply paralyzed with fear, lost in ambiguity. This book was designed to meet you where you are and arm you with the tools to propel you forward, meaning helping you better identify opportunities and at the same time mitigating or eliminating risk.

According to volume 2 of the *Economic Impact of Franchised Businesses,* a recent study commissioned by the International Franchise Association and conducted by PricewaterhouseCoopers, there were over 900,000 franchisor and franchisee-owned outlets representing more than 80 different industries in the United States alone. According to the same study, US franchises generated nearly 11% of the entire US private sector economy.

Simply put, franchising works and people just like you are winning.

Note that this book is not an unbiased source of information. I am decidedly pro-franchising because most people who employ the knowledge in this book and follow the process I recommend for selecting and investigating a franchise succeed.

Although I am unashamedly pro-franchising, I am not an advocate for all franchisors equally. Like any universe of people or entities, there is a bell curve distribution of results. Franchise brands to the left of the bell curve are high risk and low return and need to be identified as such and avoided. Franchisors at the middle of the bell curve will survive and may do well as franchisors, but the franchisees of this brand will be bypassed by franchisors of brands to the right of the bell curve. This book will be a tool to help you identify and invest in franchisors that today are or tomorrow will be to the right of the bell curve.

Three Truths About Franchising

- **Self-employment simply is not for everyone.** Starting a business is a lonely and emotionally taxing undertaking, and it is not for the weak at heart. Unless you are already an entrepreneur, you will have two learning curves. The first will be learning to shift from being an employee to being an entrepreneur. Entrepreneurship is an identity shift, not a career shift. The second learning curve will be the business you invest in. If you have never owned a business before, you are about to enter a period of deep personal growth. The good news is that this growth moves in one direction. Once you are an entrepreneur, regardless of what happens next, you will never think and act like an employee again. Or as I like to say, "Once a pickle, never a cucumber again."

- **Regardless of whether you are a serial entrepreneur or first-time businessperson, not every franchise presents a good opportunity.** Franchising is like any other industry. You will spot genius, mediocrity, and incompetence. If you are a great entrepreneur who makes an unfortunate investment decision in a bad or mediocre brand, eventually your business will go in the direction of the brand. A franchisee can only defy gravity for so long before the business suffers.

- **Not every franchise is right for every person, regardless of how successful a particular brand is.** Just like some people are not wired to be accountants or salespeople, not everyone is wired for every franchise concept. Real success comes when you select a business that leverages your background and skills, compensates for shortcomings, mitigates some risks, and delivers your objectives with the highest degree of probability. That's a different set of variables for each reader. Secondarily, you pick a franchisor that is skilled at recruiting, training, developing, and leading a team of entrepreneurs such as yourself to dominate their local markets on the way to building a national brand. Franchising is hand-to-hand, market-to-market combat.

By reading this book and studying its contents, you will walk away with at least three positive outcomes (or more):

- If you have never owned a business before, you will know whether self-employment is right for you.
- You will learn the telltale signs of what genius, mediocrity, and incompetence looks like in franchising, giving yourself a better chance of achieving your definition of success.

- You will identify with a high degree of certainty which companies and opportunities do or do not deliver the life and rewards you want for yourself and your family.

Kissing a Lot of Frogs Before You Find Your Prince

Currently, there are somewhere between 4,000–7,000 existing franchise brands and about 250–350 new brands entering franchising each year. Not every franchise that looks like a good opportunity is. The reverse is also true. Not every business that looks like a bad opportunity is.

For instance, how would you like to own a business that has extremely high employee turnover, high overhead, high lease costs, high equipment costs, low margins, and high advertising costs? The average customer only spends a few dollars, so you are forced to do hundreds of transactions a day, just to keep the lights on. You have to move customers through your business with such feverish fury, you can't provide much in the way of customer service. As a matter of fact, extended customer interactions make the business model break down. You have got to keep your customers moving in and out, in and out. Speed is the key. Furthermore, your business is completely dependent on scores of minimum- or low-wage workers. Because employee turnover is so high, you are always on the lookout for minimum-wage workers and you are constantly understaffed. Other times, you will keep more people on the payroll than you really need because you know some people are going to quit. Would you ever want to own a business like that?

If you would be a "no" to owning this business, you just rejected McDonald's, Chick-fil-A, Domino's pizza, and just about every successful fast food and quick service restaurant chain in existence. While food service is not right for everyone, many food service brands have created multi-generational wealth and opportunities for its franchisees.

Every business has its share of challenges. When you invest in a competent brand, you invest in proven solutions to these everyday challenges.

How This Book Is Structured

This book is largely broken down into 12 chapters.

- The first nine chapters represent what thought leaders in franchising would like you to know before you start looking at individual brands. These must-read chapters offer you the backstory about franchising. This includes an overview of franchising. This content shows you how to identify and align your experience, skills, aptitudes, and capital to the owner's role in the business as a way to maximize rewards and minimize risk. In other words, it helps you shine a light on what you should be doing and should be avoiding because you are uniquely you. Read this part before you look at brands.

- The final chapters show you how to find and investigate individual brands. Although you may find the right industry for you, if you pick a weak brand, you eventually will be hamstrung by the limitations of the franchisor and brand. For instance, Subway is still the dominant player in the sub category. The franchisor graveyard is littered with hopeful number two sub shop players who cratered, like Blimpie and Quiznos, sinking their franchisees with them rather than helping them build multi-generational wealth. Consider reading this part twice – once before you look at a brand, and again while you are looking at brands.

Part 1

What You Need to Know Before You Look at Franchises

P art 1 contains advice that I would tell a friend if we were sitting on big leather chairs in front of a fireplace sipping coffee and they asked me, "Leaving nothing out, before I make any investment, what is it I need to know?"

I encourage you to read Part 1 and complete the recommended exercises before you begin contacting franchisors and potentially incurring risk.

Chapter 1

Introduction to Franchising

Before I get into what it takes to invest into individual brands, I want to establish some terminology and define some terms.

Definition of Terms

According to Dictionary.com, a *franchise* is "the right or license granted by a company to an individual or group to market its products or services in a specific territory."

I find this definition insufficient to the point of being laugh-out-loud funny.

True, a franchise is a legal contract, but when a franchisor is skilled, it takes more the shape of an intangible social contract than a tangible legal contract. The social contract is simple. Franchisees agree to execute the business model to the best of their ability, to build the brand locally consistent with the intention of brand leadership, and to add more value to products and services than it charges customers in price. The franchisor agrees to continually refine processes and systems and go to work each day to add more value to the franchisees' business than it extracts in royalties.

Put it another way, the social contract says, "We each have roles and responsibilities that impact each other. We are in this together and the common bond is building value in the brand." Within this social contract, there is no assumed hierarchy, no parent company that lords over the lesser-than, childlike, dependent franchisees.

Franchisees and the franchisor only pull out the legal contract when this social contract breaks down.

Because the textbook definition of "franchise" describes what the relationship looks like when the franchisor relationship is failing, I want to take the time to create more intelligent and workable definitions.

- From this point forward, I use the terms *franchise* and *franchise system* to describe the legal and social contract binding all stakeholders of the brand, its franchisees, supply chain, and franchisor's executives and employees.

- I use the term *franchise agreement* when I refer to the actual license. I use the term *franchising industry* to describe the estimated almost $800 billion ecosystem of franchisors, franchisees, suppliers, and other stakeholders, such as the IFA.

- The Franchise Performance Group (FPG) defines *franchising* as a brand expansion strategy entailing recruiting, training, developing, resourcing, and leading a team of successful entrepreneurs in order to build a brand.

- FPG defines the *franchisee-franchisor relationship* as the totality of the contractual, commercial, and interpersonal relationships between the franchisor and franchisees.

- FPG defines *franchisor* as the company that licenses a business system and trademarks to a franchisee and the *franchisee* as the licensee of the same.

- FPG describes *the brand* as the meaning and value customers assign to a particular business. In other words, it's everything that customers, franchisees, franchisors, and suppliers perceive about a business – what the business represents, the service it offers, and the value customers receive by patronizing the business.

Franchising Is a Business unto Itself

Throughout this book, I repeat this again and again. Franchisors are in two businesses, and they need to be brilliant at both to succeed.

- **The consumer-facing model:** The brand competes in the industry in which it distributes its products and services. This is how well the brand sells its products and services to the marketplace.

- **The business of franchising:** I define the business of franchising as "recruiting, training, developing, resourcing, and leading a team of entrepreneurs to successfully build a brand." Notice the product or service is not mentioned in the business of franchising. The business of franchising is about delivering effective training, coaching, and expertise of the consumer-facing model to new franchisees who presumably are new to the industry and business model.

I briefly describe these two businesses and continue to develop these important themes throughout the book.

The Customer-Facing Model

For simplicity, I call the end user "the customer," whether the business is business-to-business or business-to-consumer. Virtually every brand is faced with stiff competition within their respective industries. This appears self-evident. However, what does it mean to compete effectively?

A brilliant franchisor will have built a consumer-facing business model, which on balance should receive high marks on all the following criteria:

- **Their consumer offer is unique** (or copycats will crowd the market and drive down revenues and margins).

5

- **The business model is profitable** (delivering acceptable returns for franchisees).

- **Their offer is defensible** (so franchisees can carve out and defend a position in their marketplace and distance themselves from copycat concepts).

- **Their business is resilient** (so franchisees can weather any coming economic storms).

- **The business is replicable and scalable** (so an average franchisee will predictably earn an acceptable return on their time, money, and energy, regardless of whether they are opening in existing markets or pioneering a new market).

- **The business offers long-term sustainability** (so once the brand is built, the business creates a flywheel that generates predictable and recurring income for franchisees).

The following sections look at each of these points in more detail.

The Consumer Offer Is Unique

Businesses that offer commoditized products and services will ultimately engage in a war of convenience and price. If the customer can't distinguish one brand's offer from the next, then ultimately business will be won by which brand offers the lowest price, is nearest to the customer, or can get to the customer the fastest. The market becomes a war of price and convenience and franchisees struggle to remain profitable.

As a franchisee, you never want a business involved in a price war. Years ago, Subway offered $5 subs. The brand essentially trained the customer to spend no more than $5 on their product. As proteins, commodities, and labor costs increased, franchisees had a brutal time trying to pass these costs to their customers, who wanted $5 subs. Margins shrank. Franchisees became less profitable. The goals of the franchisor – who makes their money on the top line revenue and not on the bottom line cash flow – were not aligned with their franchisees, and thus were slow to respond. Franchisee dissatisfaction soared. Many franchisees started diversifying into other food concepts rather than reinvesting into opening more Subways, to the detriment of the brand.

The Consumer Model Is Profitable

A small business exists for the mutual benefit of the customer and the business owner. Whether the franchisee is an owner-operator or runs an empire, the business needs to consistently hit their financial objectives or it's a bad investment. The franchisor does not get to say what is or isn't a good investment any more than the business owner gets to tell a customer what they should value. The franchisee alone determines what is and isn't an acceptable return on time, money, and energy.

The Offer Is Defensible

One of my favorite brands is Sandler, a business training franchise operating inside a nearly $80-billion industry where more than 60% of businesses outsource their training. While their franchise agreement is only five years, many franchisees have a 15–20 year tenure, meaning they keep renewing their agreements and doing business with the brand. Franchisees love what they do. Since the brand markets sales knowledge and experience as its core product, think about the brand's competitive advantage of sustaining a team of highly skilled and experienced Sandler sales zealots around the country.

Sandler, at the time of this writing, is one of the nation's leaders in sales training, with systemwide sales reported to be about $150 million. No brand operating in the training space appears to have more than 1% market share, so it's a dominant brand in a fragmented industry, giving franchisees a real competitive advantage over independents in the same space.

Other than Dale Carnegie, Miller Heiman, and a few other brands, Sandler franchisees compete against a cottage industry of motivational speakers and success coaches who may have personality but often lack valuable intellectual property and sales systems to impart to their clients.

Why do I like dominant brands in a fragmented market? Simple. When a new Sandler franchisee opens in a new market, what competitor can keep the franchisee out? What competitor can make it rough for the franchisee to acquire new business?

The Business Is Resilient

The business is not subject to dramatic market fluctuations, or the model is adaptable. Take hair care, for instance. Stylist.com once published a study that showed the average woman spends $50,000 coloring her hair during her lifetime. Whether the stock market is up or down or interest rates are high or low, whether it's raining or snowing, a universal truth remains. Many women don't want gray hair.

The Business Offers Long-Term Sustainability

Years ago, the market exploded with self-serve yogurt chains. Many of the emerging brands bought their product from the exact same dairy, meaning they were selling the exact same product as the brand directly across the street from them.

Brands like Yogurtland tried to capitalize by tying their brand to the product. The net effect is that the brand remains relevant only if the product remains in demand. For instance, can Yogurtland credibly sell ice cream or Italian ice? Ultimately, the brand becomes directly tied to the product lifecycle. As demand for the category decreases, so does brand relevance and franchisees' profitability. It's often a bad idea to buy a brand completely tied to a product, because the product may turn out to be a short-term fad.

For many years, I was intimately involved with the market leader in frozen yogurt called Menchie's. Menchie's sold self-serve frozen yogurt, but the brand was built around a customer experience with the long game of building a National frozen dessert brand, not a frozen yogurt brand or any other particular product. While frozen products come and go, customers seemingly will always go out to eat frozen dessert in some fashion. Menchie's CEO promised all new franchisees that Menchie's would ride the wave of frozen yogurt demand to build a National frozen dessert brand and to build National distribution. As customer preferences shift, Menchie's would pivot and add and delete products to and from their menu, keeping the brand forever relevant in the frozen dessert marketplace.

The strategy was the right one. Smart franchisees flocked into the brand by the hundreds, and Menchie's became a rocket ship of over 500 stores.

As demand for frozen yogurt cooled (pardon the pun), the CEO froze (pardon more puns), never fulfilling his promise to diversify the menu. As a result, sales suffered. The CEO stayed on his collision course with failure, despite all evidence the ship was sinking. Many stores closed. Menchie's killed the golden goose and franchisees suffered. As I was intimately involved with the brand, Menchie's remains one of my biggest career disappointments. I could not impact the poor decision-making of the CEO.

Menchie's original strategy appeared bulletproof. They executed well during their emerging growth stage. If I knew then what I know now, I would have spotted that the CEO was *never* going to navigate change, which ultimately would have cratered the brand. A franchisee can outperform a brand for only so long before the poor performance of the brand creates a ceiling. While much has been written about how to find the right business for you, in my opinion not enough has been written about how to spot a poor franchisor or a self-sabotaging leader, especially when they are flying high and there appears to be evidence to the contrary.

The industry of franchising has never done for the franchisor what successful franchisors do for the franchisee, which is to define, document, train, and support on a proven franchisor model. *There is no documented franchisor model in existence.* There is no manual, no book, no integrated business format in existence to show a franchisor how to go from one unit to a National brand of 1,000 units or more. Every franchisor has to create their own franchisor model through trial and error. That's why I specifically call out franchising as a business unto itself and present it as a potential limiting factor to would-be franchisees.

The Business of Responsible Franchising

Earlier I defined franchising as "recruiting, training, developing, resourcing, and leading a team of entrepreneurs to successfully build a brand." Let's look at each of these tasks individually.

Franchisee Recruitment

Franchising has largely embraced recruiting of entrepreneurs into the brand as a sales function. Many if not most franchisors consider you a "lead," and if you go further as a "prospect" they will discuss your "hot buttons" (reasons for buying). I see it as talent acquisition. My company (FPG) has mystery-shopped and trained hundreds of franchisee recruiters working for many brands you would recognize. Over the last 20 years of mystery, we have *never* been effectively interviewed by a brand. Most brands fail at knowing what the qualifications are on the franchisees they onboard, which adds substantial risk to your investment. An officer of the company would typically put a prospective administrative assistant hire through a more intensive interview process than they put franchisees through.

Training

Franchisors are in the business of imparting knowledge and skills of a new business to someone presumably from the outside of that business or industry as quickly as humanly possible. In other words, they must be adult education experts. As you research a brand, see if the people overseeing training have a corporate training and curriculum development background or whether they simply promote a manager or family member into a role they aren't qualified for.

Developing

Training is not a one- or two-week event, although that's how many franchisors treat the learning process. I have two brothers who were educators, so I know that educators have a saying: "I haven't taught until they've learned." In Malcolm Gladwell's book *Outliers*, he describes the 10,000-hour rule, meaning it takes 10,000 hours (approximately five years) to master something. While I have no research other than my nearly 40 years of observation, my experience does mirror Gladwell's research. With many business models, it takes two to three years to reach competency and five years to achieve mastery. Many franchisor training programs are one to two weeks, and ongoing support means "call me when something breaks or you have a question."

Sandler is a franchisor of selling sales training and coaching services, and are adult education experts. They apply the same level of care to a franchisees' training and development as franchisees do to their clients. That's why they have been successful for 50 years and their average franchisee has renewed their franchise agreement twice.

Resourcing

A man once said, "A man is only as good as his tools." Similarly, franchisees are only as good as their tools, processes, and systems. Too often, franchisors confuse processes and systems with "helpful suggestions" and "opinions." Their systems are not fully planned out and integrated into a business unit. We frequently see this with local marketing programs. Often, their operations and marketing manuals look like menus at a New Jersey diner, meaning pages and pages of options, but fewer hard and fast systems.

Leading a Team of Entrepreneurs

Franchisors often confuse command and control techniques and compliance cultures with leadership. Too many franchisors rely on authority, meaning franchisees have to follow rather than lead, meaning they choose to follow. Too often franchisors believe it's "my brand, my customers, my systems, and my territory," thus putting franchisees in a subservient position, akin to a sharecropper. Later in this book, I show you how to spot a servant leadership culture designed to empower franchisees and lead other leaders, which works well in franchising.

The Brand as One Body

Oddly enough, perhaps the best definition of franchising was written 2,000 years ago by the Apostle Paul of Tarsus. As you read this, think of a franchise as one body consisting of several members: the franchisor (the parent company), the franchisees (business owners), and the suppliers and customers.

> The body does not consist of one member but of many.
> If the foot would say, "Because I am not a hand, I do not belong to the body, that would not make it any less a part

of the body." And if the ear would say, "Because I am not an eye, I do not belong to the body," that would not make it any less a part of the body. If the whole body were an eye, where would the hearing be? If the whole body were hearing, where would the sense of smell be? . . . If all were a single member, where would the body be? As it is, there are many members, yet one body. The eye cannot say to the hand, "I have no need of you," nor again the head to the feet, "I have no need of you." On the contrary, the members of the body that seem to be weaker are indispensable. . . . But God has so arranged the body, giving the greater honor to the inferior member, that there may be no dissension within the body, but the members may have the same care for one another. If one member suffers, all suffer together with it; if one member is honored, all rejoice together with it.

While many franchisors may embrace this definition, not all do. The founder and CEO of a successful national franchisor recently spoke at a national convention for franchise executives. During his presentation, a member of the audience asked, "How do you resolve conflicts with your franchisees?"

He proudly threw his shoulders back and chest out and proclaimed, "When push comes to shove, the franchisees know this is my company!"

This CEO was a type A, confrontational personality. He had little awareness that his approach to franchising actually causes the pushing and shoving he spoke of. In these tough economic times, franchisees and franchisors need to fight the competition for market share, not each other for power and control.

The Business of Franchising: The Bottom Line

A franchise agreement does not define franchising any more than a marriage certificate defines marriage. A franchisor or franchisee feels compelled to pull out their franchise agreement only when trust breaks down. Franchising only works when both franchisees and franchisors share a deep concern about the other's interests. Franchising is as much about committed interpersonal relationships as it is business systems.

I believe the business of franchising is a two-metric business:

- The strength of unit-level economics and consistency of franchisee profitability
- The quality and trust level of the franchisee-franchisor relationship

These themes are fully described later in this book.

Why Do Companies Franchise?

There are several reasons why companies choose to franchise. This section discusses them at length.

Franchisors Taking the High Road

Responsible franchisors who take the high road possess multiple options to expand their business. They had a proven business model that produced great results, including replicating their success in other markets. Possible expansion strategies included bringing in investors, raising capital, and expanding through the chain method (where the parent company would own all the individual distribution points) or restructuring their companies and expanding it through franchising.

They chose franchising because franchising could provide them with advantages that the chain method could not.

The first competitive advantage that franchising can offer companies is stronger tactical execution of their business model by having highly skilled and motivated entrepreneurs run point on the implementation rather than perhaps less skilled, less invested company managers. An entrepreneur with their dreams and money at stake will usually try harder and therefore produce greater results than an employee with a bonus and job security at stake.

Second, franchising is a financing vehicle. Rather than having to raise millions of dollars to expand their business, franchisors leverage the franchisees' ability to raise their own capital through the SBA (Small Business Administration), home equity, ROBS (401K rollover), family, and other sources.

Third, a franchise is typically better positioned to grow more quickly than a company that chooses the chain method of expansion. It's been said, "Timing is everything." Good businesspeople know that when a market opportunity presents itself, it must be seized. Franchising offers a brand greater speed to market, which is important if the brand stands the risk of losing a beachhead to local or regional competitors starting copycat concepts.

Fourth, franchising can be lower risk for the brand. Franchisors earn fees (royalties) that are paid by the franchisees typically from gross sales, not cash flow. Additionally, the startup capital of the new business is the franchisees' risk, not the franchisor's. Although the franchisees assume much of the financial risk, the franchisor is dependent on the continuing royalty stream paid in by franchisees. Additionally, franchisors will not grow if the franchisees are not making money and achieving great results. Therefore franchisors have a vested interest in helping the franchisees become profitable, but they don't take the hit if they fail. The franchisor's revenue stream is diversified by collecting royalties off the top line of many franchisees rather than the bottom line of fewer controlled investments.

Fifth, they want to share their successes and make a difference in the lives of others. Most franchisors are deeply committed people who love to see their teammates win.

Lastly, franchisees have a collective genius that is hard to replicate in a chain method. For instance, a McDonald's franchisee thought of the Big Mac. Co-founder of Jiffy Lube and current president of Babson Business School Stephen Spinelli talked about how a franchisee solved a major problem for Jiffy Lube, which at the time was inventing the fast oil lube category. Labor cost fluctuated all over the place, depending largely on how easy it was for the technicians to remove the existing oil filter. Some filters were screwed on too tight from previous auto service providers, making it very difficult to remove, driving labor costs up and destroying margins. When examining labor cost, one franchisee seemed to show more predictable and acceptable labor costs than other franchisees experienced. Jiffy Lube support visited his location. They found he had invented a wrench with a canvas strap that the technicians would slide over the auto filter and pop it right out, regardless of how it was previously installed. The wrench was patented and distributed to all the other franchisees and added to the required equipment list for all new franchisees. Without the strap wrench, Jiffy Lube might never have gotten to the size and scale it is today.

The Low Road to Franchising

Many unethical and irresponsible franchisors get into franchising because some consultant or attorney in a blue pinstriped suit and a snappy red power tie told them that they could get rich using other people's money. And for only $150,000 to $250,000 they will show them how!

You can spot a "low road" franchisor by the following indicators:

- They are undercapitalized. Their financial survival of their company is completely dependent on the short-term revenue from selling franchises instead of long-term revenue from collecting royalties. There appears to be no other source of expansion capital available. They have to sell you a franchise to survive.
- They have not been in business more than five years or do not have a proven business model. They expect you to invest your money for the privilege of proving their business model for them.
- They have never expanded in multiple units and therefore have not proven they can replicate their success. They are expecting you to jump at the opportunity to let them experiment with your money while their cash sits in their bank – assuming they have cash at all.
- Their unit economics do not provide them with a healthy enough return to expand by investing their own money. Yet somehow they believe it is good enough for you.
- They don't interview you for the franchise to determine the fit as they would if they were making a key management hire. They sell franchises as if they were selling a car or vinyl siding.
- They are hyper-focused on selling franchises rather than making franchisees profitable, with the intention of selling to private equity and securing plum speaking slots at franchising conferences and events.

One time the founder of a fitness franchisor was looking for assistance in recruiting franchisees. When I reviewed the franchisor's financial statement, it showed the franchisor had a corporate worth of $25 – no kidding, 25 bucks! I have lost more money in my sofa cushions than the franchisor had in their whole company. Surprised, I asked, "Does this financial statement accurately reflect your financial position or do you franchise under a shell corporation?" Keep in mind, many franchisors are private companies, and as such their attorneys and accountants advise them not to keep large assets in their corporations. That is why many franchisors are actually stronger financially than they appear on paper.

However, this man responded, "That is all I have." Sadly, I rejected this good man because he was already out of business. He was not in a financial position to be able to support franchisees and grow his company.

This franchisor only had 25 bucks because some consultant clipped him for all he had to set him up as a franchisor. The founder had the noble intention of curbing the out-of-control obesity rate in America and promoting active and healthy lifestyles. This did not happen. Saint Bernard of Clairvaux once said, "The road to hell is paved with good intentions."

Many franchise consultants and attorneys are respectable people and good at what they do. Just as there are a small number of franchisors who prey on the dreams and best intentions of gullible prospective franchisees, there are a small number of consultants and attorneys who prey on the dreams and best intentions of prospective franchisors. Both predators are a stain on franchising.

Spotting a Responsible High-Road Franchisor

Ask a franchisor what business they are in. While every franchisor distributes its own brand of products and services, as I said, the franchise business model is a business unto itself.

My first job in franchising was in 1985 when I joined Subway. At that time they had fewer than 400 restaurants and were open in about 20 or so states and had no international units. Subway is in the business of selling sandwiches. However, didn't thousands of restaurants, diners, and delis across the United States also make sandwiches a staple item on their menus? Think about it. Any of these restaurants could have been "Subway." The difference was that Subway founder Fred Deluca saw sub sandwiches as an opportunity to build an international brand and change the way the world eats. Others simply saw sandwiches as meat between two slices of bread.

As you investigate franchises, you will find that brilliant business models are a dime a dozen. However, brilliant franchisors are few. It takes a brilliant franchisor to build a strong regional or national brand.

If you were to ask CEOs of franchise companies, "What business are you in?" you'd probably hear about the products and services they distribute, such as "I'm in the auto repair business" or "I'm in the business of home furnishings." You'll seldom hear, "I'm in the franchising business."

Before investing your savings in a franchise, you may want to make sure you're doing business with a franchisor who knows they are in the business of recruiting, training, developing, resourcing, and leading a team of entrepreneurs to build a brand. Most people investigating franchises examine the franchisor's effectiveness in distributing their products and services, but few people look to determine whether the franchisor is skilled in the business of franchising, and wind up licking their wounds later.

How Franchisors Make Money

A typical franchisor makes money two or three different ways:

- **Franchise fee revenues.** The franchisor charges franchisees upfront fees typically ranging from $35,000 to $50,000. This is not a big moneymaker to most franchisors. For the vast majority of franchisors, this fee doesn't cover, or barely covers, the cost of running their internal franchise sales departments. In other words, awarding you a franchise is often a break-even proposition for the franchisor. By the time you write the franchisor a check for your franchise fee, chances are they have already spent that money in advertising and departmental costs trying to find you. Franchise fee revenue is nonrecurring revenue, meaning the brand only realizes this revenue once, where royalties are recurring. The enterprise value of any franchisor is tied to the predictability of their recurring royalty streams. This means franchisees must be successful so they keep paying royalties, which creates some financial alignment. Be wary of franchisors that take big upfront fees (over $50,000), but do not produce the results or provide services to justify this investment.

- **Royalties.** Franchisees pay franchisors a percentage of their gross revenue typically ranging from 5 to 8%. Fees could be higher, but higher fees should reflect more services. Express Personnel, for instance, charges higher fees; however, they manage the entire backroom payroll operation for their franchisees. So a portion of these royalties minimize your risk, simplify your operations, and reduce your labor cost. On the other hand, some franchisors make more of their money selling inventory and proprietary products to franchisees and less on royalties. This is common in the frozen dessert category and franchises with patents and proprietary products like Chem-Dry Carpet Cleaning. Continuing fees, such as royalties or product purchases, are the lifeblood of a franchisor's business. Brilliant franchisors are in the business of maximizing continuing fees, *while at the same time maximizing franchisee results*. To maximize revenue from continuing fees, they must first be brilliant at developing peak-performing franchisees. This means they win big when you win big.

- **Products.** As I touched on, some franchisors are also vendors, selling proprietary products and services to their franchisees at a profit. Companies like Ben and Jerry's have exclusive vendor relationships with their franchisees. Having a franchisor who is also an exclusive vendor is not necessarily a bad thing, but it can be. Once, co-founder Ben Cohen did a national tour called the "Pants on Fire Tour" where he traveled the country accusing then President George W. Bush of being a liar. I would not have wanted to be a franchisee operating in the same city as one of his tour stops when he was indulging in political controversy.

- **Miscellaneous fees, such as technology fees and marketing fees.** These fees can either deliver high value such as creating media co-ops and purchasing advertising no one franchisee could afford on their own, or these can create operational burdens. One national convenience store chain once required all franchisees to implement a broken POS system that was proven to lose customer transactions to pad the president's resume so she could get promoted to another division. Franchisees were forced to comply, and customers received free gas as a result.

Out of these revenue streams, royalties and (for those franchisors who are also vendors) product sales should be most important to the franchisor. Again, be wary of franchisors whose financial statements show they need the upfront franchise fee revenue to survive. They will be tempted and probably will succumb to the financial pressure of awarding franchises to marginal candidates who have a higher probability of failure. Franchisors whose franchisees fail will probably not survive as franchisors. A franchisee failure is a black mark against the brand for customers, suppliers, and other surviving franchisees.

The Only Way for Franchisors to Maximize Recurring Revenue

If a franchisor is truly in the business of maximizing royalty and product sales revenue, how will they accomplish this? Who are they counting on? Don't peak-performing franchisees sell the most products and services to their customers, and therefore pay the highest royalties and purchase the most products from the franchisor? Don't peak-performing franchisees do a better job at making money for themselves, creating job satisfaction for themselves and their employees, and taking care of their customer needs? For these franchisors to be successful, doesn't it mean they must dedicate themselves to driving your competency and productivity? Can you see the potential for a win/win? However, don't assume because franchising works best as win/win, that franchisor executives in authority are always operating from there or have the skills and experience to deliver.

Irresponsible Franchising: A Failed Philosophy

Once, I huddled with a bunch of veteran franchisee recruiters to talk about franchising. A vice president of franchise sales from a large national automotive franchisor shared his views.

He boldly proclaimed, "It is not my job to qualify any franchise candidate looking to invest in my brand. I will give anyone their God-given right to fail." This person thought it was his responsibility to take money from anyone with the financial capital and interest in opening a business, regardless of their background, skills, and aptitudes. He absolved himself of all personal responsibility for how well the franchisees he recruited performed; instead he believed it was God's job to sort it out. This is a violation of the sacred trust that is franchising.

Later in the conversation he was whining about not being able to find a competent administrative assistant. I asked him why he didn't just grab the first person off the street and give them their God-given right to fail. He didn't think it was funny, but I had a good laugh at his expense.

You may be surprised to learn how many franchisors award franchises to franchise candidates whom they wouldn't hire to manage the same business. And in tough economic times, sometimes franchisors need the money from the upfront franchise fee to sustain their operations and make payroll and will deal with what they call "operational problems" later. Keep in mind that "operational problems" is franchisor-speak for failing or underperforming franchisees.

Ultimately, if your investment as a franchisee is going to pay out, you must successfully accomplish two things:

- **Find the right franchise** for you that best utilizes your skills, capital, and experience and helps you actualize your potential and delivers the results you are looking for.
- **Find a successful franchisor** who possesses the capital, vision, commitment, culture, and talent to build a meaningful, sustainable brand that customers and suppliers believe delivers high value.

Finding a Responsible Franchisor Who Gets It

You should get a good indication of whether a franchisor has your best interests in mind by the quality of their franchise opportunity website and the quality of your interactions with the brand's franchisee recruiter.

- Their franchise opportunity website has enough transparent information to help you understand what the business is, what the brand stands for, what it takes to win, what the financial commitment is, what average returns look like, and the work history of those running the show. The information isn't riddled with unsubstantiated claims like "Other brands can't compete with us" or "We are the best in our industry," with no data to support these self-serving accolades.

- Franchisee recruiters possess a clear understanding of the individual traits, background, and capital franchise that candidates must have to succeed in their business model. They conduct a thorough interview with you to determine how closely you fit their profile of a successful franchisee. They educate you online and/or through conversations about what you need to be prepared to do each day to succeed as a franchisee. The recruiter doesn't sell the opportunity. They interview, qualify, and educate you. You should not be faced with high-pressure sales techniques or with wondering if the recruiter is someone you can trust.

- Recruiters work with you to follow a clear, step-by-step franchisee investigation process. Both you and the franchisor know where you are in the process and what additional steps need to be taken. If they don't have a clear step-by-step recruitment process, they probably don't have a clear, well-thought-out, easy-to-follow business model either. Dismiss them as an option.

- When you ask franchisees, "Knowing what you know now, would you make the same investment decision again?" more than 80% of franchisees should answer a definitive "yes." Otherwise, my research shows this company will soon be a turnaround brand, which is not where you want to put your time and money.

Chapter 2

Special Advice for the First-Time Entrepreneur

According to a fact sheet from September 21, 2023, on the Center for American Progress website, a Current Population Survey reports that only about 16 million Americans, or 10% of the working population, are currently self-employed, and another 10 million have side hustles, meaning they filed some form of self-employment income or loss on their taxes while at the same time reporting they had jobs (www.americanprogress.org/article/understanding-the-self-employed-in-the-united-states/).

In any given year over multiple surveys, anywhere from 40 to 60% of Americans or more hope to start a business someday. But the data shows that someday never comes. Franchisors report that out of 100 people who directly request franchise information about their brands, 1% or less move forward.

The Path of the 99%

Purely statistically speaking (and nothing personal intended), you will not make an investment in a franchise either. Yes, you will engage in the typical complaints of corporate America, such as "I'm tired of placing my future in the hands of others," or "I do all the work and shareholders make all the money."

You will Google different franchise opportunities, visit franchisor homepages, print out stacks of information, perhaps talk to people and professionals you trust about their opinions of certain brands or industries, and even engage in conversations with franchisors. At the time you are researching, you will feel empowered. You'll tell your friends you're considering buying a business. Chances are they thought about it too. Some will be happy for you, some will be jealous, and some will be afraid for you. Virtually everyone will share their opinions with you. You'll dream about what it would be like to be your own boss. You'll think about your customers and employees. You will make clever little charts such as Benjamin Franklin's t-chart, where you neatly list all the "Pros" on the left side of the page, balanced by the "Cons" on the right side. Then the time will come to make a decision. To you it may look like a rational decision. But this decision will often be clouded in fear, doubt, negative self-chatter, and head trash. Eventually, you probably will make a fear-and-doubt "No" decision, backed by the logic of your neatly listed "Cons."

"The business has fatal flaws," you think. "Employee turnover is too high. Competition is too fierce. The business is too risky. Sure, it may work in some areas, but everyone knows my town is different. And with everything going on in my life, the timing couldn't be worse. Financial resources are scarce and hard to come by. I need to be responsible and not take risks. I didn't work this hard and long and sacrifice this much to lose what I have. I can't put my family in any financial danger. Plus if I leave my company, I'll lose my insurance and benefits. What if someone in my family had to go to the hospital? How would I survive those medical bills? Plus, my industry is changing so fast, in a few years my expertise would be obsolete and it would be impossible for me to regain entry if the business didn't make it. I would lose my position and have to come back perhaps on a more junior level. I can't take that risk either."

Certainly almost every reasonable person armed with the same research and faced with the same personal challenges you have would naturally come to the same conclusion. And you're right; 99% of the people who reach out to franchisors come to this same conclusion.

But that's not how entrepreneurs think. You may be entrepreneurial, but if you've never started a business before, you aren't an entrepreneur.

Being an entrepreneur is not a change of location or external circumstances; entrepreneur is an identity. It's a way of being and a way of thinking and acting that is distinctly different from the way those with an employee mindset think and act. An employee is not better or worse than an entrepreneur, just different. The economy needs both to thrive. But they approach their life, career, and investment decisions differently.

The Way of the 1%

The 1% and the 99% all start in the same place in the franchise investigation process, but not in the same clean mental place. Truth be told (and this is going to make some people crazy), the 99% have consistent and persistent career complaints like the complaints I outlined earlier, but no real intention of ever doing anything about it. That's why the percentage of Americans who wish to start a business and those who actually do are materially different. The 1% have the same complaints as the 99%, just different future intentions. The 99% investigates franchises with some underlying intention of disproving different franchise opportunities so they can dismiss self-employment as a career option. Conversely, the 1% makes a firm commitment to put the past in the past and alter their future.

Starting any full-time business seems like an unreasonable and unnatural undertaking. But the 1% refuses to live a reasonable, natural, and compromised life. Their circumstances aren't usually different than yours. Many have similar backgrounds, finances, experience, education, and training to yours. They are your age, have the same family challenges, and even live in your neighborhood. They don't have more confidence, skills, education, experience, or capital than you. Perhaps they are more committed to their dreams. Perhaps they simply have more pain. Perhaps they just can't keep repeating the past anymore. The risk and disappointment of leaving things the way they are appears bigger than the risk of starting a business. That's their math.

Whatever their reason, they have come to a place in life where they would rather take a shot rather than sit in the bleachers and wonder what it's like to play.

However, the 99% are more likely than the 1% to listen to the lies of their "inner critic," giving into self-limiting beliefs. Your inner critic is that little voice in your head ready to emotionally hijack you at your weakest moments and seize control of your decision-making capabilities, by hurling accusations such as:

- You aren't good enough.
- You aren't smart enough.
- You will go broke.
- You can't trust anyone.
- You will never get what you want.
- You don't deserve what you want.
- You don't belong.
- You don't make a difference.
- There's something wrong with you.
- It's all your fault.
- You can't do it.

And in the end, instead of buying a franchise and pursuing a life and career you desire, you buy the lie and relive some version of the same old past you expressed a sincere desire to leave behind. You will compromise on your future and a small part of you will die.

You back up the self-limiting beliefs with what appears on the surface to be airtight logic, such as "I need the security of a job until my kids go to college," or "This business has too much competition."

But you don't do the math about how much the business predictably generates, how much working and transition capital you need to ramp up the business, how the right debt strategy reduces risk, and what the probability is that you can achieve both outcomes of ramping up a business *and* sending kids to college.

And you don't talk to existing franchisees of the brand you are looking at who may be in similar competitive situations and discuss what they do to compete and thrive. Instead, you hold onto two thoughts that still appear to be true:

- If I could only find the right business, I could become successful.
- If I am to succeed, I have to launch my business when the time is right.

Let's look at these potentially self-limiting beliefs individually.

Finding the "Right" Business

You know the right business – the one with low startup costs. You could start it with the loose change you found in your sofa cushions. There is no inventory. Or if there is inventory, customers will pay you first, and then you go out and buy your inventory with your customer's money. There are no contingent liabilities such as real estate or equipment leases. There is little risk, a big return on investment, and fast equity buildup. You parley your sofa cushion money into a million-dollar enterprise.

Although there's no competition, there's lots of demand for your products and services all year long. People will walk through snow drifts in bare feet just for the opportunity to buy from you. Your products and services are so unique they can't be found anywhere else. Banks think the business is so hot that they're lined up to offer you money on a signature with no collateral. However, you don't need banks. Just more old sofa cushions to rummage through.

And think about your customers! They're happy, repeat customers – the kind of customers who walk into your place of business with hundred-dollar bills hanging out of their pockets and buy every product you offer. Plus they bring other customers with them. Of course they seek you out based on your reputation alone, so there is never a need to advertise, network, sell, or even leave the comfort of your home to find them.

What about your employees? There are no employees needed! Or if you do need employees, they punch in exactly when they are supposed to and do what you tell them, exactly the way you told them to do it. Therefore, they need little supervision. They open, close, and maintain your operation while creating complete customer satisfaction. You only need to show up to empty the cash register. Unfortunately, the register fills up so often, this may require you to make several trips a day to the bank, which can interfere with your golf game.

If by some freak chance you do have to replace an employee, it will be a breeze because responsible, clean-cut potential employees with positive "can do" attitudes are always knocking on your door, looking to come to work for you.

What's more, this business is easy to learn and to run. You come out of initial training as a master. You make no costly mistakes. You work nine to five with no weekends, with long extended lunches. You finish one year making the same or more than you are earning now. And next year you will double your income.

Any business not possessing the characteristics described appears to be the wrong business.

Finding the "Right" Time to Start a Business

The 99% live with this illusion, believing the universe consists of two time periods: the right time to start a business and the time period they are currently living in, which of course is the wrong time.

The wrong time looks like this:

- Your kids have to be "the right age." This means they aren't too old and they aren't too young. Or they need to get older and then move out. Or you think, "If only I didn't have kids I would start a business." On some level, you believe nobody has ever found a way to succeed in franchising with your family situation.

- You may believe you have to be the right age to start a business. You must be older, more financially secure, and have additional money to risk, or else you have to be middle-aged, a good earner, and at a pivot point in your life. Or you wish you were younger, and therefore had nothing to lose and a lifetime to earn back. On some level, you believe it's harder for someone your age to start a business.

- You have to have the right spouse. They earn enough to meet your household expenses and wholeheartedly support whatever decision you make. Or your spouse will help you in business to keep your overhead down. You may believe it's harder for anyone in your current marital or relationship situation to succeed in franchising.

Looking for the *perfect business to start* and *the perfect time to start a business* is the franchising equivalent of going on a "snipe hunt." Remember snipe hunts? For those of you who don't know, on camping vacations and family picnics, sometimes the adults send kids out to find *snipe*, a quest designed by adults to get rid of kids so they can drink beer, play poker, and swear like sailors.

For those first-time entrepreneurs who have children, it will look like this. When you first think about having kids, you have certain triggers. You want to be at the right level in your career, living in the right house, in the right neighborhood, in the right school district, and with the right nest egg for emergencies. Over time you find you never quite get to that level or the level moves, your house always needs something else, the neighborhood lacks something, the schools may not be what you thought they were, and your nest egg never looks big enough. Then you sit down with your spouse and decide you can always find reasons not to start your family and your clock is ticking. So eventually you decide now is as good time as any, and then you go to work to make yourself right. Because you are you, it all works out in the end.

The Bottom Line

The 99% try to wait for uncontrollable external stances to align before they start a business, while at the same time complaining that they don't have enough control. They suffer from circular logic and self-limiting beliefs, like fear of failure.

The 1% declare that now is the right time and then actively go to work to make themselves right. At the end of the day, that's the difference.

The 99% desire more control as long as uncontrollable events magically line up and offer it to them on a silver platter, which of course seldom happens.

I can sum this up in two ways:

- Those who are prone to make things happen possess an entre-preneur's mindset and probably would be happy as entrepreneurs if they aren't that already.
- Those who are prone to let things happen have an employee mindset.

If you have an employee mindset, there is nothing wrong with that. Those with an entrepreneurial mindset often need the great employees to achieve their objectives. You are a mission-critical component in most entrepreneurs' plans.

> If you wish to be self-employed yet you have an employee mindset, buying a business will be risky unless you change your mindset. Transitioning from employee to entrepreneur is not a change of scenery. It's a change of identity or mindset; it's an inside-out job.

The difference between those first-time entrepreneurs who pull the trigger and start a business and those who watch from the sidelines shown in this table.

The 99%	The 1%
Waits for the "right time" to start a business.	Declares "now is the time," and then works to make it the right time.
Tries to find the perfect business.	Tries to find a solid business with strong economics and does the work necessary to succeed.

(continued)

33

Special Advice for the First-Time Entrepreneur

The 99%	The 1%
Looks for what's wrong with franchises and why they won't work, and often overemphasizes risk despite objective evidence to the contrary.	Studies a brand's historical track record of success. Talks to franchisees operating within similar markets and with similar backgrounds to predict probability of success. Has no expectation that the business will make them successful.
Is looking for a business that will make them successful, although they know there is no such thing as a job or company that would make them successful. They did the work.	Looks for franchises with a strong track record of success and studies what makes the business work and identifies what it takes to win. Then determines whether they have and are willing to do what it takes.
Is driven to avoid risk and achieve security and stability.	Possesses risk tolerance and is willing to forgo some security and stability in the short run for long-term rewards.
Allows fear and uncertainty to make the decision for them.	Makes informed decisions on what is the highest and best use of capital, skills, and effort.
Is not born into the 99%. Becomes the 99% through the decisions they make.	Is not born into the 1%. Becomes the 1% through the decisions they make.

Chapter 3

Setting Your North Star

My friend and partner, the late great business guru Harry Loyle, used to say, "A small business exists ultimately to benefit ownership." Before you begin to look at franchises, I recommend you have your goals well-articulated and prioritized. Answer this question: "What does winning look like to you?"

Starting a business is a taxing and emotional undertaking, especially for the first-time entrepreneur. For the seasoned, serial entrepreneur, not so much. Your goals need to be big enough, and the pain of doing nothing and not living the life and career you desire has to be painful enough, to endure the frustrations of the startup and propel you through the learning curve of your new business. If your stated goals aren't worthwhile or your pain is tolerable, predictably you will do nothing other than what you are already doing. You need to set your North Star.

Coming home from another long business trip, Ken dragged himself out of the car, pulled his suitcase out of the trunk, fiddled to find his house keys, and opened the door to his North Carolina home. "Home at last," he thought. As he walked into his kitchen, his two-year-old son stared at him in horror. Terrified of "the stranger" who unexpectedly broke into his home, his son ran and hid behind his mother for safety. At that moment Ken made a bold decision. "I will not be a stranger to my children." With that decision, Ken was one step closer to owning a franchise. Months later, Ken was franchisee of a home-based consulting business.

Famed author and motivational speaker Zig Ziglar said, "People don't buy drills, they buy holes." Ziglar asserts that people don't want the tool; they want the results. Carrying that point forward, it is my opinion that people don't buy franchises, they invest in a desired future. Ken didn't want a business. He wanted to be a dad.

Goal-Setting and Benchmarks

Before you research any franchises, you should set some three- or five-year goals, depending on your desired timelines. When articulating your goals and benchmarks, I recommend you think allowing the following lines:

- **Year 1:** Survival. Prepare to do what it takes. Coming into work early, working late, screwing up without guilt and despair. Learning the business. Creating a sustainable flywheel where revenue exceeds expenses. In the absence of new skills, focus on activity. You can chop down a tree with a dull ax. It takes more swings.

- **Year 2:** Growth and efficiency. You should start to feel more competent and confident, understand the business at the core, identify and adeptly pull the key levers of the business that seem to drive everything about the business, such as sales and marketing. During year two, you should possess a line of sight between the potential of the business and your desired outcomes when you started the business.

- **Year 3:** By the end of year three, you should be materially achieving your must-have, non-negotiable objectives or have a clear line of sight as to when your desired outcomes are within reach.

Most high-value franchises will help you achieve your objectives by the end of year three, assuming your goal isn't to build an empire. Rome wasn't built in a day, or even three years and a day.

When goal-setting, I recommend goals be both financial and quality-of-life (or nonfinancial) in nature, incorporating the essence of what drives you. Financial goals should take into account cash flow, savings, net worth, equity buildup, and spendable income. Quality-of-life goals should take into account lifestyle issues that are important to you, such as having dinner at home some number of nights a week, being able to take vacations, attend soccer games, make a difference in the community, and so on.

American corporate psychologist Frederick Herzberg stated that money is a satisfier or dissatisfier, but not a motivator. In other words, there is a minimum threshold of earnings that is different for each person before other motivators show up on your radar screen. Let's call this your minimum acceptable earnings level. Once this level is achieved, quality of life instantly becomes more important. For instance, money alone was not enough to keep my friend Ken's interest.

Before you investigate businesses, you have to know your minimal acceptable level of earnings and other motivating factors.

Virtually all franchisors have key performance criteria that help you and them determine whether your business is winning. However, I know of no franchisors that measure and track how many meals you have eaten with your children or how many of the kids' soccer games you have attended, or how many vacations you have taken and where. Franchisors measure your success by *their definition of success*, not yours.

It is solely your responsibility to create a clear definition of the financial and quality-of-life goals that define what winning looks like for you and a plan to get there using a franchise as your chosen vehicle. The right franchise for you is the one that achieves your objectives with the highest degree of probability and with the lowest risk.

Mark McCormack, in his classic book *What They Don't Teach You at Harvard Business School*, tells of a Harvard study conducted between 1979 and 1989. In 1979, the graduates of the MBA program were asked, "Have you set clear, written goals for your future and made plans to accomplish them?" Only 3% of the graduates had written goals and plans; 13% had goals, but not in writing; and 84% had no specific goals at all.

Ten years later, in 1989, the researchers found that the 13% who had nonwritten goals were earning twice as much as the 84% of students who had no goals at all. And most surprisingly, they found that the 3% of graduates who had clear, written goals when they left Harvard were earning, on average, *10 times as much as the other 97% of graduates all together!*

Keep in mind, there are no dummies at Harvard, so students' intelligence level was a constant, not a variable in this study. The variable was whether clear, written goals were set with plans to accomplish them.

Setting SMART Goals

Clear goals, whether financial or quality of life in nature, must pass the SMART test:

- **Specific:** Goals need to be clearly articulated and written down. "Making a lot of money" is not specific. Earning $200,000 is specific. "Having more control over time" is not specific. "Going to 10 of my son's Little League games and 10 of my daughter's dancing recitals this year" is specific. Improving my net worth is vague. "Building a business asset worth $500,000" is specific.

- **Measurable:** You have to be able to create a tracking system, a method of keeping score. This lets you know whether you are on track and whether you have hit your goals. If your goal is to make $200,000 by the end of the year, on June 30 you should have earned $100,000 or you may not be on track. On December 31, you either hit your income goals or not. It isn't open to opinion or speculation. Using the previous example, if you attend 11 Little League games, you win. If you went to 6, you fell short. It isn't open to interpretation or opinion.

- **Attainable:** Goals must be considered both possible and a worthwhile pursuit, or you will not be motivated to achieve them. For instance, you may say your goal is to make $1 million a year, but if you have never made more than $100,000 a year, you may not really see this goal as possible. Therefore you won't take aggressive steps toward achieving it. These goals should be able to be attained with hard work with a high degree of probability. Creating an unrealistic goal because it sounds good will not motivate you to take committed action. For instance, I grew up in New Haven, Connecticut, only a few miles from Yale University. I was a B student. So I set my sights on the University of Connecticut because achieving a solid state college education was more realistic for me than trying for the impossible goal of an Ivy League education. But sometimes I went home on the weekends and crashed parties at Yale. For the record, UConn parties were better, but Yalies drank more expensive beer.

- **Relevant:** Goals must speak to your current situation, be consistent with your values, be worthy of attainment, and inspire you into action. As a franchisee you may want to experience a 20% increase in sales, but if you think it is going to take working 90 hours per week to achieve that goal, and the reason you started the business was to spend more time with your family, you may not consider it a worthwhile pursuit.

- **Time-bound:** Goals have to have a deadline – a hard, cold by-when date. Goals without a deadline do not inspire commitment. It is human nature not to take action on anything you wish to achieve "someday." Think of how long you have thought about starting a franchise. Do you have a deadline as to when you will be open? If not, other more urgent activities will take precedence and your dream will be pushed back further and further. Watch how fast life happens and gets in the way of your loose plans to start a business.

Activities with deadlines attached to them grab your attention and create a sense of urgency and action. For instance, you know you have to get your taxes done by April 15. If your goal is to get your taxes done on time, the second week of April will be a very productive time for you!

Setting Imminent Goals

Additionally, goals with deadlines that are too far out also do not inspire action. Think about something in your life that you wish would occur within the next 20 years, like perhaps that beach home in Florida. Are you taking action now? Goals with extended timelines are as useless as goals that you want to achieve someday because they don't inspire action. As it relates to franchising, consider setting long-term goals with a three- to five-year time limit. Once you are in business for three years, revisit and perhaps reset your goals based on your new track record as an entrepreneur.

Making Your Desired Future SMART

Use the following table as a worksheet to start designing your future. Prioritize according to a five-point scale.

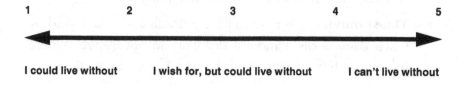

1	2	3	4	5
I could live without		I wish for, but could live without		I can't live without

My Future Desires (Goals) Make SMART	Rate from 1 to 5	Timeline (3–5 Years)

When goal-setting, start with the end goal in mind, and then back up the train and layer in benchmarks. For instance, let's say you want to earn $200,000 by the end of year three. Well, if that's where you want to be in year three, how do you know you are on track by the end of years one and two? These become your benchmarks.

Identifying Your Skills and Aptitudes

This section helps you accurately assess which one or two of the four possible behavior styles you use to produce results. This in turn will help you predict your areas of genius as well as weaknesses and potential threats before you invest in any franchise opportunity. This will also help you quickly identify whether a particular franchise will employ your particular brand of genius.

Identifying Behavior Styles

In the early 1920s, one of the pioneers of behavior profiling, American psychologist William Moulton Marston, sought to create a reliable model that would allow him to predict and explain how emotionally healthy people react to both situations and other people. To test the accuracy of his new theories of behavior, Marston needed to create a system of measurement. Incorporating some of famed psychologist Carl Jung's personality theories stating that there are four distinct personality and behavior styles, Marston created an assessment tool that measured the following behavior characteristics and it became known as DISC theory:

- Dominance
- Influence
- Steadiness
- Compliance

Dominance measures how people respond to challenges and problems. People who are high on dominance will attack problems head on and will seek out potential problems before they occur. People who are low on dominance will display a tendency to let events unfold and see what happens.

Influence measures how people respond to interactions with others. People who are high on influence are very outgoing and have a need to build strong personal relationships and influence others with their views. People who are low on influence will appear more distant and private, preferring more thinking and alone time.

Steadiness measures how people respond to the pace of their environment. People who are high on steadiness desire predictable and slower-paced environments where they can see projects from the beginning through to completion. People low on steadiness desire change and like rapid pace and like to multitask.

Compliance measures how people respond to structure or rules created by others. People who are high on compliance thrive in highly structured environments where they know exactly what to do and what is expected of them. People low on compliance like to make their own rules and prefer to be self-managed. Take a wild guess where entrepreneurs are on this scale. Most entrepreneurs are a "don't tell me what to do" waiting to happen. That's where self-awareness comes into play. Entrepreneurs who are low on compliance are wired to resist external controls and processes they didn't create for themselves, adding risk if they don't put these tendencies in check.

It is from these four characteristics that the DISC theory and assessment tool was named, covered in the next section.

Using DISC Theory

DISC (dominance, influence, steadiness, and compliance) theory has become one of the most widely used, statistically validated, and universally accepted behavior assessments that companies use to help determine whether the skills people possess match what is required for particular positions, including franchised ownership. I believe that DISC theory is among the best available tools to help you evaluate how your skills match a franchisor's profile of a successful franchisee. Franchisors find that the most successful franchisees of particular brands often fit common profiles that can be measured and predicted using DISC theory and instruments.

As you contact different franchise companies and get further in their franchise sales process, you will find that some highly skilled and sophisticated franchisors use DISC or a similar instrument to statistically measure and help create their composite profile of a successful franchisee. They have statistically figured out who predictably wins. They will profile you on the same instrument and compare your results against their composite of a successful franchisee and examine the deviations. They will discuss the deviations with you and talk about how these deviations may play out positively or negatively in your own business. For instance, they may see that you are more introverted than their profile of a successful franchisee, and they may discuss whether you are willing to cold-call for customers. Some franchisors put so much emphasis on these instruments that they will use them as a qualifier or disqualifier for a franchise. Other franchisors take a more balanced approach, using their findings alongside other information they gather, such as interviews, applications, past results, resumes, and financial statements.

Many smaller chains have too few franchisees to make a statistical sampling relevant. Larger, more unsophisticated franchise chains may assume they already know and therefore may not see the value in using instruments. Expect them to supply you with anecdotal evidence, which I urge you to listen to, but not entirely trust. Not that these franchisors are knowingly misleading you or doing anything wrong, it's that they are making educated guesses using observational data that may not be accurate. Create your own profile using the information in this chapter, and when you talk to successful franchisees of brands, you can start easily profiling them if the franchisor doesn't.

DISC theory states the obvious: normal and healthy people display consistent and predictable patterns of behavior. Taken one step further, people with similar styles within the same franchise system have a tendency to produce similar results. Put another way, the top performers generally display one style and underperformers display another. Seldom will you find style similarities between top performers and underperformers.

Before I get into styles, understand that I am not saying one particular style of performance is better than another style as it relates to franchising in general. I am, however, asserting that franchise systems are typically set up to support certain styles of performance and not others, which is one reason why franchisees' performance varies within the same franchise system.

Think about it. Franchise systems are typically created by the successful entrepreneurs who invented these systems. Every franchise system at one time was an entrepreneurs' personal system, usually started with a single business unit. Unless the franchisor's systems have undergone years of development, evolution, or transformation, the franchise system will still be somewhat reflective of the entrepreneurs' original personal system. Since each entrepreneur will be dominant in one style or another, it stands to reason that franchisees whose behavior styles most resemble the original entrepreneur's style will also be the ones most likely to master this system. Additionally, many franchisors simply don't take into account style differences when they create systems and develop training programs. They create, train, and develop according to their own dominant style the same way other people act according to their own dominant style.

Certainly, there are other mitigating factors that impact a franchisee's performance, which you will also need to take into account, such as demographics, market penetration, brand awareness, competition, location, capitalization, and general economic conditions. Do not discount style but don't overemphasize it either. Behavior styles provide a piece in the overall success and performance puzzle. If your style more closely matches the profile of an underperformer rather than a performer, all other things being equal, regardless of your past successes, you run a high risk of being an underperformer yourself. Why? Because the role the franchise plays in a particular business may not offer you your ideal work environment or the highest and best use of your talents.

Use the information in this section to help you determine whether a particular franchise opportunity will provide an ideal work environment, setting you up to win.

While your performance style can't always be relied on to pick which particular industries you should be looking at inside of franchising, your style will help you determine which specific companies, cultures, and work environments you should and should not consider. Put another way, you can't use this information to determine whether you should be in the food service or hair care industry, but it will help you determine whether you are a fit for such specific chains as Subway or Great Clips.

How DISC Works

As mentioned, DISC validates that people are very consistent in how they speak, listen, and react to people and situations. So consistent, in fact, that people have essentially become typecast actors in their own movies, playing the same character again and again. Although people and events are not predictable, the way people react to other people and events is predictable and can even be measured with a shocking degree of accuracy. To assist you, I have applied movie characterizations to each of the four styles.

In this section, you will identify which one or two of the four possible typecast characters both you and others play. This will help you predetermine which characters excel and which underachieve in any given franchise system.

The four typecast actors (DISC profiles) are as follows:

- The Action Hero
- The Comedian
- The Faithful Sidekick
- The Private Eye

You Are an Action Hero If . . .

You are an outgoing, hard-charging, risk-taking, task oriented, efficient, disciplined, organized, results oriented, and "take charge" character. You make quick, emotional, instinctual, or gut-based decisions rather than information-based or logic-based decisions. Attaining goals, assuming control, achieving results, accepting personal challenge, and creating efficiency drives you. You speak pointedly and directly, telling it like it is. You possess strong opinions and are often closed to any new facts and information that may contradict your formed opinions. Because Action Heroes do not need or seek much information to make quick decisions, you have difficulty listening to details, preferring instead to listen to headlines, highlights, or the bottom line. Therefore, Action Heroes are often perceived as poor listeners. Since you are such a strong personality, you can easily bowl over weaker personality types, creating conflict in the process. Since you may fear being taken advantage of, you may often question the personal motives, integrity, and loyalty of others, creating issues around trust.

The Action Hero's value in the business:

- You are results oriented and goal focused. You seldom lose sight of your goals or the big picture. You know what they are looking to accomplish and generally are keyed into how to get there. You seldom deviate from your stated objectives. You get others around you focused and organized.

- You are strategic and tactical. You know to chunk problems and situations down to their simplest forms and create a plan of attack quickly. You effortlessly know how to simplify everything.

- You are visionary. You can see past the minutiae of the day-to-day operations of a business and hold on to your original vision. You are excellent at stating your vision to others in simple terms so they get it. You always seem to have one eye on what is occurring and another eye on the bottom line. Others follow you because of your commanding presence and clear and simple ideas of what is required to win.

- You are an efficiency expert. You know how to trim the fat and cut the waste. You are always identifying and pushing for the quickest, easiest, simplest, and most efficient way to produce results. You quickly identify and spend time executing the activities that drive results. You know which buttons need to be pushed and when, and can be counted on to push those buttons.

- You are responsible, self-directed, and self-managed. You do what you say you are going to do. As long as you know what the results need to look like at the end of the day, you have an uncanny ability to make things happen. Against all odds, you seem to invent ways to produce results and win.

- You are a natural-born leader. You have a forceful personality and others see you as an authority figure. People naturally follow your lead.

- You get involved. You see it as your duty to look beyond what is occurring in your little franchise and contribute on a regional or national level. You desire to be heard and your opinions are generally worth listening to.

- You maintain a strong operational focus. You know how to implement processes and systems that produce results.

- You possess excellent multitasking ability. You know how to juggle people and tasks without dropping any balls. You have a natural ability to keep multiple ideas front of mind without having to write things down.

- You create win-win solutions. You are very skilled at identifying what winning looks like for yourself and others and will work to create solutions where everyone gets what they want.

- You have great problem-solving ability. You don't shrink from, avoid, or deny conflicts and challenges. You attack head on without reservation. You will be the first to identify where potential breakdowns are occurring or may occur in the future and are often ready with a solution.

- You are action oriented and quick to implement. Once you decide what to do, you don't let any grass grow under your feet. You are in perpetual motion. You get more done than most people in less time.

- You aren't afraid to take risks. As such, yours is the most entrepreneurial behavior style. You aren't afraid to spend time or money when necessary to create long-term gain.

- You are a strong decision-maker. You move quickly and decisively and are not prone to second-guess yourself or waffle in the face of making important decisions. Once you decide, it is full steam ahead.

- You have a commonsense approach to business. You can easily frame any given situation and quickly formulate a plan of attack. You are brilliant at looking past symptoms and getting to the heart or source of the matter.

- You put forth a heroic effort and play to win. You expect and demand the same of others. No one working with you is allowed a free pass.

Risk factors of the Action Hero:

- You have a tendency to resist external controls. You may not value being held accountable to follow a system. You resist following certain operational procedures if you deem them inefficient or cumbersome. You will be tempted to deviate from a franchise system, increasing your risk and decreasing the franchisor's ability to offer you meaningful support. You don't always respect boundaries.

- You form strong opinions and resist checking out perceptions against the facts. You may make poor decisions because of lack of information. You aren't always open to receiving information that is contrary to what you believe. Because you like to rally others to your point of view, you can be labeled by the franchisor and other franchisees as a "rebel" or "troublemaker" and lose credibility with the franchisor. Because you stop listening once your mind is made up, it can be difficult for a franchisor to train and support you and point out problem areas in your business.

- You seek control of a situation or interaction. You struggle in following and often resist following other leaders. You may butt heads with franchisor leadership and alienate yourself from the franchisor and other franchisees.

- You attempt to gain the upper hand in negotiations. You may be perceived as selfish and not a team player, which can get in the way of others wanting to help you.

- You tell others what is on your mind without thought about how it might land. You can damage key franchisee-franchisor relationships if others aren't comfortable with your directness or bluntness.

- You have a tendency to challenge, confront, and make others wrong, which again can diminish your franchisor's ability to provide you with leadership.

- You possess a tendency to change systems, processes, and procedures you did not create or that you do not agree with. You run the risk of changing the franchise system before you ever learn the system, which could create costly mistakes and extend your learning curve.

- You are a notoriously poor listener. This can get in the way of your training and development and create personality conflicts with the franchise support staff.

- You are a strong leader and have a tendency to bowl over weaker personalities. Many franchise support and training professionals possess those weaker personalities, damaging key relationships.

- Since you are more about achieving great results than building powerful relationships, you will at times risk damaging key relationships to get what you want.

- You have a tendency to dominate and micromanage others, which may create employee turnover, halting forward momentum.

- You have a tendency to delegate without effectively training others, setting employees up to fail.

- You have a temper. Employees with weaker personality types may hide mistakes and information that indicates problems to avoid setting you off. You are so intolerant of mistakes, you may not give your employees the safe space necessary to make mistakes and learn their roles.

- You like to be in control and make decisions with little feedback. You may not effectively harness the collective genius of your employees.

- You take a "ready-fire-aim" approach to business. You may act impulsively without thinking about all the ramifications of your actions.

- You are a natural risk-taker. You may take foolish chances, which can hurt you.

- You are impatient and want things now. You sometimes will force a result rather than let it naturally happen. You err on the side of aggressiveness.

- You forget to give others positive affirmation for a job well done. You have a tendency to communicate to your employees only when you spot a problem, giving some the experience of being unappreciated, which will create turnover.

The Action Hero's ideal franchise:

- Provides freedom to make unit-level strategic decisions. The franchise system isn't completely buttoned down and handed down from the top.

- Contains clearly articulated, efficient, and well–thought out business systems.
- Offers a work environment that is efficient and well organized.
- Involves multitasking and change. Every day is a bit different.
- Includes work days that allow for flexibility.
- Requires great personal challenges and working on the big picture. May appreciate a smaller franchisor who doesn't have it all figured out yet. Would appreciate a smaller, more entrepreneurial franchise where they have direct access to the decision-makers.
- Is a proven, replicable business model, not just a good idea.
- Has strong management information systems and clear key measures of success.
- Isn't loosey-goosey, where key management doesn't have the skill or experience to continue on a growth track.
- Offers customers a unique product or service that demonstrates value, one that will produce great results for customers or clients and something they can sell with integrity.
- Is cutting edge or leading edge.
- Is a system that provides easy access to data and key indicators of the business.
- Offers access to the franchisor's decision-makers and a forum to voice opinions.
- Can continually be grown.
- Is run by executives with a participatory leadership style.
- Leaves franchisees alone and will not be overly involved in the business.
- Fits the profile of a higher-risk franchise

- Provides you with the possibility for growth and higher return.
- Gives you choices and flexible "wiggle room," not mandates.

You Are a Comedian If . . .

You are fun-loving, outgoing, empathetic, risk-taking, people oriented, charming, affable, creative, enthusiastic, talkative, optimistic, trusting, and highly influential. Like Action Heroes, Comedians are also instinctual, emotion-based, or gut-based rather than information-based decision-makers. However, where Action Heroes are more task oriented, Comedians are more people oriented. Building quality relationships, having fun, and attaining social recognition drive them. Comedians look for reasons to believe in, trust, and like others. Like

Action Heroes, they listen more attentively to headlines, highlights, the bottom line, and the big picture rather than the details. They have trouble saying "no," and have a tendency to overpromise. They struggle with detail, are known to become disorganized, and have trouble managing their time effectively.

The Comedian's value in the business:

- You have creative problem-solving ability. You are an out-of-the-box thinker. You can find new ways to look at problems and find solutions. You are resourceful and can find what has worked in other businesses and industries and synthesize a solution for your business.

- You are visionary; you see the big picture. You can look beyond the status quo and see what is possible. You are skilled in enrolling others in your vision of the future.

- You build consensus and will work hard to avoid conflict and build powerful relationships with the franchisor and other franchisees.

- You are goal oriented. You will work hard to attain your goals.

- You influence others. You know how to rally the troops and inspire others into committed action.

- You work well with others and function well on a team. You will work to build synergies and bond with the franchisor's employees.

- You are a great communicator and are easy to talk to and relate to. You know how to make customers and employees feel right at home. You build trusting relationships with customers and employees.

- You are optimistic and put forward positive energy. You maintain a healthy can-do attitude in the face of adversity.

- You are trusting and can create trust in customers and employees.

- You are outgoing and exhibit mastery in sales and marketing. You are a natural-born salesperson and promoter. You aren't afraid of getting out into the community and telling others why you should be doing business with them. You know how to drive sales.

- You make work and shopping fun for employees and customers. Your energy is contagious.

- You have good customer service skills. You know how to keep customers satisfied and coming back.

- You are a democratic manager and good at soliciting feedback. You will work to create a positive experience for clients and customers.

- You are entrepreneurial and a risk-taker. You aren't afraid to spend money to achieve your objectives.

- You are quick to make decisions or to implement ideas.

- You like change and moving quickly, and can get much done in a short period of time.

- You possess high confidence in your abilities.

Risk factors of the Comedian:

- You move quickly and don't always think about the total impact of your actions before you take them. You are a "run out in traffic before you look both ways" decision-maker, which can cost you precious money and time. You need to learn how to solicit feedback from the franchise support staff so you don't get flattened in traffic.

- You may resist following processes, which can dramatically increase your risk in business. You would rather be unrestricted in your movements to create a result. This will make it difficult for the franchisor to be able to support you properly, as you would rather create your own system.

- You seldom do the same thing twice. You are so creative that you are constantly inventing new ways to serve your customers. You run the risk of changing the winning formula, making yourself less effective. You need to learn how to create a business rhythm.

- You form strong opinions and resist checking out perceptions against the facts. You just assume you are right and then take off.

- People may take advantage of your trusting manner.

- You are optimistic and may overlook information that indicates a problem. Therefore you miss opportunities to head off problems before they occur. You can confuse "feeling good" with creating great results.

- In order to avoid a conflict, you don't always say everything that is on your mind. You have a tendency to hold back "negative" information from people who can help you.

- You make "gut-based" or "feelings-based" decisions and may dismiss facts if facts contrast with "feelings." You don't always check opinions against facts.

- You will go off on tangents and waste time. You are so creative that you can lose your focus.

- You are probably highly disorganized and typically weak with details and financial numbers. Your motto is "Data, schmata! Let's go sell!"

- You know how to spend money and may struggle with budgeting and containing costs.

- You may have a tendency to focus on the top line (revenues) and ignore the bottom line (cash flow).

57

The Comedian's ideal franchise:

- Gives you ample opportunity to network with and learn from other franchisees.

- Offers a product or service that you are passionate about, which you can enthusiastically market and sell.

- Leverages your creativity and ability to build repeat customers.

- Is your idea of a fun time.

- Is informal in nature and highly entrepreneurial, possibly resembling the culture of a family business.

- Is led by a CEO with a democratic leadership style, where you have the opportunity to voice your opinion.

- Isn't a low-margin/high-transaction business "penny profit" (such as fast food), which relies on an owner's ability to tightly manage the cost side of the business. Your strengths are driving sales, not efficiently containing costs.

- Is simplistic, structured, and methodical, compensating for your weak organizational skills.

- Possesses a competitive point of difference that relies on your natural abilities to sell, promote, and network within the community (such as the "quick sign" industry).

- Is "flashy" with great "country club" appeal, which appeals to your ego.

- Offers freedom from tight external controls and lets their franchisees find their own way while at the same time maintaining the integrity of the brand.

You Are a Faithful Sidekick If . . .

You are warm, dependable, good-natured, structured, methodical, systems oriented, open-minded, consistent, persistent, level-headed, pragmatic, objective, sincere, and an empathetic team player. Like Comedians, Faithful Sidekicks are people oriented, but unlike Comedians, they are more introverted and less emotional. Where Comedians are driven by having fun and attaining social recognition drives, Sidekicks are driven by the need for security, stability, and belonging. Sidekicks need to see how they fit into the inner workings of a franchise and what role they will play. Resistant to change, they make slow, informed, and emotionally agonizing decisions about whether to start a business. Having a natural tendency to "play not to lose"

rather than "playing to win," they seek to eliminate risk and miss opportunities in the process. They are known to be highly detailed, organized, slow-paced, and patient. Having the gift of objectivity, they can see both sides of an issue.

Faithful Sidekicks are the best listeners and the easiest to get along with of all the four characters. Since they are introverted and prefer a predictable environment, they are often seen as timid, possessive, risk-averse, and resistant to change.

The Faithful Sidekick's value in the business:

- You are very objective and can see all sides of issues. You make level-headed and carefully thought-out business decisions.

- You are very methodical and process driven. No one has probably ever accused you of being a rebel. You will spend more time memorizing a franchisors operations manual than trying to rewrite it, which will be welcomed by most franchisors.

- You function well within a structured environment. You will follow the franchise system as it was written.

- You have great listening skills and a good memory.

- You are empathetic and people like you.

- You are a team player and an excellent team builder. Members of your team see their own value.

- You are a communicator. You keep others in the loop.

- You are a servant leader. Customers will go away satisfied and happy.

- You are easy to talk to and to relate to.

- You are highly analytical and you will study the numbers and performance criteria of a business.

- You are very persistent and consistent. Once you tap into the "winning hand" of a business, you will play that hand again and again, without getting bored or feeling like you have to change it.

- You know how to build quality relationships with your customers, employees, and franchisor.

- You have strong customer skills or aptitudes. Being good at soliciting feedback, you will listen to your customers' needs.

- You are a "steady Eddie," and your business will function with precision.

Risk factors of the Faithful Sidekick:

- You struggle with multitasking. You like to do one thing at a time and complete tasks before you start the next one. Unfortunately, small businesses are typically not linear and new stuff happens every day. You have to be able to change your daily action plan on the fly, which doesn't play into your strengths.

- You experience a high degree of fear of the unknown. Fear can sometimes paralyze you. You have to learn how to walk with fear as a companion much in the same way a recovering alcoholic walks with urges to drink but doesn't act on them. You will need to learn not to make fear mean anything or allow it to stop you from plowing forward.

- You have high security and stability needs and are uncomfortable in ambiguity. In business, you will face many ambiguous moments requiring you to assume more risk than you are comfortable facing.

- You need time alone to decompress. You may find it hard to decompress.

- You prefer a slow-paced environment. The goal in business, however, is to create a fast paced environment where the cash register is ringing constantly.

- You can be overly persistent and possessive. You have to learn that there are times to cut and run.

- You are quiet and diplomatic. With most franchisors, the squeaky wheel gets the grease. If you aren't receiving the support you need, you will need to overcome your natural tendency to avoid conflict and either get loud and angry like an Action Hero or get up on your soapbox and preach like the Comedian. Franchisors, of course, don't like this, but many franchisees do this because it works.

The Faithful Sidekick's ideal franchise:

- Is a stable business and not prone to dramatic swings because of seasonality, the economy, or other conditions outside your control.

- Sells products or services that are necessities rather than luxuries and are stable rather than trendy. Examples include such things as house cleaning and dry cleaning.

- Plays in to your customer service strengths, like specialty retail.

- Is a repeat customer business, allowing you to build rock-solid relationships, like hair care.

- Allows you to pace your day, like automotive care, and isn't prone to customer rushes, like flower shops on Valentine's Day.

- Has an established and identifiable brand. Let's face it, you aren't a promoter. You are more comfortable behind the counter than outside on the sidewalk. Look for a business where the Comedians and Action Heroes have already built the brand and you do what you do best – maintaining the integrity of the brand.

- Has an outstanding reputation for maintaining excellent franchisee-franchisor relations. You enjoy being a member of a high-performance team.

- Generates fewer transactions but high ticket/high margins. Because you may not multitask well or fare well in a fast-paced environment, you need a "tortoise business" where slow and steady wins the race.

- Creates happy customers. You may not enjoy a business such as transmission repair where many customers feel like they are being ripped off. You would do better with a business like ice cream where everyone is smiling all the time.

- Is either advertising- or location-driven, meaning your customers come to you. You aren't exactly the type who will wear holes in your shoes from beating the streets cold calling.

You Are a Private Eye If . . .

63

You are precise, exact, focused, detailed, neat, systematic, polite, logical, professional, open-minded, and slow paced. You are the most analytical, compliant, and methodical of the four characters. Private Eyes are driven by an internal need for perfection and want clear instructions about what is expected of them. Their motto is "Tell me how you want it done and I'll do it." They are very task oriented and once they are clear about what is expected, they become very self-directed. Unlike Action Heroes, who seek control over others, they prefer to work alone. They pride themselves on being informed, poring through information and analyzing data prior to making any type of decision. Because Private Eyes are introverted and prefer to work alone, they can be seen as aloof, critical, and antisocial. And because Private Eyes need more details and information than the other three characters before being able to make a decision, they also can be seen as missing the big picture, fearful, risk-averse, and resistant to change.

The Private Eye's value in the business:

- You are objective and open to new information.

- You are very methodical and process driven.

- You are quality driven. Your customers will be amazed at your level of conscientiousness and pride of service. They will have a hard time finding a business that cares about each transaction the way you do.

- You function well within a structured environment. You will follow the franchise system, even if you are not in total agreement with the structure or system. You adapt well. No one has probably ever said about you, "You know that [insert your name] – always bucking the system!"

- You have great listening skills and you remember details. You are a genius with detail. You categorize everything like the library's Dewey Decimal System and know where everything is.

- You seem to know everything about everything. And what you don't know, you know where to go to find out.

- You will find holes in any system and have the uncanny ability to spot what is missing. You are brilliant at creating processes and procedures that plug these holes.

- You are diplomatic. You walk and speak softly.

- You are highly analytical and an Einstein with numbers.

- You are very persistent and consistent, and people can count on you to do what you say you are going to do when you said you were going to do it.

- You work at a steady pace and are self-directed.

- You gather information and make data-based decisions.

Risk factors of the Private Eye:

- You will struggle with many of the same issues as the Faithful Sidekick, so refer to their list.

- You prefer to be alone. Your ideal franchise business might be "lighthouse keeper," but that doesn't exist. Being alone means you are the business. If you aren't working, you aren't getting paid. And when you are working delivering a product or service, it means you aren't marketing for new customers. By your nature, you resist building a team.

- You also struggle with multitasking. You like to do one thing at a time and complete tasks before you start the next one. As with the Sidekick, small businesses are typically not linear and new stuff happens every day. You have to be able to change your daily action plan on the fly, which doesn't play into your strengths.

- You struggle with fear. You have to learn how to walk with fear as a companion much in the same way a recovering alcoholic walks with urges to drink but doesn't act on them. You will need to learn not to make fear mean anything or allow it to stop you from plowing forward.

- You need time alone to decompress. You may find it hard to download during the day.

- You can get so caught up in the details that you miss the big picture. You can lose sight of what the details add up to and what the details mean.

- Because you are a perfectionist, you can spend too much time on a given transaction. You need to learn what is "good enough to satisfy the customer" rather than always trying to achieve inner perfection. Once you have the quality required to satisfy the customer, move on. It is better to be high volume and excellent than low volume and perfect.

- You may be seen as aloof, antisocial, and difficult to do business with.

The Private Eye's ideal franchise:

- Is highly structured and systematic. All you need to do is execute.

- Is advertising driven, not direct sales driven. Let's face it, you aren't going to cold-call. You need a business where customers are finding you through advertising, the internet, or the yellow pages.

- Has few or no employees. You prefer to work alone.

- Has limited customer interface. As long as you get the job done well and on time and on budget, that is enough. You're not the one who is going to schmooze with your customers at the bar during happy hour.

- Gives you the down time you need to decompress and allows you to mentally prepare for each customer interface.

- Differentiates from competitors by the quality of products and services offered. You are meticulous and quality driven.

- Tracks and offers easy access to all key performance indicators of the business. You manage by analysis. You need the data to analyze.

- Specializes in one product or service. You pride yourself on being an expert, not a generalist. Find a franchise that is well known for one particular product or service.

- Is technical in nature. You are a technical genius – make it work for you.

- Has fewer transactions, but high price points and high margins. You are built for taking the time necessary to produce high quality, not for speed.

Which Character(s) Sound Like You?

I described these typecast actors as if you were all one character and none of the others. Although most people tend to act according to one dominant style, they typically exhibit blended characteristics of two styles. Also, people's style will vary in intensity from individual to individual. Chances are when you read the descriptions, you found at least one character you completely identify with and another that you sometimes do and sometimes don't.

People whose styles are different from ours have skill sets (or a particular genius) we don't have. If you start a franchise, it is wise to surround yourself with different actors who possess different skills and have a different take on the business. They will contribute to you in a way you cannot begin to imagine.

Summary

Note that there are no right or wrong styles for franchising in general, but there are right and wrong styles for individual franchise opportunities. As you investigate franchises, you will see that top performers have similar styles as other top performers and underperformers have a tendency to exhibit similar styles as other underperformers. One predictor of how you will perform in any given franchise system is to determine how people just like you perform. You will have a high probability of achieving similar results.

Many franchisors use behavior or values profiles to help them evaluate whether a candidate fits the profile of a successful franchisee or is a culture fit for the company. Don't be surprised if you are requested to complete a profile. Others use gut instincts or simply don't care either way. Let the buyer beware. When talking to franchisees of the systems you will be evaluating, use the information in this chapter to help you identify the commonalities between yourself and top-performing franchisees.

Chapter 4

Matching Your Skills and Aptitudes
to Opportunities

As you research different franchise opportunities, you are faced with the difficult task of answering five questions with great clarity:

- What are the key ingredients in the franchisor's recipe for success?

- Which of the key ingredients do I possess?

- Which of the key ingredients am I missing?

- What is the franchisor's track record of helping others like me acquire these missing ingredients?

- Am I willing to do what it takes to acquire these ingredients?

This requires great discernment on your part. As you investigate franchising, you will most likely work with a franchise sales representative (or development representative as they are sometimes called) who may not know all the ingredients needed to succeed in the particular franchise you are investigating. Few have actual experience operating the brand they represent, meaning they are theorists. That doesn't mean their feedback isn't useful and shouldn't be trusted, but it does mean you need to conduct a thorough investigation on your own and to test the recruiter's opinions and theories against franchisees' opinions and experiences.

Understanding the Franchisor's Motives

The franchisor representatives will generally know enough about operations to be competent in their roles as ambassadors to people investigating their franchise, but not to the extent where they could train and support new franchisees or run the franchise business competently themselves. While they can explain on a high level what it takes for you to succeed as a franchisee, they may omit, gloss over, or not take into account certain skill sets or required habits required for your success. Again, it is your responsibility to conduct a thorough investigation.

Often franchise sales representatives do not invest enough time in interviewing and screening you properly to accurately determine both the transferable skills and abilities you possess and those you are missing. If you were to examine the background of franchise salespeople, most are indeed salespeople and approach their positions as a salesperson would. They will push the features and benefits of their franchise, deemphasizing or ignoring what the salespeople may see as flaws or risk factors in order to quickly move you toward closure, meaning signing a franchise agreement and paying your initial franchise fee. Franchise sales representatives know that the longer you take to move through the process, the less likely you are to move forward. "Time kills deals" is their mantra. As a result, sometimes you will feel pressured to make decisions before you feel you have conducted a reasonable investigation.

> Keep in mind, only 1 or 2 out of 100 people who inquire about a particular franchise actually move forward. The others fall away for reasons discussed in earlier chapters. Franchise sales representatives are under enormous time pressure to expeditiously sift through the 100 to find the 1 or 2 who will move forward in order to spend most of their time with them.

You must beware. Earlier, I told the story of the vice president of franchise sales who once said, "It isn't my job to qualify franchise candidates. I will give anyone their God-given right to fail." If your skill sets do not line up with the core competencies required to be successful in the business, some will turn a blind eye and attempt to coerce and manipulate you through their sales process anyway. They do not express concern with your heightened risk or how financial failure may impact your family. Nor are they concerned with how your failure will impact customers or their brand. They are more concerned with "closing the deal and getting one on the scoreboard."

However, *ethical and responsible* franchisors hire franchise recruiters who have the ability, vision, discipline, and integrity to get to know you and compare your skills and aptitudes against their profile of a successful franchisee. They will communicate exactly what it takes to win and check to make sure you understand you have what it takes and you are willing to do what it takes. If your skills don't completely match up, they may not immediately disqualify you from the process. Instead, they may inform you of your areas of risk and how those weaknesses may impact your business. They may ask you what training you will take or what you are committed to do to improve in those areas prior to becoming a franchise to mitigate your risk. These are the true professionals. Unfortunately, in my opinion, they are in the minority. I hope more and more franchisors adopt their best practices.

Another problem in franchising is that franchise sales representative compensation and bonus structures are tied to whether or not you join the franchise, not whether or not you perform well once you are open, which is incongruent with your and the franchisor's long term best interests.

For an unskilled and irresponsible franchisor, "quantity" of franchises sold versus "quality" of the franchisees appear to be opposing forces, especially smaller, emerging growth franchisors or franchisors who are trailing in their industry and are trying to play catch-up.

Experienced and skilled franchisors reject the "sell franchises as fast as you can" strategy. They know if existing franchisees are hitting their financial objectives and are content with the franchisee-franchisor relationship, franchisees will reinvest. More than 50% of their growth will come from existing franchisees rather than recruiting few franchisees. These franchisors will exhibit an operations culture rather than a franchise sales culture.

The KASH Model of Success

As you gather data, and as I discussed, you will find that successful franchisees of particular franchise systems have a tendency to think and act alike. They view their customers, employees, business, competition, products and services, and the franchisor the same way. They know the same things, possess similar skill sets, and engage in the same high-priority activities each day. Underperforming franchisees often view their customers, employees, business, competition, products and services, and the franchisor the same way also, but distinctly different from those peak performers to the right of the performance bell curve.

The winning formula for success for every franchise opportunity is composed of four key ingredients:

- Knowledge
- Attitude
- Skills
- Habits

This recipe for success has been termed KASH, after the first letter in each word. Here is how I define each KASH element:

- **Knowledge:** Peak performing franchisees have high levels of product, service, and operational knowledge and are students of their business and industry. They know the business model inside and out and are on top of new developments. They understand the nature, dynamics, and leverage points of their business, meaning they have identified all the activities that produce the greatest results.

- **Attitude:** Successful franchisees share a healthy view of their business and the franchisor. I define attitude as the way a person evaluates a particular external person, situation, or event. Given the same external event such as a conflict situation, some attitudes – such as win-win problem-solving – generate greater results than others – such as win-lose fighting. Few franchisees create outstanding results without first thinking about their business properly.

  Often people confuse attitude with positive thinking. That's not what I'm saying here. I'm talking about a belief system, not a value judgment. For example, successful franchisees often relate to their employees as the lifeblood of their business. Others may see employees as a necessary evil. Some may view sales as "a fair exchange of money for services," while others think sales is "manipulating someone to buy what they don't want or need." Each will act consistently with their viewpoints, achieving materially different results.

- **Skills:** Skillful franchisees exhibit polished and effective behaviors on the job. They know how to accomplish their jobs and manage their customers and employees with mastery. Skills determine a person's capacity to translate knowledge into bottom-line results.

- **Habits:** Habits measure how franchisees spend their most critical resource, time. Franchisees who spend more time on the high-priority activities that produce the most results will produce more than other franchisees do with the same time, money, and energy who get sucked into the minutiae of the business.

73

Matching Your Skills and Aptitudes to Opportunities

However, most franchisees' success or failure is not random. Success and failure is a direct result of their KASH (knowledge, attitude, skills, and habits) balance. If a wide gap exists between your personal KASH and the KASH required to succeed in a franchise business, you are at risk if you fail to close the gap. If your KASH is consistent with the profile of a successful franchisee, then most likely you are positioned to win.

Conducting a KASH Gap Analysis

Identifying whether you will succeed within a particular franchise system requires personal detachment and rigorous self-examination, which you can accomplish by following these steps:

1. Start with your existing KASH.

2. Identify the KASH required to succeed.

3. Subtract and you will know what is missing.

When your KASH deficit is too high and the franchisor doesn't have what it takes to close the gap, then your risk increases. If your KASH deficit is low, you are a more natural fit for the business and risk decreases. While franchisors have training and ongoing support aimed at building your KASH balance, they aren't miracle workers. If your KASH isn't already in reasonable alignment with a particular franchisor's KASH formula of success, under most circumstances I would recommend you take a pass. There are thousands of different franchise options available to you. You don't need to compromise. Just keep looking.

Once you have identified your KASH gaps, ask yourself, "Am I willing to do whatever it takes to acquire my missing KASH?" If you are one who works hard to achieve your goals, most likely you will work hard to acquire your missing KASH. If you are one who just likes to get by, you won't put in the extra work and your risk increases. If you like to coast, or if you simply struggle with learning new things, find a franchise whose KASH formula of success is a mirror overlay to your personal KASH balance.

Determining Your Starting KASH Balance

While you need to develop your own KASH gap analysis for each business you explore, I have included a self-assessment to help you create a baseline to use when exploring franchises.

My friend and colleague Greg Nathan, corporate psychologist, franchising expert, and founder of the Franchise Relationships Institute, helped me develop the following worksheet for you to use to identify your starting KASH balance.

Fill out the survey to the best of your ability. Don't overanalyze the questions; just go with your gut and circle the first answer that comes into your head.

My Starting KASH

Name:		Date:	

TRAINABILITY	Always	Sometimes	Never
I adapt well to change.	3	2	1
I invest money in my personal development.	3	2	1
I am open to feedback about my weaknesses.	3	2	1
I am open to trying new ways of doing things.	3	2	1
Total for section			

(continued)

Matching Your Skills and Aptitudes to Opportunities

MARKETING/SALES APTITUDES	Always	Sometimes	Never
I am skilled at influencing others with my viewpoints.	3	2	1
I am comfortable talking to strangers.	3	2	1
I am a creative problem-solver.	3	2	1
I am a confident presenter.	3	2	1
Total for section			

MOTIVATION	Always	Sometimes	Never
I have clear goals.	3	2	1
I achieve what I set my mind on.	3	2	1
I honor my commitments.	3	2	1
Faced with a problem, I can create a proper solution.	3	2	1
Total for section			

WORKING WITH OTHERS	Always	Sometimes	Never
I compromise to comply with the wishes of the majority.	3	2	1
I get along well with others.	3	2	1

My Starting KASH

I resolve differences with others without creating arguments.	**3**	**2**	**1**
I listen to other viewpoints.	**3**	**2**	**1**
Total for section			

LEADERSHIP	Always	Sometimes	Never
I achieve my goals through the efforts of others.	**3**	**2**	**1**
I will spend money developing my employees' skills.	**3**	**2**	**1**
I positively impact others.	**3**	**2**	**1**
I can get a diverse group of people moving together in the same positive direction.	**3**	**2**	**1**
Total for section			

HEALTH	Always	Sometimes	Never
I have high energy.	**3**	**2**	**1**
I know how to handle stress.	**3**	**2**	**1**
I exercise.	**3**	**2**	**1**
I eat properly.	**3**	**2**	**1**
Total for Section			

(continued)

Matching Your Skills and Aptitudes to Opportunities

My Starting KASH

PERSONAL RESPONSIBILITY	Always	Sometimes	Never
I will use my full-time best efforts to drive the business.	3	2	1
I accept responsibility for my results.	3	2	1
I accept responsibility for my failures.	3	2	1
I accept short-term pain for long-term gain.	3	2	1
Total for Section			

FAMILY/FRIENDS' SUPPORT	Always	Sometimes	Never
My family/friends support my decision to start a business.	3	2	1
My family/friends understand the risks involved.	3	2	1
My family/friends understand the time commitment involved.	3	2	1
I have stable, positive relationships with my family/ friends.	3	2	1
Total for Section			

SYSTEMS ORIENTATION	Always	Sometimes	Never
I am comfortable following processes and systems others create.	3	2	1
I adjust my methods habits to comply with existing procedures.	3	2	1
I am organized and good with detail.	3	2	1
I am willing to comply with systems, even if I am in personal disagreement with the methods.	3	2	1
Total for Section			

ENTREPRENEURIAL DRIVE	Always	Sometimes	Never
Even when at first I don't know how, I find a way to make things happen.	3	2	1
I take risks.	3	2	1
I am comfortable with ambiguity.	3	2	1
I multitask well.	3	2	1
Total for Section			

(continued)

My Starting KASH

SMALL BUSINESS ACUMEN	Always	Sometimes	Never
I create and achieve budgets.	3	2	1
I use technology.	3	2	1
I read financial statements.	3	2	1
I create and achieve strategic plans.	3	2	1
Total for Section			

TIME MANAGEMENT	Always	Sometimes	Never
I use my time wisely.	3	2	1
I do high-priority activities first.	3	2	1
I create a daily action plan and work my plan daily.	3	2	1
I guard my time.	3	2	1
Total for Section			

COMMUNICATION SKILLS	Always	Sometimes	Never
I speak clearly.	3	2	1
I say what needs to be said.	3	2	1
I listen with understanding.	3	2	1
I communicate well in writing.	3	2	1
Total for Section			

The Ultimate Guide to Responsible Franchising

Once you fill this out, you have completed the first step in assessing your KASH. Pay particular attention to any section where your or others rate you a total of 8 or below. You may be at risk in these areas. This does not mean you will not succeed in franchising, but it does mean you need to improve your skills in these areas.

Also pay close attention to particular line items where you self-rated as a 3. How can you capitalize on these strengths?

Chapter 5 covers more about KASH, in the section "Three Modes of Franchisor KASH Distribution."

When you begin contacting franchisors, consider forwarding the franchisor's representative and franchisees you talk to a copy of this self-assessment. This will help them identify who you are and whether you match the profile of a successful franchisee.

The Learning Curve and Lifecycle of a Franchisee

Just as human beings evolve as they enter different stages in life, franchisees also evolve as they enter different stages in business. In fact, franchisees move through five distinct stages in linear order: The Launch, The Grind, Winning, The Zone, and The Exit (as shown in the following image). Each stage is marked by changes in franchisees' results and satisfaction level.

This chapter helps you identify each stage and gives you proven strategies to accelerate through your learning curve. It is one of the most important chapters in this book – one I recommend you reread, mark up, and keep referring back to. I discuss how franchisees' KASH (knowledge, attitude, skills, and habits, as discussed in Chapter 4) fluctuate in each stage. I also show you how to help the franchisor tailor their support to your specific needs in each stage.

This chapter answers four important questions.

- What is the predictable learning curve and lifecycle of your franchise and what happens during each stage?

- What are the three modes a franchisor will use to support you?

- How do you accelerate through the learning curve toward The Zone?

- How do skillful franchisors help you through each stage?

Moving Through the Stages

As a franchisee, you will go through emotional fluctuations, from the joy at opening (The Launch), to the frustration of putting forth a huge effort for modest results due to the distressing frequency of your mistakes (The Grind), to satisfaction from succeeding in your business (Winning), to your eventual mastery of the franchise model (The Zone) to your eventual succession plan or exit (The Exit). The image lays out these five stages and shows what happens to franchisees' results and satisfaction in each stage. Pay particular attention to the inverse relationship between franchisees' results and satisfaction in the first two stages of the learning curve.

While franchisors train new franchisees on the nuances of their businesses, they start with the presumption that franchisees remember what it is like to learn as a beginner, from the place of incompetence.

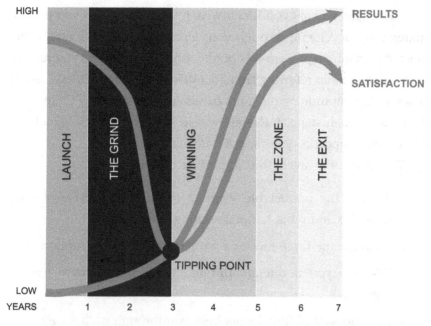

Franchisee lifecycle and satisfaction curve. © FPG/Joe Mathews.

Franchise candidates who have amassed enough wealth to start a business most likely have operated from a master or near mastery level for a long time. This chapter will *train you on how to be trained* rather than assuming you will remember.

To start, consider The Launch from the franchisor's perspective. As discussed, many franchisors make little or no money from their franchise fee. Franchise fees often cover only the cost of running the franchisee recruitment department. Your franchise fee was probably spent on salaries, recruitment advertising, benefits, supplies, and other departmental expenses and perhaps franchise broker fees for the purpose of trying to find you. Therefore, most franchisors are completely reliant on the royalty income (and product sales for those franchisors who are also suppliers to their franchisees) for the survival of their businesses. Peak-performing franchisees pay the highest royalties and purchase the most products and therefore drive the most revenue for the franchisor. Additionally, because peak performers fully realize the success formula (KASH) of the business, they also consume fewer resources than their counterparts. They pay the most and consume the least, making them (in business terms) the franchisor's highest-margin repeat customers and guaranteed sources of recurring revenue, the lifeblood of every franchisor's business.

Conversely, franchisees in The Launch and The Grind understandably generate the lowest royalty revenue and product sales for the franchisor because they are still ramping up. If they are being adequately supported, they also consume most of the franchisor's time and management resources. Looking at the franchisor's profitability on a per-franchisee basis, many franchisors lose money or break even on franchisees until they grasp the KASH success formula of the business. Established franchisees (those who are in the Winning or The Zone stage) subsidize the time and resources spent on training and ongoing support of new or struggling franchisees. Therefore, the success of any franchisor depends on their ability to give franchisees the necessary KASH as quickly as possible. If mature franchisees (in business three years or more) aren't winning, the whole franchise system may implode.

Before I dissect the five stages of this learning curve, let's look at the three ways franchisors give their KASH to franchisees.

Three Modes of Franchisor KASH Distribution

The three ways that franchisors will help you accelerate through the learning curve of your business are training, consulting, and coaching. When used in combination and at the right point in your business lifecycle, these modes will work together to achieve the same goal: your peak performance.

Some franchisors instinctively support their franchisees correctly. They may train, consult, and coach their franchisees at the right time and in the right combination without even knowing the difference or what to call it. Others understand the differences and the timing, and have a proven system for supporting franchisees. A third group, consisting of unskilled franchisors, doesn't know the differences or the timing and may never bother to learn them.

In Chapter 1, I defined "the business of franchising" as "recruiting, training, developing, resourcing, and leading a team of entrepreneurs to build a brand." Therefore, among other things, every franchisor is a training, coaching, consulting, and advisory organization. Therefore, a franchisee should expect to be trained by adult learning experts and supported by domain area experts highly skilled and trained in the area of coaching, consulting, and performance management. Since it often takes several years to master a business model, you should expect your learning path to be completely mapped out with key benchmarks and performance indicators that tell you and the franchisor precisely where you are on the learning curve of your business. However, this often isn't the case. Too many franchisors see training as an event to be completed, like a two-week initial training course, and then you are kicked out into the wild to fend for yourself. This section details the support expert franchisors routinely deliver, so when it's time to explore certain brands, you can grade their level of support when you speak to franchisees.

Franchisee Support Mode One: Training

There are essentially two types of training: information and skills. Training starts by transferring the information you need to know to be successful in the business and creating a proper context for learning. Franchisee training should be highly structured and remedial, assuming franchisees know little about the business they are entering. Many franchisors will send remedial pretraining information ahead for franchisees to digest before they come into the franchisor's training event program.

Training creates a hierarchical relationship, which a franchisee might find uncomfortable to start. The working assumption is that the trainer knows more than those being trained. This "trainer-knows-and-you-don't" dynamic creates a top-down hierarchy. This is not a bad thing, just the dynamic of the trainer-trainee relationship.

When you are being trained, communication typically flows downward from the trainer to you. Very little flows upward, and very little *should* flow upward. For example, picture being in a franchise training class where a new franchisee says, "In our CPA firm, we didn't do it your way; we did it [such-and-such way]" and the trainer responds sweetly, "That probably works great in a CPA firm, but we are learning how to run a muffler shop, not an accounting practice. Do it our way. Thank you for sharing."

You are there to acquire knowledge, not offer it. Often your past paradigms and experiences are not relevant to the new tasks at hand. It's not only important to learn the business, it's important to learn the business in its proper context. In other words, don't learn the auto business through the prism of an accountant. Learn the auto business through the prism of one who is an expert in the automotive industry. These are separate and distinct vantage points.

> During training, the franchisor will focus intently on building knowledge and skills, while providing lots of opportunities for you to practice and make mistakes in a controlled environment. Remember, practice *does not* make perfect; *practice makes permanent*. Perfect practice makes perfect. Be sure you only do business with a franchisor who regularly monitors your practice, making sure you engage in perfect practice designed to create permanent winning habits.

Skilled franchisors will help develop your business and technical skills. Remember, you are not joining a franchise to learn how to do such tasks as unclog a drain; you are joining a franchise to learn how to make money and create a desired lifestyle by unclogging drains. You need to learn how to deliver the product and market, manage, and promote a business. Only do business with a franchisor who understands that your business skills are as important as your technical skills.

Just as franchisees don't need to reinvent the wheel, neither does a franchisor. Smart franchisors may use outside vendors to deliver certain components of their training program and adapt their franchise systems to the vendors' products and training, such as sales training.

Again, the goal of training is to transfer knowledge and skills. This can be hampered by several common mistakes on the part of the franchisor:

- Systems are not properly documented, leaving knowledge gaps.
- Training programs are "data dumps," trying to squeeze too much information into too little time.

- Knowledge is offered but modeling skills are not.

- More emphasis is placed on training than on consulting, coaching, and ongoing performance management. Knowledge is overrated – on its own, it doesn't make a difference. (For instance, why do so many people smoke? Don't they know it causes cancer? Why are so many adults obese? Don't they know how to order a salad and exercise on a treadmill?) A franchisee's consistent and skillful implementation of their knowledge is what produces great results.

Franchisee Support Mode Two: Consulting

Consulting is about identifying performance gaps and fixing problems. After initial training, competent franchisors consult with their franchisees on an ongoing basis, identifying and eliminating obstacles to growth. While the same person may provide initial training and ongoing consulting, consulting and training are materially different modes of support, requiring different sets of skills, and are used at different times in the learning curve to produce different results. Consulting differs from training in the following ways.

In consulting mode, the support person's job is to identify and fix problems quickly. Since franchisees are new to the business, the franchisor should take responsibility for identifying your problems and crafting a solution, which requires more time, energy, and investment on their part. Your role as a franchisee is to execute the solution the franchisor prescribes. Often franchisors will train franchisees after the fact; helping franchisees learn how and why a breakdown occurred and showing ways to prevent a similar breakdown in the future. This is ideal because it will also help you get a deeper understanding of the subtle cause-and-effect relationships of your new business – what does and doesn't work and why.

With consulting, as with training, communications flows downward. When a franchisor's support staff is in consulting mode, they take the same directive role as a trainer. They will probably tell you "do this and that," expecting that is exactly what you will do, even when your past experience tells you otherwise, because your past experience may not be relevant to this particular business.

As with training, when a franchisor is operating in the mode of consulting, there is a hierarchy. They are the domain area experts and the new franchisee isn't. Some franchisees are uncomfortable with this hierarchy and push back.

Franchisor Support Mode Three: Coaching

Coaching is about pure execution. Coaching is similar to consulting, except for one key differentiator. The mode of coaching assumes you already know what to do and you know how to do it, whatever "it" is. In coaching mode, the franchisor will prompt you with questions to help you identify your own gaps and problems and prompt you more to help you craft your own solutions. When coaching, the problem identification and solution resides with the franchisee. When consulting, these reside with the franchisor. Therefore, coaching is ineffective and is thus a poor mode of producing results the earlier you are in the learning curve of your business.

Coaching is also about accountability. An effective coach will ask smart questions to determine what you will do and by when, and then follow up to listen to the outcomes and ensure you fulfilled the action plan you designed for yourself. Dr. Robert Cialdini, psychologist and guru on influence, discovered that people are most likely to take an action when they make a verbal promise to another with a clear deadline about when something will occur. Accountability works. Some franchisees resist accountability, again thinking,

"If I wanted a boss, I would take a job!" This is poor judgment on their part. Accountability is a key part of the performance equation and a major benefit franchisees have over independent businesspeople.

- When the franchisor's support staff is in coaching mode, they address situations in which a franchisee knows what to do, but isn't doing it or is stuck about identifying the best course of action. The franchisor will ask probing questions, such as "What do you see as your best options?" and "If you took option 1, what is the likely result? If you took option 2, what is the likely result? Which takes you closer to your goal?" These probing questions help franchisees cut through the noisy self-chatter and make emotionless, rational decisions aimed at achieving an objective. Strong coaches will immediately schedule a follow-up call or meeting to determine the outcome, and if the outcome falls short, ask more questions to get into more problem-solving.

- When coaching, franchisor support staff operates in partnership with franchisees. There is no hierarchy. The coach's job is to coach. The franchisees' job is to execute. Each has clear roles and responsibilities.

- In coaching, the solution always resides with the franchisee, not with the coach. This distinction is different than consulting, where the solution resides with the franchisor.

Head-to-Head Differences Between the Modes

How else do these three modes differ? The following example assumes a franchisee isn't growing their sales as budgeted. The franchisee says, "My sales are off this month. . . ."

91

The Trainer	The Consultant	The Coach
"Let's hold a sales training program for your salespeople."	"Let me follow your salespeople around and hear what they are doing wrong and figure out a solution."	The coach asks, "How many calls are you making? What are customers telling you about their reasons for not buying? What changed from last month? What do you need to be doing differently?"
It is assumed if the salespeople knew more, they would perform better.	The consultant assumes the salespeople or franchisee cannot identify the problem or craft a solution.	The coach assumes that by prompting the franchisee with questions, the salespeople or franchisee will identify their own problem and create their own solution.
The solution resides with the trainer.	*The solution resides with the consultant.*	*The solution resides with the franchisee.*

The point is this: if you are to be successful, the franchisor needs to be prepared to mix and match training, consulting, and coaching at the appropriate times of the learning curve. Your role as a franchisee is to internalize the training and execute the consulting and coaching as it is offered. Let's now look at how to successfully navigate the learning curve.

Stages of the Franchisee Learning Curve and Lifecycle Explained

This section now explains in detail each stage of the franchisee learning curve and lifecycle: The Launch, The Grind, Winning, The Zone, and The Exit.

In Chapter 4, I discussed the KASH model of success. KASH stands for knowledge, attitude, skills, and habits. I asserted that successful franchisees usually seem to possess the same level of KASH as other successful franchisees in the same franchise system. Many underperforming franchisees become arrested in their KASH development, never acquiring the necessary KASH to successfully navigate the learning curve into peak levels of performance. In this section, you'll see how your KASH fluctuates during each stage of your franchisee evolution, and learn what it takes to successfully graduate into the next stage.

The Launch

When a franchisee signs their franchise agreement, they are filled with mixed emotions. While there is some fear of the unknown, they are mostly filled with a sense of joy and empowerment. It's like they can look out across the learning curve and see the life they are designing for themselves and their families, as if it is already occurring and they just took the necessary step to make it happen. Their sense of almost certain success fills them with awe. They move feverishly through startup activities such as setting up a corporation, securing financing, finding and securing a location, purchasing inventory, and so on. They hang on to the training instructor's every word during initial training. They leave training charged up and ready to make their mark.

Eventually the franchise opens, and they wake up every morning ready to take on the day. They eagerly serve customers and treat themselves and their employees gently, seeing rookie mistakes as productive learning opportunities. While money is tight, they prepared for it to be tight.

However, because they are not yet skilled at what they do and customers may not know the brand, their results are as poor as they will ever be. Despite the weak initial results associated with starting a business, they recognize this is temporary and they give themselves permission to learn. They know their results will be there eventually if they diligently do what it takes to learn the success formula of the franchise.

Knowledge

When you invest in a franchise, you invest in the right to be incompetent for a short period of time. The Launch is a short-term time of intense learning.

Attitude

Your outlook toward your learning curve remains positive. The grass looks a little greener and the sky a little bluer. Your days appear filled with excitement, adventure, and awe. For the first time in a long time, you feel as if you are being called forward into action. Instead of throwing shoes and curses at your alarm clock, you often wake up before it rings, charged up with the electricity of an exciting new day. Work becomes play. Although your business may not yet be making money, you experience peace. People in your life may start complaining about your frequent gleeful whistling of "Zip-a-Dee-Doo-Dah" and the theme song to *The Andy Griffith Show* while they're trying to work.

However, earlier I defined "attitude" as how you view the business, and not in terms of "good" and "bad" attitude, which is how the motivational speakers may lump it. For instance, you may still think like an accountant or sales rep although you invested in a home healthcare business. You still need to gain the vantage point and business distinctions of a home healthcare professional to succeed in the role of the franchisee.

Skills

Let's face it. During The Launch, you will probably stink. This is not a bad thing because, as discussed, you know you have invested in the privilege of being incompetent for a short period of time. You have to give yourself permission to learn. A motivational speaker once said, "Anything worth doing is worth being lousy at for a little while." Unless you are one of those rare prodigies or your background closely matches the skills required to succeed in your new venture, your skills at best will be unrefined. Some skills will transfer over from your past career and some won't. The Launch is a time for deep personal and professional development. Aside from learning a new business model, if you are a first-time entrepreneur, you will be experiencing a second learning curve, which is transitioning from the employee mindset to the entrepreneurial mindset of self-directed self-sufficiency, where you eat what you kill.

Sometimes franchisors are not well refined as professional development organizations, and make the rookie mistake of overplaying imparting knowledge, but ignore franchisees' skill development. Remember, skills by definition determine your capacity for transforming know-how into results. Therefore, if you align with such an organization, you may be left on your own to develop your skills.

While you will find many franchisors who have correctly documented systems and processes, you will find fewer franchisors with the ability to correctly identify your missing personal skill sets and have programs in place to fill in your skill gaps to help you attain mastery level execution of processes. For instance, I don't know of any franchisors who have training programs that teach franchisees how to make good strategic decisions under time pressure and with imperfect and incomplete information or improving frustration tolerance, all marketable and necessary skills entrepreneurs must possess. If you have deficits in this area, you are most likely going to be left on your own to develop that skill or will have to find third-party providers and make investments outside of the chain.

Habits

The second you open your doors, your habits will start forming. At the beginning of The Launch, you will either begin the good habit of spending more time executing the high-priority activities that generate the most results or formulating the bad habit of wasting time on busywork that produces little. Carefully document and observe where you spend your time. In a learning curve, budget time for learning and skill development. How quickly you develop KASH will determine how quickly you ramp up your business and generate positive cash flow. Until you have refined on-the-job skills, it's important to develop a habit of creating high levels of activity. You can still chop down a tree with a dull axe; it just takes more swings.

Strategies for a Successful Launch

Many franchisors' initial training programs are typically done in the vacuum of a classroom setting, with perhaps little real-world experience. If the franchisor does not offer continuation training three to six months after you open your doors, I recommend asking to take the initial training program a second time, even if this means paying additional fees. Once you are in the real world executing the business model, you develop the context you didn't have in the initial training program. Context in a learning curve is *everything*.

> When you launch your business, do not focus on profitability. Instead, focus on learning moments and generating activity that produces results.

You will know you have completed The Launch when you start becoming frustrated and disillusioned with the learning curve of your business. Put another way, your attitude may sink. Instead of whistling "Zip-a-Dee-Doo-Dah," you now hum B. B. King's classic "The Thrill is Gone." Don't despair. The thrill isn't really gone; it just appears to hide for a little while.

The Grind

Think about the last time you picked up a new hobby. Let's use golf as an example. Adults who picked up golf later in life are thrilled with the decision to learn the game. They get fitted with clubs and shoes, go to the driving range, sign up with a teaching pro, and learn the basics of the game. Some are so giddy, they even buy silly hats, bright sweaters, and loud plaid pants. Learning is fun, and they don't take mistakes so seriously at first. They let themselves hit popups and ground balls, and take out Texas-sized divots. Hitting into the woods, trap, or lake, although not desired, is really no big deal; it is a given part of the learning process.

Somewhere in the learning process, golf stops being fun. The permission they had given themselves to make mistakes is revoked, replaced by a demand for results equal to the money, effort, anguish, and gaudy trousers they invested in. For instance, my cousin once gave my older brother Paul a near perfect free set of irons. Oddly, the 9 iron had been bent into a hook, rumored to have happened by being slammed shaft first into a tree.

This phenomenon also occurs in franchising, primarily with first-time entrepreneurs, but hopefully with less violence. As these new franchisees move through the learning curve, they often revoke their own learning privileges and demand a return on their investment that they don't have the KASH (or capacity) yet to produce, creating a sense of helplessness and frustration.

Serial entrepreneurs have a different take because they experienced it before. They often see The Grind as a sign of progress, because after The Grind comes Winning. They understand that producers, who are used to creating more results than most, don't often jump from The Launch to Winning without experiencing some Grind.

Some franchisees may even produce a false experience of failing. As long as the franchisee has cash reserves in the bank, these experiences can't be trusted.

Once, I was training a class of franchisees consultants of a business service franchisor. I saw a particular franchisee who looked distraught and had mentally checked out. Picking up on this, I called for a break and took the franchisee aside to see what was happening. The franchisee confided, "I'm upset because I know the other franchisees are getting the business quicker than I am. I'm behind the rest of the class."

I asked the franchisee, "Do you think that when you leave here, you are going to know everything you need to know to become successful or do you think your real training begins when you leave here?"

"I know I will have a ton of work to do when we leave here," replied the franchisee.

"Will you do what it takes?" asked the trainer.

"Absolutely!" declared the franchisee.

I then confided, "Consider for a second that not only are you not behind the rest of the class, *I am secretly declaring you the valedictorian!* Everyone else is relishing the joy of their startup. You have already moved into the frustration of the learning curve. Congratulations. You are at the head of the class."

Consider for a second that there are two types of pain. The first is like a headache. We relate to this pain as if it is something bad – something that shouldn't be. We then do whatever it takes to make this pain go away.

However, there is also a second type of pain, like exercise pain. During exercise, muscle burn or fatigue becomes the desired result. We take steps to manifest this pain. We invite it into our bodies. "No pain, no gain!" we say. We relate to exercise pain as a sign of progress – a sign of winning and getting more resilient and stronger. This pain has a goal, requires effort, increases pain tolerance, demands delayed gratification, and builds character.

For whatever reason, a franchisee often experiences the pain of the learning curve of a business as headache pain rather than exercise pain.

The Learning Curve Can Be a Blind Curve in the Road

When my oldest son, Michael, was four years old, I taught him how to ride a bike. The first time I let him go, he pedaled hard and then dumped the bike, skinning his knee. The second time he pedaled farther, dumped the bike, and bruised his shin. After the third fall, he said to me in anger, "If I lived on a different street, owned a different bike, and had a different father, I would be riding a bike right now! When he was sprawled out on the driveway, what would lead him to believe that in the next ride he would get balance? But then, one magical, unpredictable time, this is what happens. While baby-soft skin may seem to be preferable to cuts and bruises, you can't get balance without falling down. It may also be difficult to predict exactly when you will get the business on a deep experiential level. So you have to blindly trust the learning process and just keep pedaling.

The Grind ends with an empowering "now I get it!" series of experiences. Just like the kid who gets "balance" when learning to ride a bike, once a franchisee gets the business, they will always get it. The KASH formula becomes part of their identity.

Let's take a look at a franchisee's KASH when in The Grind.

Knowledge

Knowledge is steadily increasing, but gaps still exist. Franchisees are still dependent on the franchisor, because they don't know what they don't know. Where The Launch is a time of unconscious incompetence, meaning franchisees don't know how bad they really are, The Grind is a time of conscious incompetence. They get how much further they need to go to win. This change of experiences can be scary and intimidating.

However, fearing The Grind is like fearing the Boogey Man. When a child realizes there is no such thing as the Boogey Man outside their own imagination, darkness loses its power over the child. When franchisees get that there is no such thing as The Grind outside their own imagination, the disempowerment, fear, and frustration of the learning curve also dissipates.

Attitude

Most franchisees are results oriented and often results simply aren't to the franchisees' satisfaction or expectations. This is where franchisees and franchisors disconnect. *This disconnection occurs when franchisees need franchisors the most.* An objective look at results may show a steady increase in franchisees' performance. Franchisees will typically produce marginally better results week after week, slow and steady. However, franchisees often get caught up in the frustration of the almost superhuman effort it takes to produce those results. Most franchisees have been solid producers in the past. Producers like to produce. They forgot how hard they had to work early in their careers. They only remember and still relate to their past mastery. Because they are struggling to achieve the results they achieve, many get sucked into *the false experience of failing*, although they may actually be on or ahead of plan.

Franchisors don't measure false experiences, just results. Many of the franchisor's support personnel have never owned a business before and don't get what it is to be in The Grind. Therefore, they do not offer the emotional support franchisees desperately need to successfully navigate this stage.

Franchisees react to The Grind in four ways:

- **Fighters fight.** These franchisees create monumental problems where either no problems or perhaps tiny problems exist. They blame the training, products, competition, support, marketing, pricing, and even their customers. They think, "I am working the system, but the system isn't working."

- **Optimists get caught up in false hopes.** They engage the power of positive thinking, layering positive thoughts of prosperity on top of "stinking thinking." When the franchisor calls asking, "How are things going?" the franchisee responds, "Just peachy!" A business coach once told me, "Hope is a beautiful thing but a lousy business strategy." Many franchisors are going to assume when you say you are "peachy," you are indeed peachy, instead of pretending to be peachy when you are really petrified. If you are prone to false positive thinking, learn how to shoot straight and say what you are really experiencing so the franchisor can offer you emotional as well as operational support.

- **Pessimistic franchisees think the sky is falling.** These franchisees begin expecting failure, and can easily gather the data to support their conclusions. "Just look at my past results!" they say.

In a learning curve however, past poor results are not irrefutable proof of future failure, because every day new franchisees acquire new KASH, which alters the existing state of their business and what they are capable of achieving in the future.

Unlike The Launch, where a franchisee can clearly see across the learning curve into the land of milk and honey, during The Grind, the learning curve becomes a blind curve in which franchisees cannot see past the bend.

- **Emotionally mature franchisees give themselves permission to learn.** Although they are not crazy about mistakes, they learn their lessons and move on. They know mistakes are part of the process, and they build safeguards to avoid making the same mistakes twice. They know they will feel anxiety from time to time. But they also know they will survive the fear because they remember being afraid of other things in the past, and they didn't die from that fear either. They know there will be frustration, and their frustration won't be fatal. They take their learning curve one day at a time with a full understanding that whatever happened yesterday is already in the past and can't be changed, and they maintain an intense focus on making today pay out.

In a learning curve, past poor results are not irrefutable proof of future failure, because every day new franchisees acquire new KASH, which alters the existing state of their business and what they are capable of achieving in the future.

A vast majority of franchisees of a vast majority of franchise systems will succeed if they commit to acquiring the necessary KASH it takes to win.

Skills

Throughout The Grind, franchisees are usually getting better at what they do. But because progress may be slow, steady, and many times undetectable, they may lose sight of the progress they are making.

Skill development is what carries franchisees past The Grind and into Winning, by eventually producing greater results with less effort and fewer resources.

Habits

In The Grind, habits begin to form. This is a critical time in the learning process. Remember the old adage "Practice doesn't make perfect, practice makes it permanent." Bad habits form as easily as good habits. Each business has high-priority activities that produce most of the results. Each business has minutia – those activities that suck a franchisee in, chew up time, and ultimately don't make a difference.

Forming winning habits will propel franchisees to a breakthrough in results and into the stage called Winning. If the franchisee forms bad habits, they continue to "grind it out," feeling decreasing satisfaction and dramatically increasing their chance of failure. Most franchisees get into the flow of the business, find the right rhythm, and acquire the necessary KASH to experience Winning. But don't leave it to chance. Keep reading!

Strategies to Successfully Navigate The Grind

- **Work on your business one day at a time.** Plan your day and work on your plan. Forget what happened yesterday. Deny yourself your right to worry about tomorrow. As Jesus said when delivering the Sermon on the Mount, "Do not worry about tomorrow, for tomorrow will worry about itself. Each day has enough trouble of its own." Focus today on developing the necessary KASH you need to succeed. Once today is complete, make a commitment to wake up tomorrow and do it again.

- **Get emotional support.** Find someone in your life who instinctively knows how to pick you up when you are down.

- **Stay out of "survival" mode.** Make decisions you would make if you were playing to win rather than circling your wagons and cutting costs to avoid failure.

- **Conserve your cash.** Let the franchisor know exactly your cash balance and what your plan calls for that month.

- **Treat yourself gently.** You are supposed to be learning. If you aren't making mistakes, you aren't trying hard enough.

- **Be humble.** Reach out for help and support. Let the franchisor earn their royalties by contributing to you, helping you fix your problems quickly.

- **Trust the learning process.** Remember, you weren't born competent in your last position. No doctor ever removed anyone from their mother's womb, spanked their little butt, wrapped them in a blanket, and handed them to their mother proclaiming, "Congratulations, you just gave birth to an eight-pound, three-ounce vice president of marketing."

How the Franchisor Can Help You

More training: Have the support people watch you, monitoring your on-the-job performance. Have them focus on developing good habits, improving skills, and continuing to develop your knowledge base.

More consulting: Don't be afraid to burn up the franchisor's phone lines. Keep close track of the key performance measures of your business such as labor cost, cost of sales, lead-to-close, cost of acquiring a customer, and so on. Get these measures to the franchisors' support staff. Ask them what it means and get strategies to fix problems fast. If you disagree with the franchisor's solution, execute it anyway. Remember, your disagreement may be coming from a past business paradigm that may be irrelevant to your new business model. Follow the franchisor's instructions closely until results prove otherwise.

More coaching: You may need constant reminders of your goals and why you started your business in the first place. You may need help moving through worry. The franchisor's support team should help you move through your stress in order to make better business decisions.

Winning

As franchisees acquire the necessary KASH to succeed, they begin to experience the ability to create positive outcomes with less assistance. In The Grind, franchisees understandably act as a person pumping water from an old hand-operated iron pump. They spend a tremendous amount of time, money, and energy, pumping and pumping, disheartened by the mere trickle of water their pumping creates. What they don't sense or see is the pipeline full of water that has yet to make it to the nozzle. Once the water starts flowing, it takes less and less energy to keep the water going. Less pumping produces more water. This is what Winning looks like. Winning is not produced by a singular event, just like water doesn't flow by one mighty pump. Winning is a process. Franchisees enter Winning through many little victories, by learning to do the little things right, and by steadily acquiring the KASH formula of success.

Franchisees enter Winning as a combination of their own personal effort and the franchisor's skill in imparting their KASH formula of success. However, these franchisees are not yet out of the woods and can still fall back into The Grind. How? By folding their winning hand.

A franchisee of a fresh juice franchise once told a funny story about some of his customers. "When my new customers start drinking green juice, they feel 10 times better. Some think, 'If I take 10 times that original amount, then I should feel one hundred times better!' But instead of feeling better, they throw up and never come back."

It can be the same with franchisees in Winning. Many feel compelled to make "minor adjustments" like emphasizing certain aspects of their business and deemphasizing others. Because they have not completely grasped the KASH success formula of their business, they may not fully realize the synergistic cause-and-effect relationships and see the full impact of these decisions. They tamper with the Winning formula and sometimes disrupt the rhythm of their business, creating a setback.

When franchisees enter Winning, a sophisticated franchisor will shift their support strategies to making sure franchisees change nothing, drumming the Winning formula into the franchisee's memory through sheer repetition. Franchisors should keep a watchful eye on these franchisees, but many franchisors do not understand this dynamic and do not remain vigilant. These franchisors assume their job is now done and winning franchisees will just keep doing what works and the world will be as it should be.

Because many franchisors do not understand this dynamic of human performance (the winner's unwitting drive to fold the winning hand), they are not on the lookout. Therefore, as you enter Winning, make sure someone is watching your back, documenting what you do, and holding you accountable for not changing anything!

Knowledge

Franchisees in Winning are consciously competent. They know what they are good at and what they need to do to produce results.

They are empowered with the experience of being able to make things happen.

Attitude

Winning franchisees are empowered franchisees. They are achieving their goals or have a clear line of sight toward them. They have successfully navigated their learning curve and can see the finish line. All they need to do is to keep their foot on the gas, keep the wheel straight, and keep driving.

Franchisees in The Grind drive their businesses by looking in their rearview mirror, fretting about costly mistakes in the past. Franchisees in Winning spend more time looking through the windshield, focused more on the road ahead.

Skills

Winning franchisees have developed and refined their personal skills. They are good at whatever they need to be good at to win. They have the ability to produce positive outcomes and handle whatever the business throws at them. Their next step is to become skillful trainers and leaders, having the ability to successfully impart the KASH formula of the business to their employees.

Habits

Winning franchisees know the high-priority activities that produce the greatest results and spend their time engaged in these activities. They have gotten into the rhythm and the flow of the business. They are generating greater results with more ease and a higher degree of predictability. One habit they probably need to drop at this point is self-reliance. It's time to include professional development and nurturing of staff into their day and groom themselves as a manager – transitioning from doing to delegating.

Strategies for Successfully Navigating from Winning to Peak Performance

- **Don't fold the winning hand.** Train and develop your staff, giving away the KASH success formula of the business, making sure everyone has the Winning hand. Refine your systems and document your processes and procedures. Let employees step up and contribute. Decrease your value so your employees may increase their value.

- **An out-of-the-box strategy to drive performance is to volunteer to mentor another franchisee or to act as an assistant trainer in the franchisor's initial training program.** Medical school professors have a saying: "See one, do one, teach one." They teach surgery by first letting the medical student observe (to build their knowledge), then they do (to build their skills), and then they teach (to build winning habits). Just as a medical student will not teach what the medical student is not already executing, you will not teach what you are not executing. This is a brilliant way to permanently cement the Winning KASH formula in your memory.

How the Franchisor Can Help You

Less training: You already know what it takes to win. Now it's about executing what you know. You do, however, want to be trained as a trainer so you can develop your staff. You also want to make sure you have a solid understanding of all the key performance indicators of your business and what they mean.

Less consulting: You want to start developing a healthier sense of independence from the franchisor, building your skills in diagnosing your own problems and having both you and your staff creating your own solutions. The knowledge is now within you. Exercise it.

More coaching: Work with the franchisor to help with goals and strategic planning. Use the franchisor as your accountability structure, holding you responsible for executing your plan and systematizing the business to create a flywheel of perpetual forward momentum. Give them permission to challenge you and confront you when you are off track.

The Zone

When franchisees enter The Zone, they produce outstanding results as if they were on auto-pilot. They have fully committed the KASH success formula to memory. They are unconsciously competent and brilliant execution has now become a habit.

> Most of what franchisees are looking to accomplish with their business will occur in Winning. Many Winning franchisees will not enter The Zone, nor is it a requirement for success. Peak-performing franchisees are far to the right of the franchisor's performance bell curve.

Transitioning from Winning into The Zone is often not about doing more of what it takes to get into Winning. The difference is attitudinal. When in Winning, franchisees need to think about what they must do to win, create a plan, and then they must execute their plan. In Winning, franchisees still invest a ton of mental energy thinking about what they should or shouldn't be doing. Franchisees in The Zone act more automatically, with less thinking and less energy spent.

Knowledge

Peak-performing franchisees are walking encyclopedias, experts in their field.

Attitude

Franchisees in The Zone are empowered with the sense of being able to design positive outcomes at will. Some become humble, attributing their success to the franchisor, their employees, and their Creator, instead of their own personal greatness. Others become puffed up, reveling in their "rock star" status given to them by the other franchisees.

For some, their relationship to their business evolves again – no longer are they focused on just making money. They are now thinking about how to benefit others and the community. Their desire for success may be replaced with a new desire for significance – profits for purpose or a transformation in how they view success. Others get caught up in the trappings of success, such as bigger houses, fancier cars, expensive toys, and luxurious vacations.

Skills

Franchisees in The Zone expertly execute their knowledge. They have highly defined personal and organizational skill sets, being able to produce outstanding results with seemingly little effort.

Habits

These franchisees know what activities produce the greatest results and structure their day to expertly execute these activities. Peak-performing franchisees are not without risk, however. Believe it or not, their greatest risk comes from success.

You may be asking incredulously, "Success? How does success create risk?"

After conquering the last known civilization, famed military leader Alexander the Great cried out in anguish, "Alas, no worlds left to conquer." Alexander won. What was Alexander to do next?

The thrill of living and working occurs in playing to win, not in the actual winning. Winning is overrated. Playing to win is juicy.

Have you ever climbed a mountain? How long did you hang out at the top before you were bored out of your mind? Isn't it more thrilling to climb?

How the Franchisor Can Help You

More training: Not for you, but get training for your staff and offer to train other franchisees. Volunteer to help train other franchisees, giving you an experience of greater purpose. Allocate some time to mentor employees and at least one other franchisee who is mired in The Grind.

Less consulting: Start relying on and challenging your staff to identify their own breakdowns and create their own solutions. Give them decision-making power. Use the franchisor's operational audits as their scorecard, an objective measure as to how your staff is doing.

More coaching: Get agreement from the franchisor's support staff to never let you win, to create new goals worthy of being achieved that keep you motivated and in the game. When it looks like winning is inevitable, have them challenge you to design larger and loftier goals – goals so large you may never win or lose, but keep you in the game.

The Exit

If you have contemplated buying a home, did you think, "This is a house I will live in for the rest of my life," or were you thinking shorter term? When you took your first job, did you think, "This is a good place to work for 40 years and then retire," or did you think it was a good place to cut your teeth, with thoughts of eventually moving on? People who invest in franchises often exit seven to ten years out.

Many consultants will tell you the time to sell the business is when a business is at its peak market value. This doesn't always hold true in most franchises. That's like saying to a homeowner, "The time to sell your house is at peak market value." From a financial perspective it's true, but from a practical standpoint it's naïve. What if you have kids in high school? Do you pull them out and put them in a new school because your house has hit peak market value? What if you simply enjoy your neighborhood and living in your town? Do you sever these relationships because the real estate market peaked? "Who cares about peak market value?" the homeowner thinks. "I like living here."

Just as there is a time to sell your home and change jobs, there will be an appropriate time to sell your business, and it may not be when it hits peak market value. There are other considerations.

To simplify The Exit, there are two basic times to sell, and one is not necessarily better than the other. It's your business, so you get to choose.

- When you have accomplished what you originally set out to accomplish and there is nothing more you want to accomplish with the business.

- When you know you will accomplish everything you are looking to accomplish, although it hasn't all been accomplished yet. It's just a matter of time, just around the corner. Sure, you could wait around for those results to occur, but work has lost its challenge and you don't feel like waiting.

Sell your business when there are no worlds left to conquer, when you have nothing left to prove. Don't prolong the decision or you will have the same dissatisfying experience that Alexander the Great had after the last civilization fell.

I always found it interesting how many franchisees hang on too long and become bitter. They engage in nasty gossip with other franchisees and end up destroying the integrity of the franchisee-franchisor relationship. Regardless of their age, they become like the crotchety old neighbor who sits on their rocking chair on the front porch, yelling at people who walk past. Not that the people walking past are doing anything wrong, but because the crotchety neighbor has nothing better to do. The franchisor becomes a frequent and convenient target for franchisees who have nothing left to win and nothing better to do.

I am not asserting that these franchisees are necessarily doing anything wrong, the same way rocks aren't doing anything wrong when they hit the ground after being dropped. Rocks simply obey the laws of gravity. Franchisees are obeying the laws of behavior. To interfere with the law of gravity, the rock has to be caught before it hits the ground. To interfere with the law of behavior, franchisees must either catch themselves or be caught by the franchisor before their attitude hits bottom. Because few franchisors understand the dynamics of normal human behavior, few look out for Winning or peak-performing franchisees to fall. Asking franchisees to catch themselves is almost like asking the rock to catch itself.

Knowledge

Franchisees in The Exit stage of their business often have expert knowledge. They have seen it all.

Attitude

During The Exit stage, there is a slow and steady erosion of desire to achieve operational excellence. The business has lost its challenge, and these franchisees are no longer inspired. Where work was once play, work is once again work.

Most franchisors report significant sales increases when such a business transfers to a new owner, often in double digits. What do these new franchisees have that the old franchisees don't? More knowledge? More skills? Better habits? Certainly not. They have a more productive energy. New franchisees act inspired; old franchisees act tired.

Skills

Exiting franchisees develop a new skill for cutting corners. They know how and where to cut back on the effort and still achieve some minimally acceptable performance. However, eventually cutting corners plateaus results and, when left unchecked, will negatively impact performance and eventually their resale value.

Habits

Many of these franchisees start walking the path of least resistance. Often, they have gotten out of the habit of personal development and continual improvement. They have gotten into the habit of minimal acceptable performance, meaning doing just enough to pay the bills and maintain their current lifestyle. As they are no longer focused on perfectly executing the high-priority activities that drive results, results will eventually flatten or track downward.

Franchisees in The Exit stage often say long, long goodbyes. They are like the last guests to leave the party, oblivious to the fact that the party is over. Because they have no other party to go to next, they just hang out, overstaying their welcome.

The Business Seller's Mindset

When selling a business, there appear to be two types of franchisee responses to the resale process. The first group are mature businesspeople who may have sold businesses before or know others who have, and thus have a realistic idea of what their business is worth and what happens next. They sell a business the way others sell used automobiles. They know the business has a certain fair market value, and they research what it is. They calmly contact the franchisor's franchise sales representatives and alert them of their intentions. They also enlist the services of a business broker to generate leads. They exit with dignity and grace.

The second group dismisses the notion of fair market value, assuming this concept does not pertain to their unique circumstances. They assign a monetary value to their pain and suffering in The Grind and add that to the asking price of their business, like they are suing the new owners for damages. When the prospective buyers do their due diligence and question them about the business, they experience it as a personal attack. "More pain and suffering," they think. "I am going to have to raise the price of the business."

How the Franchisor Can Help You Sell a Business

More training: Get training on how to value a business and what happens before, during, and after the resale.

More consulting: Find out what businesses have sold for in the past. What is fair market value for your business? What terms should you consider? How will the franchisor support you and the buyer during the resale and transition of your business?

More coaching: Selling a business is an emotionally taxing process. By then, you have so much mentally and emotionally invested in the business, separation is difficult. Coaching helps prepare you for an exit and transition into what is next.

Summary

Just as human beings evolve as they enter different stages in life, franchisees also evolve as they enter different stages in business. This evolution occurs through five distinct phases in linear order: The Launch, The Grind, Winning, The Zone, and The Exit. The franchisees' results and satisfaction level fluctuate from stage to stage. During each stage, franchisees' results are directly tied to the KASH they acquire.

None of these stages are better or worse than any other stage; they simply are. Many franchisees, however, resist The Grind and attempt to leapfrog right into Winning. They demand results of themselves they have not yet acquired the KASH to produce, increasing daily frustration. With an intelligent learning strategy and close contact with the franchisor's skilled trainers and operational support personnel, franchisees can accelerate their learning curve and compress their learning curve time frame from The Launch to Winning.

What Insiders Want You to Know About Franchising Before You Invest

Franchising has evolved quite a bit over the last 50 years. Franchisors can be lumped into three basic schools of thought that I call Franchising 1.0, 2.0, and 3.0 and will describe in this chapter. Do not invest in 1.0 and 2.0 franchisors. That isn't to say they don't or can't make money, but that they don't assign the proper value or respect to what you risk and bring to the table as a franchisee and it's reflective in the culture of the organization. It's more of a quality of life decision – a "life is too short" decision.

Franchising 1.0

Visionaries and pioneers like Ray Kroc (McDonald's), Fred DeLuca (Subway), and William Rosenberg (Dunkin' Donuts) created what FPG (Franchise Performance Group) defines as Franchising 1.0 (1960–1990). It's "the original franchising strategy," as a "better, faster, and cheaper" distribution model to get their products to market using other people's money and effort. The franchisees assume the financial risk and the franchisor realizes almost risk-free recurring revenue streams.

If you could look into the heads of the franchisor's ownership and leadership and hear their thoughts, you would see how often they took the position that they owned the brand, product, supply lines, and customer relationships. The following image illustrates this relationship.

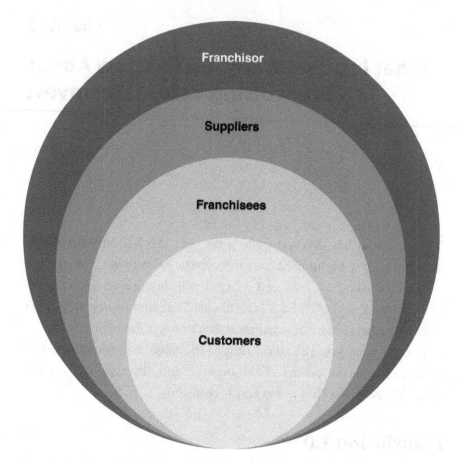

Franchising 1.0: The franchisor asserts dominance and control.

Franchisees were simple points of distribution, not stakeholders in the brand, as it is thought of today. My first boss, Subway founder Fred DeLuca, used to say, "I could own them or I could franchise them. I franchise them." In Franchising 1.0, franchisees substitute as managers, allowing the franchisor to make money without having to build the significant organizational hierarchy the typical centralized chain model is faced with. My generation of franchisor leaders almost uniformly began our careers inside this franchisor-centric leadership paradigm. As my generation of franchising leaders continued to evolve, we thought this franchising paradigm was too simplistic and we adapted, changing the way many franchisor leaders thought about the business of franchising.

Franchising 2.0 (Current Era)

The era that FPG defines as Franchising 2.0 began in the early 1990s and continues to this day. Almost every tenured franchisor leader (VP of a franchisor or above) stumbled into franchising by accident, fell in love with it, and stayed in it for the long haul. *This first-ever generation of career franchising professionals emerged and shifted the paradigm from franchising as a distribution model to franchising as a business unto itself.* My generation of franchising career professionals saw that franchising, regardless of the investment level or business category, seemed to operate under its own set of rules, separate and distinct from other forms of business. Through the coordinated efforts of the International Franchise Association (IFA), event promoters, and media companies like Franchise Update and Franchise Times, career franchising professionals shared best practices. Leaders published books such as *Franchising for Dummies, The Educated Franchisee,* and my first franchising book, *Street Smart Franchising.* They also produced some standardized franchising education like the Certified Franchise Executive (CFE) program, where I taught two classes: one on franchisee recruitment best practices and another on franchisee training and support best practices.

What I am about to say may shock you. Franchising has never done for the franchisor what franchisors have routinely done for franchisees, which is to document and codify their business model. A complete franchisor documented business model *does not exist* in the same way franchisee business format models exist.

Every franchisor is left to their own devices to invent their own franchising model, which I defined earlier as "recruiting, training,

119

developing, resourcing, and leading a team of successful entrepreneurs in order to build a brand."

Companies like mine (Franchise Performance Group) have systematized components of the franchising model, such as our domain area of expertise explaining how franchisors should recruit top franchisee talent. But no one has yet designed an end-to-end franchising roadmap that shows Early Stage and Emerging Growth franchisors how to take a brand from a small local or Regional chain to a large National household name with a high degree of probability. However, I believe the Franchising 2.0 model is playing itself out, thus paving the way for the next generation of thought leadership, called Franchising 3.0.

Franchising 3.0: The Era of Responsible Franchising (Evolving Now)

FPG asserts that Franchising 3.0 will be about responsible franchising, defined as maximizing franchising as a strategic advantage in the marketplace, accomplishing that by perfecting and documenting franchising as a business format.

Despite the size, reach, and revenues generated, the franchising ecosystem has not evolved with the level of intricacy, standardization, systemization, elegance, education, and sophistication one would expect from a high-stake, multi-billion-dollar industry. While individual brands within franchising have certainly elevated – category killers such as Domino's and McDonald's – franchising itself hasn't innovated, codified, or matured as other $100 billion–plus industries have.

According to *2022 Franchising Economic Outlook* by the IFA and FRANdata, there are 775,000 franchised establishments in the United States, representing $787 billion in economic output. To put this in perspective, in 2018 according to the IFA and IHS Economics, there were about 760,000 franchised establishments in the United States representing nearly $757 billion in economic output (see the image). Franchising has an enormous impact on the US economy and is one of the most successful business expansion strategies ever invented. However, franchising is very mature and not as rapidly growing as a franchise investor might think.

If you aggregate the revenue of franchised establishments, it is almost twice the size of the nearly $400 billion automotive aftermarket industry (2023 estimates by AutomotiveAftermarket.org).

Let's highlight the auto industry for a second. The car was invented in 1885 by Karl Benz, a full 30 years after Albert Singer of Singer Sewing Machine fame was reported to have invented franchising. Look at how the auto industry has evolved since then.

The automobile industry is studied in universities (mechanical engineering, electrical engineering, and business). One can earn a PhD in automotive engineering. In addition, there are technical schools and certification programs for both mechanical and auto body repair.

There are trade associations (Alliance of Automobile Manufacturers, National Automobile Dealers Association), government oversight (Federal Trade Commission, US Department of Transportation, National Highway Traffic Safety Administration), consumer rating systems (Consumer Reports, JD Powers), case studies (Harvard Business Review, KPMG) and transparent and trusted sources for consumer information (Consumer Reports, NADA guides, Kelley Blue Book, CARFAX, TrueCar).

The automotive industry has created an entire ecosystem of auto-related providers that support, sustain, and innovate on behalf of customers and the industry itself. For instance, banks and company-sponsored financing programs make automobile ownership possible for almost all socioeconomic classes. Gas stations, auto repair businesses, auto body shops, tire shops, auto parts stores, and other service providers exist to extend the useful life of automobiles.

What Insiders Want You to Know About Franchising Before You Invest

A Dearth of Support for Franchising Models

Franchising as a brand strategy or entrepreneurial path (on the franchisee level) is largely ignored in entrepreneurial studies programs in business schools. In addition, there is little consumer advocacy, few franchising business analysts, and scant transparent third-party information about franchise brands that either a potential franchisee or a private equity firm looking to purchase a brand can trust to help them make more informed investment decisions and mitigate their risk. There are also few comprehensive rankings or scoring systems that franchise candidates, private equity firms, or lending institutions can count on as an unbiased source of information. Franchising 2.0, relative to other similar-sized industries, remains the Wild West.

However, given its vast size (nearly 800,000 franchise units, 4,000-plus brands, and estimated $800 billion–plus in output), inefficiency, opportunity, and unmitigated financial risk, franchising is now experiencing the kind of market disruption that forces self-examination and eventually leads markets toward innovation, reinvention, and transformation.

This section details what I believe Franchising 3.0 should look like on both an ideological and a strategic level. I detail what I believe to be the telltale signs from which business paradigm franchisors are operating from so you can align yourself with a franchisor evolving into a 3.0 brand.

I invite the current and next generation of franchising leadership and stakeholders to advance this work, build on these concepts, and continue to share what works to the combined benefit of the franchisor, franchisees, strategic suppliers, and the brand's customers.

It's my hope this work will push franchisors toward Franchising 3.0, which I refer to as "responsible franchising" and which I believe will lead to a mastery level understanding of developing franchise brands through expert execution an overall strategy to recruit, train, develop, resource, and lead a team of successful entrepreneurs in order to build an iconic and valuable national brand.

For franchisors who have already transcended to the Franchising 3.0 "responsible franchising" mode of thinking, if you could look into their heads to find out how they're thinking, you might see something like the image shown here. In this model, the brand is a separate and distinct entity from the franchisor. Suppliers, franchisors, and franchisees each have mission critical roles and responsibilities to add value to the brand, as I will describe.

The franchising flywheel. © 2020 FPG and Joe Mathews.

What Insiders Want You to Know About Franchising Before You Invest

Franchisors with responsible franchising thinking would say that franchisors and suppliers exist to ensure the success of their franchisees and to add more value to the franchisee than they extract in royalties and fees. They would also say franchisees exist to add more real and perceived value to the customer than they extract in price. As long as this value chain exists uninterrupted, the brand will experience positive forward momentum and brand growth will take on a life of its own, akin to a flywheel. And like anything in nature with forward momentum, bodies in motion stay in motion until interfered with by outside forces. These outside forces can include a disruption in the franchisee-franchisor relationship, a change in leadership or ownership resulting in a change in culture, a change in customer preferences leading to a decline in sales, or a crafty competitor who out-positions the brand. As long as the 3.0 franchisor succeeds in navigating the brand past these challenges and hurdles, the brand will achieve iconic brand status.

Iconic Brand Franchising Defined

In classical business terms, iconic brands possess all of the following:

- **Strong brand identity.** Customers acknowledge and appreciate the brand's uniqueness, genius, or excellence.

- **Clear brand promise.** No matter what, the customer can seemingly always count on these brands to deliver a consistent product, service, or customer experience that exceeds customers' needs and expectations, solves customers' problems, and delivers real and perceived value that exceeds what the customer is spending, leading to customer satisfaction and loyal customer relationships.

- **High perceived value offering.** Customers consistently walk away thinking, "That was a good use of my time, energy, and money, and the value (real and perceived) exceeds what I spent."

- **Consistency.** Customers know what they're getting before they get it. The brands deliver value with a high degree of regularity and predictability.

- **Uniqueness.** The business has to offer customers something different, better, and more valuable than comparable businesses in their space. If not, the market will quickly become inundated with copycat concepts, commoditizing and devaluing the products and services, killing opportunity for franchisees, and perhaps forcing them to compete with no real competitive advantage. Dan Cathy, CEO of Chick-fil-A, is reportedly fond of saying, "Every business has to have its chicken sandwich." However, people don't go to Chick-fil-A just for the chicken sandwich. The company offers a unique customer service experience called "polite," which no other company seems to be able to pull off at a Chick-fil-A level. Their hiring and training methods for rank-and-file workers is best-in-class. Christian-owned, they are public with their beliefs about treating customers and employees with courtesy and respect, and the market continues to reward their values on unprecedented levels.

    Do not confuse "unique" with "first-to-market." "Unique" as I am defining it strictly means "difficult to copy." Several years ago, self-serve yogurt became the frozen dessert customer experience of choice. Brands copied each other's colors and store designs, bought yogurt from the same dairies, and ultimately created a mass commoditization of the segment. Thousands of frozen yogurt shops opened all over the country, flooding the market. Just like any commodities market where supply exceeds demand, the yogurt chains got into a price war, killing margins. These businesses started cutting staff, meaning they didn't have enough people on payroll to keep the toppings bars and bathrooms clean, creating a negative customer experience, eventually killing the category.

- **Defensibility.** These brands have staked out a market position or niche that is uniquely theirs, creating high barriers to competitive entry. The franchisor's consumer-facing model must present high barriers to potential competitors by being difficult or too expensive to copy. Otherwise, the market will rapidly attract new entrants, oversaturating and commoditizing the franchisees' product or service offering, driving down the price and eroding margins, and devaluing the brand. Some franchisors confuse such things as "first to market," "largest brand," or "fastest growing" with a defensible brand position. "Defensibility" answers the question "How well will this brand hold up to the inevitable onslaught of competition?"

For example, in the past, category-leading remedial education chains like Sylvan and Huntington were profitable because the high hourly teacher's labor expense was spread out over the three or four students each teacher tutored at one time. However, in-home tutoring chains emerged offering one-on-one tutoring. As in-home and one-on-one tutoring became an expectation for many customers, it created a threat for larger, brick-and-mortar remedial education chains. These chains were stuck with the high fixed costs of an office or retail location, while competitors using the in-home model enjoyed very little overhead. To keep up with customer demand, brick-and-mortar remedial education chains offered more one-on-one tutoring, eroding their profit margins.

The next wave of tutoring will most likely be delivered virtually, which will eliminate commuting and overhead expenses even further. There may emerge lower-cost providers who pass some or all of these labor savings to customers, thus creating a pricing advantage and putting even more of a squeeze on the higher fixed-cost remedial education models. The more established brands have difficult positions to defend.

- **Profitability.** The model must consistently exceed the expectations of the franchise candidates most likely to invest in it. The CEO of an Emerging Growth brand once told FPG, "Our franchisees don't think they're making money simply because their checking account balances are declining. They don't look at the key performance criteria of the business. They're doing great!" That's what irresponsible franchising sounds like. Franchisees can't deposit key performance criteria to the bank. Right now, this chain, once a high flier, is now struggling. Given that the franchisor's definition of success is distinctly different than their franchisees, wasn't a fall from grace predictable?

- **Value as a franchise opportunity.** Franchisors create value for franchisees by perfecting a business platform that adds more perceived benefit to franchisees than it extracts in royalty dollars and other costs. The franchisor's business platform includes such things as marketing, training, processes, systems, strategic relationships, and support, all of which work in unison to create a flywheel effect. This virtuous flywheel helps franchisees deliver the customer value proposition by perpetuating a consistent brand strategy and brand identity. When franchisees are asked, "Knowing what you know now, would you make the same decision again?" a full 80% or more of the franchisees polled should answer "yes." If not, the franchisor almost certainly suffers from a franchisee-franchisor relationship problem, a unit-level economics problem, or both.

Why 80%? Franchise candidates should not expect 100% of people to be satisfied 100% of the time. Franchising, as I have said before, is often a never-ending series of franchisee-franchisor negotiations and compromises. It's often said a good negotiation results in not everyone getting everything they want, meaning both parties may be dissatisfied.

- **Long-term sustainability.** The brand that has proven it is defensible against competitive threats such as disruptive technologies or similar business models in the short run may not experience the same success in the long run. To achieve long-term sustainability, a brand's product and service offering must continue to stay relevant well into the foreseeable future.

For instance, Midas Muffler used to make their money exclusively by marketing replacement automobile exhaust systems. At one time, due to rust and corrosion, auto exhaust systems often needed to be replaced every five years or so. When automobile manufacturers started making exhaust systems from stainless steel or aluminum, exhaust systems gained greater durability, threatening and disrupting their core businesses. They were eventually forced to pivot into becoming a general maintenance and repair business (rebranding as "Midas"), going after lines of business the brand was historically not known for, such as replacing brakes and rotors, fan belts, and oil changes.

Fitness and weight-loss brands often start up trying to capitalize on the latest fitness trends, worrying more about making quick money rather than creating a sustainable brand. The franchisor graveyard is littered with the bones of brands that made the mistake of tying the brand to a particular trendy product or service – such as cupcakes, frozen yogurt, home-meal assembly kitchens, and "sell-it-on-eBay" stores. By doing so, they inadvertently attach the brand to that product's or service's lifecycle. This means that as demand declines, the brand becomes irrelevant, creating the strong possibility of a premature franchise demise. Unless these brands pivot like Midas did, they will sunset and franchisees will lose their investments and livelihood.

How Franchisors Think Determines How Franchisors Act

How the franchisor leadership values franchisees ultimately translates into policies, systems, and procedures that will be designed either to unlock the franchisees' (and therefore the brand's) full potential, or to attempt to contain and control franchisees.

A franchisor's leadership tends to think of franchisees in one of two ways:

- Franchisees are a strategic asset, leading to better execution and a competitive advantage in the marketplace.

- Franchisees are a brand liability, posing a potential downside risk that needs to be capped.

The outlook that is chosen dictates corporate culture. If the franchisor sees franchisees as a liability, they will often respond by creating a highly legalistic, compliance-driven, and top-down command-and-control structure that diminishes and devalues the contributions of skilled and experienced franchisees, creating unnecessary stress. Franchisee stress and dissatisfaction often lead to a decrease in the quality and consistency of their execution, negatively impacting the customers' brand experience. I explain the telltale signs of toxic franchisor cultures later in this chapter.

A franchisor's self-sabotaging beliefs over time will create a snowball effect that stops forward momentum, destroying the aforementioned flywheel effect, ultimately necessitating a turnaround.

Leaders who treat franchisees as assets possess the highest probability of building an effective high-performance franchisee community, becoming a market leader, and creating a valuable and iconic national brand.

Conversely, leaders who see franchisees as a brand liability often breed distrust, leaving the brand exposed and vulnerable to an iconic or soon-to-be-iconic franchise brand operating from the first philosophy.

Franchising 3.0 Fundamentals

As I stated, every company that elects to use franchising as their go-to-market strategy ultimately engages in two separate and distinct businesses. The first business is its customer-facing model. The second business is franchising. Franchising is a business unto itself.

Every franchise system is ultimately supported by two broad brand pillars:

- **Franchisees' profitability.** Franchisees must achieve their income and ROI objectives with a high degree of probability. The primary job of the franchisor is to create, refine, and perfect a business model that works.

- **Trusting and workable franchisee-franchisor relationships.** The foundation of trust is built on franchisees' predictable and acceptable financial returns and transparency of information.

The Greatest Predictor of a Franchise Brand's Success

FPG asserts that a brand's current and projected franchisee-level profitability and the trust built into the franchisee-franchisor relationship are the two greatest predictors of the brand's near-term and long-term success.

Franchisees' profitability expectations vary by franchise buyer profile, investment size, business type, where the brand exists in its growth cycle, and other mitigating factors I have yet to describe. I discuss this in detail throughout the book. However, franchisees' satisfaction with ROI and relationships are ultimately determined by their expectations going in, which are highly subjective.

The 80% Rule

Regardless of the brand or industry or franchisees' expectations going in, my research and nearly 40 years of experience shows that if approximately 20% or more of a brand's franchisees are not content with their financial returns or business trajectory, as well as the quality of the franchisee-franchisor relationship, left unaddressed, the brand will most likely break down and head into a *turnaround situation,* where the brand has lost forward momentum and now needs to be fixed. over the next one to three years. This is true regardless of whatever success the brand has experienced in the past. Conversely, once 80% or more of a brand's franchisees are happy and profitable, the franchise is most likely positioned for continued growth and success as long as leadership and franchisees don't rest on their laurels and lose their competitive advantages.

Furthermore, *for every year* a franchise brand is in turnaround, it is my experience that *it will take the brand three years to dig out.* Brands that are in turnaround are easy to spot, as a disproportionate share of franchisees will be looking to exit and existing franchisees will not keep reinvesting in the brand to open more locations or territories.

Turnaround or soon-to-be turnaround brands often share the following characteristics:

- **Inexperienced leadership.** The brand leaders have never built a brand that size in the past and are engaged in system-wide, on-the-job training on every level.

- **Hubris.** Their success has gone to their heads, and they are starting to believe they are infallible.

- **Loss of initiative (in particular founder-led businesses).** The founders or ownership are finally getting a strong payout after years of living lean. They are slow to reinvest as they start taking money out of the business.

What Insiders Want You to Know About Franchising Before You Invest

- **Materialism.** Ownership starts investing in the typical trappings money presents, such as bigger houses, more expensive cars, planes, and posh office buildings, and start taking their eye off the ball.

- **Self-deception.** Brand leadership can no longer objectively look at the strengths and weaknesses of their operation and threats the industry poses. They believe they have achieved some level of market dominance and are now positioned to constantly defy gravity. And those who have not lost objectivity and voice weaknesses and threats are culturally ostracized by leadership as "naysayers," until these voices are silenced either through culture pressure or exits, leaving in positions of authority only those brand leaders who drink the Kool-Aid.

Declining Franchisee-Franchisor Relationships

Regardless of whether both the franchisees and franchisor are meeting or exceeding their financial projections, if the franchisee-franchisor relationship becomes strained, they will each find that they invest more time and resources into trying to control or avoid being controlled by the other and less on collaborating to drive profitable growth, creating breakdowns.

Many breakdowns originate because of win-lose financial dealings between the franchisees and franchisor. Once trust is lost, it takes a long time to restore, often requiring outside intervention to re-create workable relationships.

Franchisees are entrepreneurs and, as such, are also rugged individualists. They are generally best led through influence and not top-down, command-and-control authority. Franchisees work best when they have the positive experience of being heard, resourced, and empowered. They resist being controlled and contained. They are generally big-picture thinkers who can relate to the franchisor's CEO and ownership, because they are also CEOs and owners.

As a brand grows, adds more franchisees, and builds more franchisor infrastructure to support these franchisees, the natural progression of the franchisee-franchisor relationships evolve from informal and casual personal relationships to formal business relationships. But the basic underpinnings of trust should remain the same.

The franchisee-franchisor relationship begins with a commercial foundation, but with iconic brands the relationship often remains highly personal, with committed working relationships operating within a tight-knit brand community. Franchisees, franchisors, and key strategic vendor partners operate like a tribe, with the brand values at their core and profitable brand growth and protection of franchisees' profitability as primary motivators.

The relationship melts down into a cold commercial relationship only when the informal and trusting relationships break down, core values are not being upheld, or contributions by brand stakeholders are not being honored or valued.

The relationship further disintegrates into a legal relationship when such things as the franchisor's professional boundaries and franchisees' investment dollars aren't being respected.

Successful and iconic franchisors honor and nurture these bonds of trust by providing franchisees with consistent transparency and open lines of communication.

Bottom line: Franchising operates according to an unwritten social contract, not a written legal contract. The social contract requires responsible franchisors to act as follows:

- Ultimately, the franchisees' job is to serve their customers to the best of their ability consistent with the values, standards, and original intent of the franchisor and to add more perceived value to the customer than the customer pays in price.

- The franchisor's job is to maintain the integrity of the brand and create processes, systems, structures, products, marketing, and other resources that drive profitable revenue growth, and to add more perceived value and tangible financial results to franchisees than franchisees contribute to the franchisor in royalty dollars.

As long as each is honoring their commitment to the other, the brand will elevate, creating a flywheel effect, as depicted here.

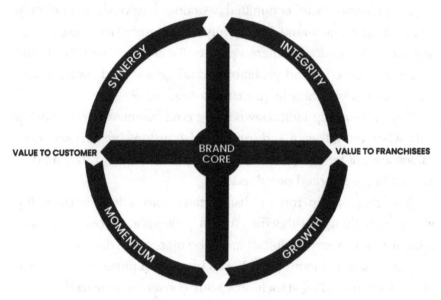

The brand value flywheel.

When one party believes that the other is not delivering its fair share of value, parties frequently invest more energy into assigning blame than competing for market share.

When franchisee-franchisor relationships break down, parties tend to make their disputes antagonistic. Typical rules of civil business discourse may go out the window.

Franchise systems with consistently strained franchisee-franchisor relationships should consider third-party interventions to help restore trust and workability.

Marketplace Movers

The primary brand accelerator can be summarized in two words: *added value*. Franchisors must add more real and perceived value to franchisees in customer perceived brand equity, marketing, tools, tactics, brand position, product/service advantage, best practices, training, and support than it extracts from them in royalties or the brand runs a high risk of slipping into a turnaround stage.

Customers must almost uniformly believe they receive more value in their commercial dealings with franchisees than franchisees extract in price, or the brand will be the next turnaround.

Importantly, the franchisor's leadership has no say about how franchisees define and measure value. Nor do franchises have any say in whether or not customers get their value.

To maximize the value creation within their areas of responsibility as depicted on the flywheel, franchisors must collaborate and communicate with their franchisees on meaningful levels. The franchisor's perceived value cannot be sold, mandated, manipulated, or forcefully jammed down within the organization or outside to the franchisee level. How franchisees measure value and whether the franchisor routinely delivers it resides entirely within the minds, hearts, and business checking accounts of their franchisee community.

In turn, franchisees also must be keenly aware of how their customers measure value. Franchisees do not get to say whether or not value was added and delivered on the consumer level. Ultimately, customers will vote with their checkbooks and on social media platforms the brand does not control.

When each party masterfully and habitually adds more value to its constituency than it extracts in fees, the flywheel turns, creating forward momentum. And like any object with forward momentum, it takes less energy and resources to maintain forward motion than it does to create it.

When the brand constituents systematize and commit to the habit of delivering added value, the flywheel will continue turning, creating exponential growth with greater achievements and fewer spent resources than in the past to achieve these results. Momentum reduces effort and makes everyone's job easier and more efficient.

Once the flywheel is turning, the momentum seems to create its own momentum. *This does not mean the franchisor won and is now on a straight path to iconic brand status.* This only means the brand is winning relative to where they are in the lifecycle (Early Stage, Emerging, Regional, National, Iconic, Turnaround, or Resurgent). Chapter 9 explains the lifecycle of a franchise brand in detail.

How Do You Know the Flywheel Is Slowing?

When the flywheel is spinning, it feels like the brand appears to be on one continuous cycle of forward momentum. When the flywheel is slowing and a negative spiral is approaching or already on hand, the brand feels like a never-ending series of one-off problems and catch-up days. Strategy goes out the window and everyone gets preoccupied daily with their version of emergencies or breakdowns. Unlike the flywheel – which occurs to leadership as one large continuous cycle with its own head of steam – in a negative spiral, leadership feels like a plate-spinning circus act. Leadership exhausts itself running helter-skelter from plate to plate, not with the goal of maximizing available opportunity or implementing brand strategy, but with the frenetic and frantic goal of not letting the brand fall apart. The plate-spinning act will look different at different stages of the brand lifecycle, and I get into the telltale signs of each stage in Chapter 9. Regardless of where a brand exists on the lifecycle, winning brands often exhibit the following 15 key indicators.

15 Indicators the Flywheel Is Spinning

- Visionary and discerning leadership
- Open channels of communication for employees, franchisees, customers, and suppliers
- Solid unit-level economics that deliver franchisees consistent and expected returns
- Workable and trusting franchisee-franchisor relationships
- A business model that is unique, profitable, sustainable, and occupies a defensible position in the marketplace
- Customers who place a high value on the franchisees' product and service offerings
- Franchisees who place a high value on what the franchisor offers
- Mastery-level understanding of their customer-facing model
- Mastery-level understanding of the business of franchising, namely recruiting, training, developing, supporting, resourcing, and leading highly skilled franchisees
- A solid strategic plan for moving the brand to the next stage of the franchise lifecycle
- Discipline, capital, skills, and experience necessary to execute their strategic plan
- A franchisor belief system that states franchisors exist to add more value to franchisees than franchisees pay in royalties
- A franchisee belief system that they exist to add more value to their customers than they extract in price

- A steady stream of satisfied customers who value the brand promise, positioning, and products and services
- Total brand buy-in from the franchisor, franchisees, suppliers, and customers

If a brand is missing more than one of these attributes, the brand is at risk of becoming mired in a turnaround, and actions need to be taken.

Franchisors often fear, ignore, devalue, or misinterpret the flywheel because it shows that the brand is bigger than and different from the franchisor itself, with a large portion of the brand's potential and added value lying outside the franchisor's control. It shows franchisors that, regardless of the language in their franchise agreement, the brand exists as community property, where all brand constituents (brand ownership and leadership, brand employees, franchisees, suppliers, and customers) possess some level of brand ownership and influence. Customers step up as if they were duly appointed brand ambassadors to their communities and networks, introducing others to "my brand," "my place," or "my people."

The simple formula of adding more value than received in fees creates an unwritten noble obligation among customers, suppliers, franchisees, and employees to return the favor and reciprocate in some way. They give back some version of money, time, and energy to the brand that added value to them, ensuring it survives and thrives well into the future.

The Responsible Franchising Paradox

In the final analysis, the franchising flywheel creates a paradox. Everyone gives more than they get, and in the end everyone gets more than they give. What they ultimately receive in the end is often abundantly more than the constituents predicted or imagined when they invested in or became involved with the brand.

For instance, the spiritual values of the leadership and store managers of Chick-fil-A shape their business model. "The Chick-fil-A culture and service tradition in our restaurants is to treat every person with honor, dignity, and respect and to serve great food with genuine hospitality," CEO Dan Cathy told the *Atlanta Journal-Constitution* in 2014. The brand is famously closed on Sundays so employees can honor the Christian sabbath. Despite restaurants operating just six days a week, customers have rewarded the brand with the highest average volume sales in the QSR segment, although other restaurant chains are open seven days.

Back in 2012, an advocacy group planned a nationwide brand protest at Chick-fil-A restaurants across the United States because of the company's stance on same-sex marriage. Media commentator Mike Huckabee, a longtime customer and brand advocate, decided to make an effort to protect the brand by declaring August 1, 2012, Chick-fil-A Appreciation Day and posted it on social media. Customers turned out in record levels. Drive-thrus in some locations became a mile or more long with more than two-hour wait times. Police had to direct traffic in many locales because of the number of cars blocking the ingress. After Chick-fil-A tallied their end-of-day sales, they announced the single greatest revenue day in the history of their company.

For a moment, leaving politics and religion aside, isn't it interesting that the most successful single-day promotion in the history of QSR was started by a customer and had nothing to do with the parent company, its marketing department, or its franchisees or licensees? Arguably, the most successful promotion in the history of food service can be sourced back to the franchise flywheel, created by the brand ecosystem in response to a perceived existential brand threat.

Conventional franchising (the way most brands currently execute the franchising model) appears to ensure that the flywheel never spins under its own power. Franchisors discuss the brand in terms of "my brand, my system, my customers, and my suppliers," but it's the franchisors' possessiveness and need for control that is one of the primary reasons most franchise brands never flourish. Franchise brands are launched inside an ideology or paradigm that virtually ensures the brand eventually engages in the type of self-limitation, self-sabotage, and parochial possessiveness that creates headwinds and drag the brand down.

When brand constituents experience a brand value chain defined by giving more than you take, the recipient is prone to giving back to the giver and brand in meaningful ways. It's this elegant reflex reaction and good nature of humanity to give back to those who give first that moves the flywheel, producing results and outcomes that the brand stakeholders and constituents could never have predicted.

The flywheel will keep spinning and the brand will flourish under its own power, growing exponentially in both unit count and unit-level profitability, until something disrupts it. Eventually, like Chick-fil-A, habitual winning becomes ingrained in the corporate culture and the brand performs well much in the same way that winners naturally win.

Predicting a Vicious Cycle Before It Shows Up in Results

Franchise brands seem to follow Newton's first law of motion, creating and sustaining either a virtuous cycle (flywheel) or a vicious cycle downward. Bodies (or brands) in motion will continue in their current trajectory (growth or decline) unless acted upon by a disruptive force. Business seems to also abide by similar laws. For instance, authors Clayton M. Christensen and Joseph Bower determined how category and industry disruptions are often caused by strong external forces rather than the current market leader, like Uber and Lyft disrupted the taxi industry.

High-growth chains with well-executed franchise models outpace themselves year after year with seemingly less energy and effort than it took to produce results from the previous year. It's my experience that brands with forward momentum (the flywheel effect) keep their momentum until something disrupts it.

In his book *How the Mighty Fall: And Why Some Companies Never Give In*, author Jim Collins studied how a brand's vicious cycles are often caused as a byproduct of the leadership's internal blind spots and hubris. So, major disruptive forces can also germinate from inside the brand.

Collins saw a linear progression of common mistakes successful company leadership makes after first achieving a virtuous cycle and flywheel effect. For greater readability, FPG altered the names of some of the stages but kept their meaning intact:

Stage 1: Excessive pride
Stage 2: Undisciplined and irresponsible pursuit of more
Stage 3: Denial of risk
Stage 4: Decline in results
Stage 5: Brand irrelevance or turnaround

The first three stages start as leadership character flaws that manifest as "the truth" ("We really *are* the smartest people in the room!"). These attitudes eventually become ingrained in the company's leadership culture and management philosophy, which in turn impact decision-making, strategy, goal-setting, risk tolerance, and resource allocation. Dissenting opinions are ostracized out of the corporation or shut down until there is no disagreement. This creates an authoritarian command-and-control culture or a group-think environment that ultimately leads to nonstrategic overreaching (i.e., new product or service extensions, brand acquisitions, taking on ill-advised debt) and tactical misfires, ignoring information, ultimately translating into an unexpected decline in results, transforming a virtuous cycle into a vicious cycle. The brand will continue its vicious cycle decline (or negative flywheel effect) until it develops the organizational backbone to acknowledge and execute a turnaround. (In franchise brands, these breakdowns occur at predictable inflection points along the franchise brand growth cycle, covered in detail in Chapter 9.)

Because it is my assertion that the entire brand ecosystem moves or disrupts the flywheel, the brand's disruptive forces can include leadership, franchisees, and suppliers – not just external competitive forces. Once the franchisor's flywheel slows or stops, it becomes a turnaround brand.

Any unidentified and uncorrected breaks in the value chain (recall that the *value chain* is a collaboration between customers, the franchisor, the franchisees, and the suppliers where each feels they extract fair value from the brand consistent with their investment) will eventually create more stress fractures, eventually leading to multiple failures and a downward spiral. The longer the spiral, the more difficult it is to course-correct and move the brand into a Resurgent stage.

Success Begins and Ends with Corporate Culture

In an article published in *Investopedia* on April 25, 2023, business author Evan Tarver describes "corporate culture" as "the values, beliefs, and behaviors that determine how a company's employees and management behaviors interact, perform, and handle business transactions." Simply put, it's how companies knowingly and often unknowingly train employees to think and act.

Behavior always starts with beliefs. Responsible franchising pioneer and my first mentor, Paul Pieschel, used to tell me, "How you define the problem determines how you solve the problem." He used to spend an exorbitant amount of time ensuring he was defining problems properly. What Pieschel and experts in behavioral psychology say is that either on an individual or organizational level, beliefs birth actions. Actions create results. Therefore, all results can be tied back to the quality of thought and beliefs that were the genesis of actions, as shown in the image.

How beliefs impact results.

What mires individuals or organizations in a downward spiral is the inability or unwillingness to rigorously examine and alter the self-limiting and self-sabotaging organizational beliefs that proved to be the genesis of the behaviors that created the downward spiral. New ways of thinking create new ways of doing things.

Common Franchisor Corporate Cultures

How one individual franchisor employee views franchisees or how an individual franchisee views the franchisor speaks more about the individuals than the brand. However, the prevailing common *collective* beliefs and attitudes about franchisees and the franchisor determine corporate culture. Once culture is determined, it is difficult to change. Why? The existing culture always protects the existing culture and resists and ostracizes those who desire change until the dissenting forces give up and either fall in or move on.

The core elements that appear to drive brand cultural beliefs are as follows:

- **Unit-level economics.** Are franchisees' financial returns meeting their expectations? If not, how are the franchisor and franchisees working together to define and address the issues?

- **Franchisee training, support, and resources.** What is the quality and effectiveness of the franchisor's training, support, and performance management systems? Would franchisees say the value of the tools and support they receive is greater than or equal to the royalty dollars invested? How are the franchisor and franchisees working together to enhance brand value and drive franchisees' profitability?

- **The trust level and workability of the franchisee-franchisor relationships.** Do franchisees, employees, and franchisor leadership trust each other and work toward crafting mutually profitable campaigns, offers, and solutions? Do franchisees feel they are heard and understood? Does information routinely flow up and down the organization or just funnel down from on high? Would franchisees say they are informed about issues important to them? Would they say they feel like an integral part of a team or more like the low man on the totem pole?

How franchisees and the franchisor answer these questions speaks volumes about the culture of the franchise organization. Strong financial returns go a long way to satisfy franchisees' concerns, but ROI alone is not a substitute for trusting franchisee-franchisor relationships, mutual transparency, and collaborative problem-solving. Enduring franchise brands offer franchisees both.

Franchisors with a collaborative, franchisee-friendly corporate culture will attract more sophisticated and talented franchise candidates than more heavy-handed franchisors who resort to threats, punishment, and coercive command-and-control techniques to try to keep franchisees in line.

Types of Franchising Cultures

Dr. Jay Hall, PhD, who passed away in 2011, spent a lifetime studying the impact of corporate culture on individual performance. Dr. Hall identified four prevailing corporate cultures, which FPG modified to reflect what occurs in franchising.

For simplicity's sake, I grade franchisor cultures by two distinguishing characteristics: the franchisor's organizational concern for franchisees' results, and the franchisor's organizational concern for quality franchisee-franchisor relationships. At any time, any company can exhibit traits from any one of these cultures. However, over the long haul, franchise organizations tend to exhibit a dominant pattern of beliefs and behaviors, which predicts which pattern of beliefs the organization will revert to.

This section looks at these cultures in a progression, starting with the least effective and progressing toward the most effective and desired. The image here shows this system of cultures.

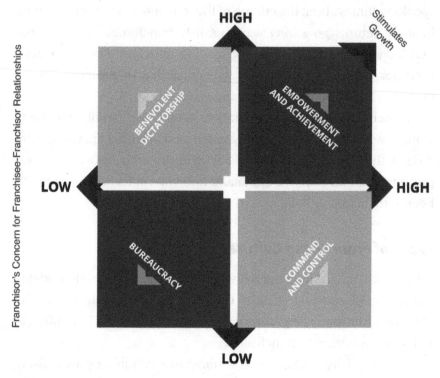

Common franchisor cultures. Joe Mathews, 2020/Franchise Performance Group.

The Bureaucracy

Bureaucracies are highly legalistic, multilayered companies where the lower you go in an organization, the less decision-making responsibility and authority an employee of the franchisor has. The organization seemingly exists to maintain the status quo, avoid accepting personal responsibility, and elude being held accountable for producing results. When a franchisee is faced with a unique challenge or makes a special request, the knee-jerk reaction throughout the layers of management is "No, we don't do it that way," regardless of whether what the organization is currently doing actually works or remains in the franchisees' or customers' best interests. Change is met with stiff resistance, and management frowns on individual initiative. Employees and franchisees are expected to follow the rules, do what is expected, and resist original thinking. Policies and procedures are set to control employees to ensure compliance, not to drive results.

Impact on Franchisor's Employees and Franchisees

Ponder the type of corporate employees and leadership that would survive in this franchise culture in the long term. Those franchisor employees who are dedicated, results oriented, efficient, entrepreneurial, visionary, big-picture thinkers, or out to make their mark in the world would be ostracized, and then would quit or be fired. Only those who simply want to earn a steady paycheck while hiding out and avoiding personal responsibility would want to stick around for the long haul in this environment. Think about the type of person whose goal in life is to secure a good job with the post office or motor vehicle department. Are you picturing a real go-getter and risk-taker?

Because bureaucracies value sameness and security over performance and efficiency, they remain a breeding ground for underperformance.

Now think about the quality of the interactions between the bureaucratic franchisor support staff and the franchisees under their charge. Would these conversations and communications pertain more to tactics and strategies about how to drive franchisees' sales and results, or would the conversations tend more toward what franchisees must do to continually stay in compliance?

Once, a bureaucratic retail chain that I worked with forced its franchisees to adopt a proprietary point of sale (POS) system at a cost to its franchisees of tens of thousands of dollars per location. Franchisees who beta-tested the system reported that the system had bugs, routinely lost customer transactions (meaning revenue to the business), and was not ready for a national rollout. Brand leadership ignored the franchisees' warnings and forced franchisees at threat of default to adopt the new system. It was more important to the franchisor that all franchisees operate from one flawed standard system that made the company money than several working systems where the license fees went to the vendors. One year later, their newly adopted system still corrupted data and transaction information, making many reporting functions meaningless. The CEO was promoted and transferred within the larger organization, distancing herself from the wreckage she created.

Impact on Results

Franchising works because it makes businesses more decentralized, flexible, and nimble by completely empowering and creating ownership to those closest to the customer. Bureaucracies create the opposite effect. Therefore, bureaucratic franchisors have little staying power in today's competitive commercial marketplace. This is why most surviving bureaucracies exist in the public sector where people have no other alternatives with regard to corporate cultures.

Benevolent Dictatorship

Benevolent dictatorships are typically informal, folksy, low-stress companies where much attention is paid to making people feel good. Feeling good, being appreciated, and loyalty to leadership are more important than bottom-line results. This culture is commonly found in small, privately held franchisors where the founder or owner places friends and family in key management positions, not because they are the most qualified people for their jobs, but because they can be trusted to do the owner's bidding without pushback. Unless an employee possesses the right last name, marries into the family, or plays golf with the owner, often there is little room for advancement. The owner isn't really out to build a powerhouse brand, but a little brand fiefdom where the brand ownership, employees, friends, and franchisees are taken care of and have some fun. If you were a franchise candidate visiting the corporate office, at first glance this culture seems informal, unassuming, and perhaps attractive to a new entrepreneur.

However, often the counterproductive, underlying beliefs of leadership that permeate within the franchisor's company is "My brand, my system, my customer," and "Franchisees are like employees (or worse, children) and need to do what we say." Ultimately, this will lead to tension, fractured trust, and breakdowns in the workability of the franchisee-franchisor relationship. While personal franchisee relationships are held up as important to the brand, these relationships are skewed because they aren't marked by the typical characteristics of an adult relationship. These relationships more resemble the parent–dependent child relationship than an interdependent, synergistic commercial relationship.

Until franchisors embrace the idea that franchisees are highly capable individuals who need the tools, resources, and freedom to build strong brand value and offer the brand a leverageable competitive advantage in the marketplace, the brand may quickly plateau and then decline. Left unchecked, this culture often sprouts the next turnaround brand.

Impact on Franchisor's Employees and Franchisees

Because the brand leadership demonstrates little faith in the capabilities of managers, staff, and franchisees, power, authority, and decision-making are concentrated at the top. The brand ownership becomes like puppet masters, pulling the strings and making employees and franchisees dance to a tune only they can hear.

As in bureaucracies, within a benevolent dictatorship, information mostly flows downhill, instead of up and down the organization. Brand leadership makes strategic decisions from an ivory tower and leaves to middle management the role of the town squire to announce decisions to the lowly franchisee citizens of the band fiefdom.

Think of what happens to talented and upwardly mobile employees or talented franchisees of this kind of organization. Brand leadership calls 100% of the shots without feedback or meaningful discussion. Those high-caliber employees of the franchisor and franchisees who know their value and wish to collaborate in the decision-making process and see their ideas implemented won't last. Only those willing to keep their heads down and consistently do the bidding of the benevolent dictatorship will remain, weakening the brand.

> Highly capable franchisor employees and franchisees will find and join a culture that values performance, results, and initiative.

Impact on Results

Now think about the quality of training and ongoing support these surviving low-skilled department heads and employees can offer franchisees. Will it be enough for results- and action-oriented franchisees to win or will they find it necessary to go outside the organization for tools and support? If these franchisees complain about either the quality of support or not being invited to participate in decisions impacting them, their comments aren't often heard in a commercial context. The franchisor will often respond with, "Don't these unappreciative franchisees know how hard we work? Don't they realize we are just trying to help them?" In a benevolent dictatorship, the franchisor's intentions and franchisees' appreciation are more important to the franchisor than franchisees' performance and results.

A benevolent dictator, CEO, and founder of a multi-brand franchisor nicknamed Bud never gave officers and department heads annual operating budgets. He made decisions on how his money would be spent on a case-by-case basis without their input, always keeping brand presidents guessing. In addition, he regularly moved employees in and out of departments and brands without consulting with brand leadership or the individuals being redeployed about what they wanted and needed. Bud believed he knew best, and his employees and franchisees would understand over time, or not. ("My company, so who cares!") Among brand presidents, the corporate joke was "We don't have budgets. We have 'Bud Gets.' Because whatever Bud wants, Bud gets." The different brands eventually shuttered units and franchisees failed to renew their agreements at renewal time because of weak support and brand underperformance. Many of the franchisor's brands have now ceased to exist or are just hanging by a thread, managed by skeleton crews.

Command and Control

This is one of the most common cultures in franchising. Command-and-control companies have strong central authorities where most strategic decisions are made. While power and authority may be more diffused than in the benevolent dictatorship culture, it's still consolidated at the top. Data routinely flows up from franchisees to the corporate office, yet decisions are more often than not handed down. Franchisors may have advisory committees consisting of franchisees, but these committees aren't decision-making bodies. They exist to advise the decision-makers, who are free to accept all, some, or none of the advice. In addition, franchisor leadership isn't always transparent with information, disclosing only what they deem franchisees need to know. While the franchisor leadership may verbalize such things as "franchisees are partners and stakeholders in the company," their attitudes, actions, and private conversations tell a different story.

From the get-go, franchisors often design themselves to be command and control. For instance, almost every Franchise Disclosure Document (FDD) and Franchise Agreement, if enforced literally, perpetuates this culture. If you were to read a FDD right now, most likely you would see paragraph after paragraph about what franchisees must or must not do, along with corresponding punishments should franchisees fail to act accordingly. If you were to then read the franchisor's obligations, more than likely you would come across language such as "Although not required, the franchisor may from time to time at its own discretion choose to [fill in the blank]."

Like the benevolent dictatorship, the franchisor leadership of a command-and-control company believes, "My brand, my system, my customer," and "Franchisees need to do what we say."

These franchisors let legality and parochial interests interfere with brand strategy. From a legal standpoint, clearly the franchisor owns the brand. From a legal standpoint, it's also the franchisor's responsibility to protect the brand.

But from the viewpoint of the marketplace, franchisees and franchisors share responsibility. Look at Apple, Harley-Davidson, and White Castle. These brands have a cultlike following and the brand assumes a life of its own. These companies offer their brands to their respective communities to build relationships on their own terms. In response, customers, and stakeholders make it their responsibility to ensure the brand thrives.

In the past, I worked with Snap-on Tools. At the time of our engagement, professional mechanics exponentially preferred Snap-on Tools over any competitor's tools. To demonstrate the cultlike following of the brand, Snap-on's director of franchising produced photos of men walking around NASCAR races with Snap-on tattoos on their shoulders, backs, and forearms. Wouldn't you want to own a business whose customers are so in love with the brand and product that even if they buy another brand from another vendor, your product is the one they eventually aspire to own and are willing to permanently mark their bodies for?

Legally, this represents an unauthorized use of the brand's logo, so the company would be within its rights to force the customers to make appointments with a dermatologist to have the tattoos removed. No brand can command such brand loyalty and excitement. Such brand loyalty and following unfolds over time, taking a life of its own. Such loyalty is driven by the customer, not by the C-suite.

Conversely, Disney built an entertainment empire through creating traditional family-friendly movies, content, and entertainment experiences. Over the last few years, in the name of diversity and inclusion, Disney leadership started altering their culture and entertainment offers to the public to reflect a culture of diversity and inclusion instituted from the top down. Parents with more traditional values, concerned about Disney's shift in values, have been rejecting their movies, parks, and other offerings at an alarming rate, plummeting Disney stock 50% over the last three years at the same time the S&P 500 index increased 27%, for a 77% differential. If you were a business owner and your business was cratering as fast as Disney's, wouldn't you change something fast? But corporate culture is not designed to change fast, even when the prevailing culture is failing customers, employees, and shareholders.

Impact on Franchisor's Employees and Franchisees

Command-and-control cultures are formed from several limiting and somewhat dysfunctional beliefs about the nature of franchisees and what makes franchising work.

These self-limiting cultural beliefs often include:

- Franchisees and employees are slackers and are always looking to get away with something. Therefore brand leadership needs to stay on top of them in order to build the brand right.

- Franchisees' and employees' objectives are less important than the franchisor's objectives. They exist to serve the franchisor's interests and should check self-interest at the door.

- Franchising allows the franchisor to build the brand using the franchisees' money. Franchisees are a necessary evil, not a strategic partner in the brand's overall success.

- If you want franchisees and employees to perform, the franchisor should reward the behavior they want and punish the behavior they don't. Leadership implements a carrot-and-stick leadership model.

- Mistakes are bad. Uniformity is good. Systems exist to minimize mistakes and control behavior. Don't think. Just follow the system.

If you are a highly skilled, motivated, upwardly mobile franchise professional, would you want to work here? And if you were already working here, how long would you stay?

If you were a franchise candidate looking to invest in a franchise, would you join? If you were already a franchisee of such a system, would you sell?

Impact on Results

The core values of a command-and-control culture are results, power, and control. Here is the major disconnect command-and-control franchisors create with franchisees. When asked, "Why do you want to start a business?" almost every franchise candidate in existence repeats some version of "I want more power and control over my life, career, and investments." So you can clearly see why in this culture, franchisee-franchisor conflicts are inevitable. That's why companies exhibiting a dominant command-and-control culture are so often sued by disgruntled franchisees, or routinely have franchisees banding together to create alliances to beef up their numbers to take a stand against the company. They end up fighting each other for control (or to avoid being controlled) rather than fighting the competition for increased market share. Such brands burden themselves with the risks of franchising while at the same time negating the value.

The command-and-control founder of a food concept I once worked with walked into a new franchisee's recently opened place of business unannounced. It was a peak time and the new franchisee was struggling to handle the customer volume. The founder became angry and started barking out commands to the franchisee's employees, ordering them around. When the franchisee objected to what she believed to be inappropriate behavior by usurping her authority as an owner, she was told, "We are the parent company and franchisees have to do what they are told." When retelling this story, the franchisee said, "I already have parents and don't need more. I wish someone told me I was going to be their child before they took my money." How motivated was the franchisee after the encounter? What is the predictable impact of this encounter on her brand experience? When a highly qualified new franchise candidate is looking to invest in a franchise and reaches out to this owner asking her if the candidate should join the chain, how will she most likely respond?

Can you see how these three dysfunctional cultures mentioned here are seemingly designed to self-sabotage?

Empowerment and Achievement

The empowerment and achievement culture creates the most fertile ground for cultivating an iconic national brand by providing an inviting environment that attracts and retains highly skilled and self-directed franchise candidates and franchisor executives and employees.

Brand leadership see their jobs as facilitators. They routinely interact with the top-producing employees and franchisee thought leaders, making sure these key implementers possess the tools and resources they need to win. They identify and eliminate potential bottlenecks or barriers to forward momentum. They are not egocentric. They give the necessary power, authority, and resources to those responsible for creating results. They are transparent with information. They are clear about the individual needs of employees and franchisees and work to align their individual goals with business objectives, so everyone wins.

I once worked with a franchisor support team of a QSR (quick-serve restaurant) franchisor who made it their mission to understand who their franchisees were as individuals and what drives them. The franchisor's support team used the franchisees' stated objectives, such as taking afternoons off to attend their kids' soccer games, as a context for their support recommendations. The support team showed franchisees how they can move closer to achieving their goals by implementing the franchisor's recommendations. I helped the franchisor's support team identify franchisees' communication styles and feed them information consistent with how these franchisees absorb and process information, minimizing communication breakdowns. We discussed adult learning principles, coaching principles, consulting best practices, negotiation, and conflict resolution techniques. As a result of the outstanding training, consulting, and coaching given by the support team, the brand grew hundreds of locations in a highly competitive QSR segment.

Impact on Employees and Franchisees

Empowerment and achievement cultures attract and retain top franchisor executives and employees and franchisee talent. Leaders, employees, and franchisees thrive personally and professionally within the teamwork-driven, results-oriented culture, unlocking the best of who they are and actualizing the most of what they can achieve. The franchisor's and franchisees' experience are valued and respected. Employees of the franchisor are rewarded consistent with their performance and promoted based on merit. Instead of consolidating power and authority at the top, the franchisor's leadership manages a bottom-up company, dedicating time, money, and energy empowering franchisees to spend resources, make decisions, and ultimately produce outstanding results.

Franchisees and the franchisor enjoy rock-solid relationships. Both seem to understand that each needs to make a healthy return on their time and money and neither can perform at high levels unless all their companies are healthy and profitable. When faced with a problem, they engage in a win-win solution rather than a zero-sum, win-lose solution.

Impact on Results

Brand leadership uses their executives, employees, and franchisees as their big idea farm, implementing the best ideas from their trusted people closest to the customer. Franchisees buy into the franchisors brand vision and make it their personal mission to deliver the brand promise. The brand leverages franchisees' entrepreneurship and skilled execution into a key strategic advantage in the marketplace. Rather than battling each other for control, franchisees and the franchisor collaborate on executing and systematizing the best ways to capture market share and deliver the brand promise to their customers.

These franchisors don't look at systems as a method to control behavior and minimize mistakes. They realize every major breakthrough by definition occurs when an employee or franchisee isn't following the system. Systems exist to replicate outstanding results, not to hinder innovation and destroy initiative. The franchisor and franchisees foster a learning and continual improvement culture, constantly refining and innovating.

As a result, customers understand the brand value. Some become local brand ambassadors. Others become cultlike followers. Investors

157

take notice, and franchise interest skyrockets. The brand's enterprise value rockets as a result.

The franchise flywheel turbocharges, and the brand hits a tipping point. Winning becomes an organizational habit. Franchisees produce greater results with less time, money, and energy invested than in the past.

Eventually, private equity discovers the brand and assigns a premium enterprise value to reflect the brand's sound business model and highly predictable royalty streams driven by this community of happy and profitable franchisees.

The Evolution of Corporate Culture

Unless the franchisor is already a significant chain that enters franchising later in their lifecycle, many franchisors enter Early Stage and Emerging Growth as benevolent dictatorships. These companies are generally privately held and tightly controlled, where leaders wear multiple hats and perform functions they were never adequately trained for.

During Early and Emerging Growth stages, franchisees are often treated like family. Leaders develop close interpersonal relationships. The brand generally maintains an informal family-style relationship among its stakeholders until it becomes no longer workable. As the brand expands and the organization begins to hire middle management and domain area experts like marketing, training, real estate, and field support, those franchisees who invested during Early and Emerging Growth stages no longer have immediate access to the founder.

As the business grows, the franchisor evolves from informal management and leadership to a formal organizational structure with clear job descriptions and clear personal, departmental, and organizational objectives. The franchisees will experience a shift to a more professionally run organization with new professional boundaries.

Sometimes franchisees and/or the founder resist this shift. Many entrepreneurs initially start businesses as a rejection of the traditional corporate structure, and now the very organization they joined is beginning to feel like what they once rejected. This is a recipe for staunch cultural and organizational resistance from both brand ownership and franchisees.

Smart and adaptable brands anticipate this shift and manage franchisees' and stakeholder expectations upfront. Franchisees join because they want to participate in a successful brand. Early Stage franchisees in particular desire a meaningful role in a successful brands' history, but they may not know in advance what that looks like. Smart franchisors spend extra time communicating to franchisees who join in the Early Stage and Emerging Stage about exactly what to expect over time and how growth will change the franchisee-franchisor relationship. By securing franchisees' support, the franchisor has the freedom to grow and evolve naturally with fewer organizational headwinds and less resistance.

If growth and relationships are being managed properly, the chain will evolve into an empowerment and achievement culture. Unfortunately, these culture shifts are often mismanaged. Often, franchisors' leadership react to franchisees' pushback by creating a legalistic and authoritarian command-and-control structure or the founder cuts off growth to maintain their benevolent dictatorship.

As chains grow, the increasing demands of the roles outstrip many of the franchisor's team members' ability to keep pace. Where on-the-job training may have been enough when growth was a trickle, as the chain enters exponential growth, the franchisor should be hiring experienced high-capacity executives whose leadership capacity exceeds the franchisor's rate of growth. But that's often not what happens.

Benevolent dictators value loyalty. Sometimes they are loyal to a fault. They give their team many opportunities to step up and perform, seemingly blind to the idea that the job demands more than

What Insiders Want You to Know About Franchising Before You Invest

the team possesses the capacity to deliver. Meanwhile the system continues to break down and eventually franchisee-franchisor relationships fracture.

Because franchisees stop getting the attention they are used to, they start doing their own thing, often inconsistent with brand identity and brand standards, creating brand disconnects and confusion in the mind of the customer.

Poorly managed growth creates a brand experience of spinning out of control. The franchisor spends all of their day in a break-fix mentality, resolving one-off conflicts and issues. Work stops being fun. Strategic plans sit on a shelf while the organization spends another day fighting fires.

The franchisor knows their team is spread thin. Sometimes valued employees buckle under the pressure and quit, and the chain loses precious brand expertise at the time they need it most. The franchisor begins to hire out of desperate need, onboarding managers and leaders from other chains. These new hires embed processes, procedures, and organizational behaviors from past chains. The franchisor begins to look and operate like a patchwork quilt of stop-gap solutions imported from other brands. Because new hires are expected to build the plane while they are flying it, they often don't have the time to stop and assess or align their approach with brand identity and brand values.

Eventually, franchisor leadership gets fed up with their sense of loss of control and franchisee-franchisor friction and they start tightening the screws on the franchisee community. By doing so, they usher in a new era of command and control.

This culture does not sit well with franchisees. Franchising works through collaboration, influence, and alignment of franchisee and franchisor interests. Entrepreneurs by their very nature resist strong-arm tactics. The more authoritarian franchisors behave, the more they will be met with stiff resistance from franchisees.

The franchise agreement is written so franchisors have all the cards. Franchisees know they can't win a direct assault, so they often engage in hit-and-run, sniping, or passive-aggressive behavior. They spread negative validation, blowing up the franchisor's already declining pipeline of new franchise candidates. They stop attending national conferences, so all in attendance bow to the demands of the command-and-control leadership giving leaders a false sense of emotional engagement and buy-in. They decline assistance from field operations, or worse, enroll field ops teams in their issues, turning them against the franchisor.

Brand strategy goes out the window. The brand enters a negative, self-perpetuating downward spiral. In the process, the franchisor becomes the next turnaround brand.

How Iconic Franchise Brands Protect Culture

Iconic brands don't hire staff just to fill chairs because they are stretched too thin. Instead, they have accurately assessed who are the organization's high potentials and either hired outside mentors or budgeted time and resources to train them up in advance for success in their next role.

They also know which positions need to be staffed by bringing in talent from the outside. To avoid hiring from desperate need and requiring new employees to hit the ground sprinting, franchisors invest in the proper human capital 6 to 12 months in advance, allowing the brand to organically grow into the franchisor's increased capacity. This allows the brand to educate the new hires on how to work within the franchisor's empowerment and achievement culture, minimizing the risk of having new hires import dysfunctional organizational behaviors from previous cultures.

When done right, the culture will experience a maturity process that will look something like this image.

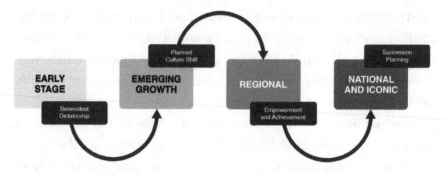

A successful maturity process.

This process reflects a learning organization with a continuous improvement mentality that adapts well to change, is interested in building something iconic, and isn't afraid of releasing the brand to the customer, supplier, and franchisees so each can build relationships and add value to the brand on their own terms.

Other franchisors, frightened by feelings and experiences of a loss of control, will circle the wagons and dig in. Leadership unwittingly believes control is more important than being iconic, resulting in stunted growth and diminished value.

Chapter 7

Assessing the Skills and Viability of a Franchisor

I've already stated that every franchisor is in two separate and distinct businesses. Business 1 is their consumer-facing business. They need to possess a mastery-level understanding of bringing their products and services profitably to market. If you shop a franchise, you should experience excellence, meaning the franchise operation delivers more real and perceived value to the customer than it extracts in price. I delve into the common value proposition of franchise brands in a moment.

Business 2 is the business of franchising, which I defined as "recruiting, training, resourcing, developing, and leading a team of entrepreneurs to build a brand." A national franchise brand is built one neighborhood or trade area at a time. The best predictor of a franchisors' success (which is worth repeating) is the franchisees' ROI and quality of the franchisee-franchisor relationships.

For a franchise brand to be viable, a franchisor must demonstrate mastery of both businesses, or eventually the brand will stagnate and decline. When a brand stagnates, franchisees increase risk that no one franchisee can mitigate. There are times when a franchisee can outperform a brand, but generally not for any extended period of time.

The Common Consumer Value Propositions of a Franchise Brand

I've identified 14 distinct ways customers perceive value, as explained in each section of this chapter. I am not asserting this is a whole and complete list, but a workable guideline for you to determine how particular brands deliver value, whether they can state it or not. My research shows that responsible franchise brands have historically staked out positions in one or two of these areas in order to dominate their competition in the marketplace. No one brand will or should be expected to deliver value consistent with all 14 customer definitions of value. However, most responsible franchise brands will zone in on one or two positions out of the 14 listed.

The following sections look at these consumer value propositions in detail.

Innovation

Customers acknowledge that these brands sell the most advanced products and services. For instance, one franchisor built a strong national brand through a proprietary technology that allowed franchisees to pinpoint and fix hard-to-find leaks in pools and spas in a noninvasive way (through a listening device), rescuing homeowners from the expense and frustration of having to rip up large swaths of their yards to zone in on leaks to resolve the issue. And Chem-Dry carpet cleaners have a patented product that uses carbonated water to lift stains from carpets much in the same way club soda lifts wine stains from a blouse.

Most companies relying on innovation depend on constant research, development, and reinvestment. Most entrepreneurs looking to start franchises resist getting into businesses that require constant reinvestment due to quick product or service obsolescence.

Franchisors who rely on innovation as their key point of difference don't seem to survive unless the franchise system holds a patent or has exclusive distribution rights for a patented product. Typically, the desire for a team of franchisees to reinvest moves slower than technology advances, meaning franchise brands can lose their technological edge in a hurry. For example, most franchisors don't penetrate 100 new markets within 10 years, yet 10 years in a technology business is an eternity. By the time an innovative company can achieve any significant level of market penetration through franchising, chances are their initial advantage will already be obsolete unless, like Chem-Dry, their technology doesn't have to be constantly updated. Innovation can come in any form.

A former professional hockey player and Stanley Cup winner of an Emerging Growth hockey school franchise developed a system to teach youth hockey players how to skate masterfully, using their skates, body, and motion to create space for passing, shooting, and controlling the puck. He opened schools across Canada and is now opening schools in cities in the United States with NHL hockey teams.

Necessary to the Customer

Customers simply cannot do without these products and services. Luxottica built a multi-billion-dollar business by manufacturing and distributing eyeglasses and contact lenses through such retail brands as LensCrafters and Pearle Vision. Beltone did the same with hearing aids. Regardless of the economy, people need to see and hear.

Price Leaders

These are brands that sell products cheaper than everyone else. Examples include Walmart, McDonald's, Taco Bell, Domino's, and Subway. Price leadership can be a real competitive advantage or a slippery slope. Well-managed brands demonstrate high degrees of operational excellence along with a competitive advantage on the supply chain. However, this strategy may also add risk, which threatens long-term sustainability since costs are usually going to increase, and brands may have already trained their customers to resist paying more. Sometimes brands inadvertently educate the market to expect a specific price point, such as Subway's once popular promotion of $5 footlong subs. When rising labor and protein costs made it unprofitable for Subway franchisees to continue with their $5 sub offering, many customers pushed back hard and rejected the higher price point or reduced their frequency of visits, leading to sales and profitability declines for many franchisees, sending the brand into a turnaround situation.

Service Leaders

These concepts include a unique customer experience or higher customer service expectation and often charge a slight premium for the value-added experience. Youth sports brand i9 Sports has designed social sports leagues that place a high value on a parents' experience as well as the children's, distinctly different from the ultra-competitive travel leagues. Re-Bath sets itself apart as a remodeler by carefully managing their customers' experience from design through installation and post-installation so they can get in and out of a customer's home in five days or less. When I asked one Re-Bath franchisee why he chose Re-Bath, he told me customers treat contractors like fish. "After a few days, we stink and they want us out." Re-Bath solves that problem.

If customers value the experience and brands demonstrate a strong ability to replicate this experience across their network, other brands will have difficulty copying their value proposition and creating a competitive advantage.

High Perceived Risk for Change

These brands have an opportunity to lock up their customer base as long as they meet their customers' minimum satisfaction threshold. Examples of these businesses include maid service brands and commercial cleaning. Maid service brands enter people's homes and therefore must earn the customer's trust by doing four things:

1. Arrive on time.
2. Clean well.
3. Leave on time.
4. Refrain from stealing.

As long as the brand meets these expectations, they will create a repeat customer with a high lifetime value. This is the same for janitorial brands who work commercial accounts. Dirty bathrooms and failure to replace toilet paper disrupt business and kill employee morale. A janitorial service that consistently keeps restrooms tidy can expect to keep clients.

Customer Intimacy

These brands build deep and committed personal relationships with their clientele. Examples include senior care businesses such as Visiting Angels, Home Instead, Comfort Keepers, BrightStar Care, and ComForCare. Others form a community or tribe, like fitness brands CrossFit and Orangetheory Fitness. Once these relationships have formed, customers find them difficult to re-create, and therefore they perceive a high risk for change.

Speed and Convenience

These brands focus on getting customers in and out quickly, minimizing life disruptions and playing off the high value their time-starved

Assessing the Skills and Viability of a Franchisor

customers place on convenience. These brands attract customers who place a high value on time. Great Clips is a great example. Customers can log onto their Great Clips mobile app and determine walk-in wait times at nearby locations. Little Caesars' Hot-N-Ready Pizza strategy capitalizes on busy customers who don't have time for a home-cooked meal. Other brands are often mobile-delivering products and services at the home or office for a premium. If the business is brick-and-mortar, companies need to be very skilled in real estate selection, as time-crunched customers look to stay in a small shopping orbit and do it all in one trip. Restaurant concepts capitalize on drive-thrus, selling more products out the window than they do from the counter.

Lifestyle

Harley-Davidson doesn't really sell motorcycles. They sell "freedom on the open road." Lifestyle brands often have high ego appeal. Lifestyle brands can also promote shared values with their customers, such as faith-based Christian Brothers Automotive. Other retail examples are Wild Birds Unlimited, which sells bird houses and bird feed to people who appreciate birds. HobbyTown owns a dominant position in the remote-controlled cars, planes, and helicopter toy business and provides customers with knowledgeable staff.

Aspirational/Luxury

These businesses sell premium services and luxury brands, such as Expedia CruiseShipCenters, which specializes in selling luxury cruise vacations.

Disruptive

These brands reinvent products and services, altering what customers value and how they shop. Planet Fitness disrupted the highly commoditized gym model through a high-value/low-cost offer designed to attract and retain well-intentioned but infrequent gym users. Jiffy Lube disrupted car maintenance service by inventing a method for oil change and basic car care in 30 minutes or less. Disruptors often give their franchisees a two- to three-year head start on the competition before copycat concepts roll out. They need to grab the "first mover" position, or they will lose to a copycat concept that accelerates past them. First-mover companies always seem to operate from the chaos of grow-as-fast-as-you-can, which means constant break-fix, a constant state of franchisor personnel flux (jobs change, people elevate, move, or quit because of the pace of the environment), and corporate culture may suffer.

Socially Responsible

These brands have a reputation for being solid corporate citizens who give back to the community or the planet. TOMS shoes is a classic example. While many franchisees give back to their local community, these brands build charity into their brand identity and tie it to their product or service offering. Many franchisors claim this brand position as a default position due to an incomplete advertising and marketing strategy. If a franchise brand's primary point of difference is responsible corporate citizenship to their local markets, the burden shifts 100% to the franchisee to build the brand on the local level rather than sharing the burden with the franchisor to wisely invest limited brand fees. While most franchise systems require responsible local community brand building, this should be an activity as it generally isn't a defensible brand position. Any brand can be a good corporate citizen at any time.

High Value/Affordable Luxury

These are premium brands with products or services still within reach of middle-income America. For instance, Massage Envy's monthly subscription model made spa services more affordable for their customers. Kilwins offers customers high-quality yet still affordable ice cream and confections.

Expertise/Thought Leadership

These brands are highly focused and have deep domain knowledge within their industry. For instance, Fleet Foot is a specialty retail store for runners. EarthWise Pet, Camp Bow Wow, and Central Bark provide its customers with expert knowledge and unique products to maximize pet wellness, relaxation, and health. GNC specializes in personal nutrition and wellness. Shoot360 is a disruptive basketball training facility that gamifies basketball drills through innovative technology.

Customization and Personalization

These brands offer customers a unique and precise combination of what they want, how they want it, and when they want it. This business model is often explained as mass customization, meaning they have developed a scalable model that allows customers to cost effectively tailor their product or services to unique specifications. Blaze Pizza, self-serve frozen yogurt chains, and Chipotle/Subway-style assembly line restaurants are all examples of this.

If poorly executed, this strategy can also backfire. For example, Cold Stone Creamery wowed customers with their system for mass customization of their ice cream, but customization also meant slower customer service times. In food service, customers don't want to wait more than 5–10 minutes for their product. As the brand grew popular and lines got longer, the increased wait times created a negative customer experience, resulting in declining sales, which leveled off at acceptable 5–10 minute customer wait times, but at a huge cost to franchisees. Cold Stone franchisees became a victim of their own success due to a flawed operating model, which, if successful, guaranteed customer dissatisfaction through long wait times.

Summary

This list may not be exhaustive. However, it is my experience that any brand that fails to build a reputation for consistently delivering the benefits as defined by one or more of these attributes will quickly see its services commoditized or create confusion in the mind of both the customer and franchisee as to the true value being offered. Brands that do not stake a claim in how they deliver value will most likely eventually enter a mostly unwinnable war fought on price and convenience, resulting in a sales plateau. They will eventually decline.

Chapter 8

The Franchisor Landscape in the United States

Franchising is looking at a possible significant near-term market correction. I've been saying this for years, and it still hasn't happened. Past history shows that as one new franchisor enters the market, another exits, for about 250–350 new concepts per year and approximately the same exiting. The franchisor economics are such that the number of franchisees looking to buy a business cannot support the number of franchisors currently in business, hence the turnstile exits. My prediction is based on multiple limiting factors working in synergy, and leads me to believe market dynamics will only become more pronounced over the next few years.

Dynamics Affecting the US Franchise Market

The factors affecting the franchise market are discussed in the following sections, in no particular order.

Oversaturation of Franchisors

In 2017, research firm FRANdata reported there were about 3,800 active franchise brands in the United States, at or near a record high for franchising. Today, many believe there are over 4,000. A partner at Princeton Equity Group, a private equity firm with a franchising thesis, once told me they had counted 7,000 franchise brands. The actual number is hard to gather because not every registered franchisor is actively recruiting new franchisees. The following image shows the distribution of franchisors by size.

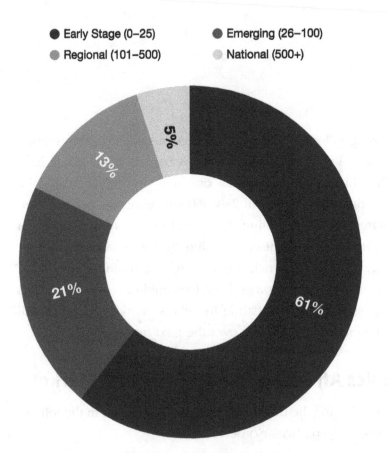

- ● Early Stage (0–25)
- ● Emerging (26–100)
- ● Regional (101–500)
- ● National (500+)

Distribution of US franchisors by size. Adapted from FRANdata.

Fewer New Franchise Candidates Entering the Market

Consulting firm Franchise Performance Group (FPG) and FRANdata both estimate that in any given year, only 13,000–15,000 franchise candidates invest in new franchises.

Hundreds of New Concepts Enter the Market Each Year

In any given year, FRANdata and the International Franchise Association report approximately 250 to 350 new concepts choose to franchise, adding more noise to an already crowded marketplace. Most new concepts do not add new buyers – instead, they further dilute the ratio of buyers to franchise brands and further disrupt the demand/supply curve.

New Low-Entry Cost Self-Employment Options

In 2022, the US Census Bureau reported five million new business starts. Most of these businesses were individual owner-operator models with no employees. Companies and employees seem to be more open to side hustles, independent contractor positions rather than employee positions. Brands like Lyft and Uber and websites like Upwork give entrepreneurs a solid low-entry cost option to start a business, which used to be limited to often disreputable multi-level marketing companies.

Lower Unemployment Leading to Lower Risk Tolerance

According to the Bureau of Labor Statistics, the 2023 unemployment rate hovered under 4%, which is considered a full-employment economy. The unemployment number drops to 2% when you consider only people with a bachelor's degree or higher, which a typical franchise investor would possess. When unemployment is high, starting a business looks more secure than the job market. When unemployment is low, to a would-be first-time entrepreneur, the job market looks more secure than starting a business. TTI Success Insights estimates 40% of the US population is primarily motivated by safety, stability, and security rather than other drivers, such as independence and control.

Stock Market Uncertainty Causes Franchise Candidates to Freeze

The US economy avoided an expected recession in 2023. Financial experts are seemingly in disagreement about a potential recession in 2024, which will or will not have occurred by the time this book is published. This level of uncertainty creates a wait-and-see attitude among franchise candidates. Smart and responsible franchisors understand this and will negotiate a better-than-expected deal with franchise candidates, offer incentives to grow, and may mitigate new franchisees' risk to stimulate growth. Franchise candidates will be in a stronger negotiating position with many brands than in normal times and should look at taking advantage of this leverage.

Increasing Costs of Business

With low unemployment comes wage increases. Higher wages and energy costs always lead to higher product and service costs, squeezing margins particularly for companies who are low-cost providers or who operate in commoditized markets. The interest rates for SBA and other sources of commercial lending are at or near 10-year highs. Franchisees may find it difficult to pass their cost increases along to their customer base, further squeezing margins, raising break-even points, and decreasing cash flow. Construction costs are up, interest rates are up, labor is up, and inflation is up. Some franchise brands demonstrate great resilience to these economic forces. Others are held hostage.

What It All Means

It is unwise for franchise brands to ignore these trends, thinking somehow the brand will remain unaffected by the broader national economy. Given what I believe to be great disequilibrium in the franchise candidate demand/franchisor supply curve, we expect to see consolidation among franchise brands, which seems to be the role private equity firms are taking in franchising.

In the short term, these inhibiting factors will make it harder, but certainly not impossible, to grow sizable, significant, and valuable franchise brands. Regardless of the economy, smart, well-capitalized, disciplined, and high-value franchisors with profitable business models continue to grow at a favorable clip and to be worthy of investment. The lower-value, undifferentiated, lower-skilled copycat franchisors with unpredictable returns need to be concerned and correct their course.

Here is the good news. In this market, you are highly valuable to a franchisor and may be in an atypically strong negotiating position when it comes time to invest in a business.

Strong Franchise Brands Will Become Stronger

Typically, economic headwinds eventually lead to a leaner, more resilient business models for the smart franchise brands who execute well. This in turn leads to stronger and more sustainable unit-level economics for many brands at the expense of weaker competitors and other franchise brands that fail to keep up. Dominant and skilled brands can expect a disproportionate share of market bounce-back, bolstering their leadership position and driving franchisees' cash flow.

In their 2018 Franchise Sales Index, technology supplier FranConnect reported that out of the nearly 500 franchisors operating on their platform, about 80% of franchisees who invest in a brand went to brands with over 75 operating units or territories, which FPG would classify as either late-stage Emerging Growth brands, Regional brands, or National brands. According to generally accepted statistical analysis, this sample size statistically creates a 95% confidence level with less than 5% expected margin of error as shown in the following chart.

Follow the math.

Category	Data (or Estimate)	Source
Estimated number of franchise brands	Approximately 4,000	2017 FRANdata study
Estimated number of Early Stage and Emerging Growth brands	Approximately 3,200+	2017 FRANdata study
Estimated number of new franchisees joining any system	In any given year, approximately 13,000–15,000	FRANdata and FPG estimates
Number of new franchisees joining Early Stage and Emerging Growth	2,800–3,000	Franchise Performance Group (FPG) estimates based on 2018 FranConnect Franchise Sales Index findings
Estimated number of new franchisees entering franchising each year	250–350	FRANdata
Estimated number of operating units needed to achieve royalty self-sufficiency	40–100	FPG franchisor financial models

Category	Data (or Estimate)	Source
Average number of new franchisees per Early Stage (including startup) and Emerging Growth franchisors	**Less Than 1**	Simple Math; 2,800 estimated new franchisees divided by 3,100 estimated Early Stage and Emerging Growth franchisors
Estimated time for Early Stage and Emerging Growth franchisors to achieve royalty self-sufficiency	40 or so territories or franchisees. Average run rate leads to 40 years to royalty self-sufficiency.	FPG models based on best available evidence

Franchising research firm Franchise Grade studied 10 years of startup franchise growth beginning in 2007. They found that over a four-year period, more than 30% of startup franchisors had 0 to 1 franchise locations. Ten years after launch, more than 50% of this group had 50 or fewer franchise locations, meaning many had not achieved royalty self-sufficiency and thus had to continue to sell franchises to make franchisor payroll, meaning they have to recruit people like you, whether you fit or not, just to keep the lights on. *Caveat emptor,* or "buyer beware." That isn't to say franchisors are disreputable or irresponsible, but it is to say there is intense pressure for franchisors to award you a franchise in order to survive, regardless of fit.

According to an October 13, 2020, article in *Franchise Times*, only 16% of franchisors have 100 units/territories or more, and a mere 4% have 500 or more, which would classify them as a large National brand.

This means that thousands of business concepts have at one time hired consultants and attorneys who communicated that if these brands would only invest $150,000–$250,000 or more into their consulting companies or legal firms, they would turn these brands into viable franchisors. *They were wrong about 80% of the time. That's worse than the odds of a coin flip.*

Also, keep in mind that Emerging Growth, Regional, and National franchisors who have been franchising for more than 10 years often did so with far less competition and disruption than the newest generation of franchisors.

Why Candidates Should Consider Avoiding Smaller Brands

Why is the available franchise candidate market rewarding larger brands rather than Early Stage and smaller Emerging Growth brands? It's not necessarily because of the size of the brand. I believe it depends on the size of the comparative risks. Smaller brands historically have proven to be less refined, less sophisticated, and produce fewer returns than larger brands. If smaller brands can't demonstrate consistency of returns, they present higher risk. **As a result, candidates' interest and investment goes to the chains with best-in-class economics with the lowest historical and perceived risk.**

Many times, when I discuss this dynamic with smaller franchisors, they come back with, "We have large territories available, therefore we have tremendous opportunity." The franchise investor doesn't define opportunity according to green grass and blue skies. They define opportunity according to the predictability and desirability of the franchisor's historical unit-level economics and the likelihood the franchisor will add more value to the franchisees' investments than they extract in royalty payments.

> Here is the bottom line. Franchise candidates will always invest in unique, proven, profitable, replicable, predictable, and sustainable models run by responsible brand leaders. This is what people have always sought by purchasing a franchise.

The best predictor of whether a franchisor may become a valuable, sustainable brand is that they already look, feel, act, support, perform, and deliver customer value like an iconic brand while still in the Emerging Growth stage. I will present the lifecycle stages of a franchise brand later in this book to give you greater context and insights.

Opportunities and Risk Factors

Franchise candidates don't invest in franchising – they invest in individual brands. This means well-run and well-executed brands with profitable business models can and will buck larger microeconomic and macroeconomic trends. They aren't necessarily tethered to franchising as a whole, *unless they make the fatal mistake of thinking and acting like other franchisors.*

Too many franchise brands think they will operate successfully on a shoestring, believing that being undercapitalized creates risk only for franchisees, but not for them. Franchisors are required to present three years of audited financial statements to every franchise candidate in a Franchise Disclosure Document (FDD). An undercapitalized franchisor is easy to spot.

Emerging Growth franchisors of under 100 franchisees or units (which represent more than 80% of current franchisors) need to possess a war chest or access to at least $1 million to $2 million of financial backing to reinvest back into their brand as necessary to perfect their business model and to build their bench strength and support infrastructure. Brands that don't have proper financial backing will either collapse, stagnate, or get picked up by value-shopping private equity turnaround specialists or market consolidators. Franchise candidates need to put as much emphasis on the franchisors' P&Ls as franchisors do when looking at a franchise candidate's personal financial statement and access to capital.

Chapter 9

Understanding Where Franchisors Are in Their Lifecycle and Learning Curve

Regardless of the service, product, investment level, or industry, all franchise brands seem to track along a common brand growth curve, with predictable stages that need to be successfully navigated in a predictable fashion to maximize opportunity.

The FPG Franchise Brand Growth Curve

The FPG Franchise Brand Growth Curve stages are linear, sequential, time limited, and highly predictable if you know where to look.

The growth curve somewhat mirrors economist Raymond Vernon's famed product lifecycle. Vernon discovered that, while the opportunity time frame and sales volumes aren't consistent from product to product, the relative path is identical. See the following image.

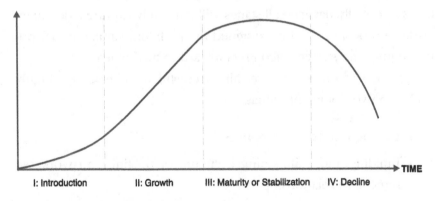

Raymond Vernon's product lifecycle graph.

The key to managing a product lifecycle is to correctly identify where the product is in the lifecycle and then employ human and financial capital relative to the needs of that particular stage.

For instance, during the introduction stage of Vernon's product lifecycle, a company needs to focus on marketing to build brand awareness, engage customer trials, grow a customer base, and gather market share. During growth, a company runs hard, seeking to establish a dominant position and maximizing the opportunity by outpacing the competition. During maturity, sales soften, companies defend existing market share, protect existing customer relationships, and seek to extend profitability by keeping products relevant as long as possible. During decline, companies phase out or sell off the declining product lines, and then acquire or create new products and services and start a new product lifecycle.

> The dynamics and demands of each stage dictate and determine the company's brand strategy.

Rather than a smooth continuous curve like Vernon's product lifecycle, I created the FPG Franchise Brand Growth Curve, which is a bit more complex. During each stage, franchisors face potential points of diminishing marginal returns, eventually leading to leveling or decline if they don't skillfully implement the strategies relevant to that stage while at the same time planning for the next stage. The franchisors that successfully navigate all stages will ultimately capture a dominant leadership position and be assigned the premium valuation that private equity and strategic acquirers reward to market leaders.

Again, I assert at its core, all successful franchisors are highly skilled in two dominant arenas:

- Driving unit-level economics
- Building and maintaining a culture of trusting and workable franchisee relationships

As franchise brands move through each stage, unit-level economics should continually improve, financial predictability increases, and risk decreases. The franchisee relationships and corporate culture will evolve from an informal entrepreneurial culture to a more formal yet collaborative corporate culture that values relationships and performance in equal measure. See the following image.

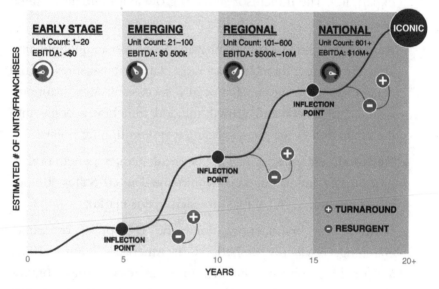

The FPG franchise brand growth curve.

FPG asserts all of the nearly 4,000 franchise brands can ultimately be bucketed into seven possible stages: Early Stage, Emerging, Regional, National, Iconic, Turnaround, and Resurgent. These stages reflect where a company is within the business of franchising and don't always reflect the lifecycle stage of the products and services they offer customers. While the franchisor and product lifecycles may be related, these lifecycles need to be considered separate and distinct.

- **Early Stage.** These are essentially startup franchisors. While they may be highly mature local or Regional brands, they have not yet proven themselves successful franchisors.

- **Emerging.** Franchisors have proven themselves on a small scale. Their initial group of franchisees are succeeding and expanding. The franchisor starts to grow at a more accelerated rate.

- **Regional.** Franchisors have proven themselves in multiple markets. Their target franchisee, by most statistical measures, would declare their businesses financially successful. More cautious, better capitalized, and growth-minded franchisees come into the chain at a faster pace, creating a system tipping point.

- **National.** Franchisors have successful market penetration in most major media markets within the United States. Brands look to achieve critical mass in each major market.

- **Iconic.** The brand, now dominant, disruptive, or game-changing, is deeply embedded in American culture. Think McDonald's, Subway, Dunkin'. In many cases, these brands define their categories, set the customers' expectations for competing brands, and determine the brand standards for all competitors.

- **Turnaround.** Franchisors that do not successfully execute strategies relative to the stage they're in, whose unit-level economics do not improve as the chain expands, and whose franchisee relationships become strained, will first experience a slow-down, and if corrective measures are not taken, sales will flatten and eventually decline, threatening the long-term stability and existence of franchisees, franchisors, and the brand.

Because of the typical one- to two-year lag time between the franchisor's strategic decisions and the impact of these decisions on the growth curve, many Turnaround brands don't yet know they are Turnaround brands. Often franchisors mistakenly think they are Early Stage or Emerging franchisors because the data hasn't shown otherwise. I will discuss this time lag later in this chapter.

- **Resurgent.** Franchisors that know they are in a Turnaround, correctly identify root causes, implement countermeasures, halt the decline, and start the slow reversal can become resurgent brands. They often present themselves to the franchisees and customers as reinvented brands. Arby's is an example of a successful resurgent brand.

Key Inflection Points

During any stage, franchisors may suffer from *The Peter Principle*. Consultant Laurence Peter coined this phrase in 1969 to describe a predictable organizational behavior pattern in which companies promote managers and employees until they fail. Peter described this as "rising to their level of incompetence." Paradoxically, Peter found the main cause of failure for a manager or employees was their past successes. When placed in a new situation, managers and employees habitually implemented what worked in their last role, regardless of the appropriateness for their new situation. Rather than acknowledge and study the changing landscape and adapt accordingly, many people simply keep going with what they already think they know. Until they fail.

Inflection points represent the point in time where franchisors start to "peter out" and have to pivot, making decisions and applying resources that address the needs and issues they will encounter during the next stage. Too often, franchisors continue to make the same decisions that worked in their current stage and eventually fall off the growth curve and become the next Turnaround brand.

Key takeaway: The same franchisor's mindset and tactics that worked so beautifully in the previous stage *become a barrier of entry to the next*. If a franchisor doesn't make at least a tactical shift and often a fundamental transformational organizational shift, they will predictably peak and then decline. Because of the common lag between the time strategic decisions are made and the impact of these decisions on the curve, franchisors need to pivot before the data proves they are "petering."

Just as each stage of Vernon's product lifecycle dictates strategy, each stage of FPG Franchise Brand Growth Curve dictates franchisors growth strategy and allocation of capital and resources. If the strategy is mismatched to the stage, the budget doesn't support the strategy, or if franchisors are slow to make new decisions, growth will peak, and sales will flatten. If the brand continues along the same course, it eventually will slip into decline unless the franchisor takes corrective action.

"Smart Growth" versus "Fast-as-You-Can Franchising"

Some franchisors think they should sell franchises as quickly as possible and then get out before operational problems surface. However, smart acquirers like private equity investors measure a franchisor's value against the predictability of future recurring revenue streams. Smart private equity firms can spot an unstable pump-and-dump, franchise-as-fast-as-you-can operation by examining sales volumes and predicting franchisees' unit-level economics. If franchisees' returns appear weak, private equity will assume these royalty streams are at risk and devalue the franchisor. The private equity market wants financially sound franchisees that will predictably pay royalties for the duration of their agreement and renewal periods.

Private equity firms look at what is called "a cohort analysis," which is comparing how comparable groups perform side-by-side. Once I was asked to look at the predictability of future revenue streams by a private equity firm looking to purchase a franchisor. I noticed as the chain grew, the new franchisees in later years were not achieving the same results as new franchisees in previous years. Keep in mind the organization would be larger, possess more capital, have a larger team, and have more opportunity to study and resource enhancements to ensure more profitable ramp-ups. But the opposite was occurring. I surmised the domain expertise could be attributed to a few key employees and not to the documented processes and systems. In other words, the franchisor didn't properly identify and document what worked best as franchisees enter training and ramp up over the first two years.

Furthermore, I identified that the key members of the leadership who possessed this knowledge were not continuing with the brand post-acquisition. I informed my client in my opinion they were at the very beginning of a systemwide breakdown. It appeared the exiting leadership team lowered its standards, offered franchises to candidates they would have said were unqualified in the past to pump enterprise value, and were looking to exit before operating problems hit the fan. My client passed on acquiring the brand.

A few years later I met the former owner of the brand. I told him I acted as an advisor to a private equity firm who passed on the deal. He asked me how I advised my client. I told him the back story I extrapolated from the numbers. Without acknowledging anything, he smiled and said, "You advised your client well."

Considering Risk and Reward by Lifecycle Stage

Generally, but certainly not always, the larger the brand, the more profitable the parent company, and the more experienced the brand's leadership, the lower the franchisees' risk. When franchise candidates investigate a smaller brand, they should default to the idea that smaller brands have greater risk outside the franchisees' control, as I describe next. That doesn't mean don't invest. It means the reward should be greater to offset the additional risks. Consider National and Iconic brands like investing in a mutual fund. Consider Early Stage and Emerging brands like investing in a new internet stock or cryptocurrency – higher risk, but make sure that is offset by a higher potential return. The reason there are more than 80% Early Stage and Emerging Brands and few grow beyond that point is that they offer franchisees higher risk and lower returns than the National brands, which makes a poor investment case.

Keep in mind you do not invest what is average for franchisors, you invest in one brand. If you invest in an Early Stage, Emerging, Turnaround, or Resurgent franchisor, their financial returns must exceed and their risk must be lower than what is pictured in the following image. I recommend you think through a model something like this as a starting point. If you invest in an Early Stage or Emerging franchisor, they must operate inconsistently with the model pictured here. In short, they should work hard to mitigate your risk and offer returns more compelling than National brands.

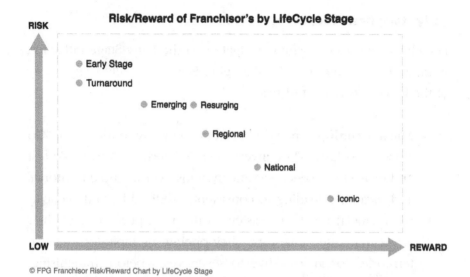

© FPG Franchisor Risk/Reward Chart by LifeCycle Stage

Risk/reward of franchisors by lifecycle stage. Adapted from FPG.

Early Stage Franchisors

Early Stage franchisors start as successful local concepts, typically with fewer than 20 operating units, locations, or territories. While they may have demonstrated proof of concept for their corporate operating business model, they struggle with establishing proof of concept as a franchisor. Better capitalized and more sophisticated franchise buyers already know about the high failure rate for both Early Stage franchisors and pioneering franchisees, and therefore sit on the sidelines and watch.

According to FRANdata, Early Stage franchisors represent more than 60% of franchisors in the US marketplace. According to the data, it would appear *only one-third successfully graduate from Early Stage to Emerging brand status.*

Understanding Where Franchisors Are in Their Lifecycle

Early Stage Best Practices

Franchisors who successfully navigate past the Early Stage inflection point and accelerate into the Emerging Stage generally share many of the following characteristics:

- **Market timing.** They do business according to the adage "Go slow to go fast." They invest time and resources to battle-test and prove their processes and systems over multiple territories and locations, leading to consistent, predictable, and acceptable financial results consistent with the expectations of their target franchisee investors. They operate multiple locations or territories for at least five to seven years before franchising, demonstrating long-term sustainability across markets.

- **They develop a brand of demonstrable value.** Because they are intelligent and sophisticated considering their size, they can entice pioneering franchise candidates to take a risk. Often these franchisees are regular customers, suppliers, or extended family, with the common denominator being that they all have strong familiarity and general affection for the brand.

- **They take the time to build a strong foundation.** They look long and award franchises cautiously, understanding that in the Early Stage every franchisee needs to win. They carefully manage franchise candidates' expectations upfront, giving them a clear understanding of what it takes to win and getting commitment that they are willing to do what it takes. Pioneering franchisees understand their place in brand history and accept responsibility for evangelizing the brand to qualified franchise candidates. The franchisee-franchisor relationship starts on extremely strong footing.

- **They are capitalized properly and invest wisely.** They have access to a war chest in the $1 million to $2 million range and understand that they may need to invest in infrastructure and brand refinements before achieving royalty self-sufficiency and organizational stability.

- **They accept and implement sound advice from franchising professionals.** Just as they tout the value of experience and the risk of doing it all themselves to franchise candidates, they in turn invest time and dollars putting together an advisory team with real-world franchising experience in growing successful franchise brands.

- **They recruit selectively.** They critically think through what it takes to be a successful franchisee and are prepared to walk away from candidates who don't measure up. On the support side, they take their time hiring the best talent, people who share their values and have documented success in supporting franchisees and adding value to their brand.

- **Leadership designs and executes their strategic plan.** Key employees and leaders often have mastery-level expertise in the multiple domains they're responsible for. If they don't, they hire consultants or advisors who bring this experience and bake this expertise into their processes and systems.

- **The new market penetration strategy has proven effective.** The franchisor has mastered and optimized all aspects of their new customer acquisition and revenue model, including necessary advertising vehicles and predictable targets for cost per new customer acquisition, customers' dollars-per-transaction, customer frequency, and customer retention.

- **Leadership is tech-savvy and uses technology to drive information and efficiencies.** The business leverages the latest and best technology effectively for their customer-facing and franchisor-related business systems.

- **They already look and act like a National brand.** Branding and systems are highly refined. Scalable strategic vendor relationships are in place. Supply lines are negotiated and scalable. Leaders are high-capacity executives. The chain grows to fill slack organizational capacity rather than always playing catch up. The organization always hires, trains, and develops team members to increase slack capacity. They resist every urge to cut corners. Instead of buying into the logic of "let's launch into franchising with what we have and evolve and develop the brand over time," they think, "Let's launch with the best version of ourselves."

- **Strong brand position.** The customer value proposition is clear. The target audience is defined and sees high value in the product or service offering. The brand has established raving fan customers in the markets it serves. Other customers are aware of the brand and appear to be anxiously waiting for the brand to enter their market also.

- **Brand identity.** The brand is well known to the customers in the markets it serves and has some reputation and awareness in contiguous markets or nearby cities.

- **One or more members of the leadership team have already been there.** One or more partners or executives have already built a regional or national chain with 200 or more territories or franchisees on their watch. They know what to expect when a chain hits tipping and inflection points.

If a franchisor successfully matures the brand, demonstrates these characteristics, and successfully recruits, trains, develops, and leads a small but elite band of 20 or so profitable franchisees, the franchisor graduates from Early Stage into Emerging franchisor status.

Franchisors who graduate will begin to attract an additional group of investors FPG labels Early Adopters. These candidates are generally more risk-averse than Early Stage pioneers but equally growth-minded. By widening its appeal to now include a strong secondary group of Early Adopters, the brand is poised to hit its tipping point.

Early Stage Risk Factors

Many franchisors fail to reach their potential, not because of competitive threats, but because of the following:

- **Self-deception.** Early Stage franchisors often view their business from an insulated insider's perspective, rather than looking at the business from a more classic supply-and-demand, industry, and franchise candidate/investor perspective. While the business format may have worked for the owner, the systems, training, or support may have undetected weaknesses, omissions, or flaws that inhibit a franchisee's ability to learn the model and aggressively grow.

- **Undercapitalization.** Franchisors often falsely believe they can grow their companies using franchise fee revenue or on a shoestring on pure hustle. Only when it is too late do many learn they will need to make significant investments in personnel or brand and system refinements prior to generating any significant return on franchise fees, royalties, or rebates from franchisees' product purchases.

- **Low will.** Many franchisors want to capture the value without doing the heavy lifting necessary to refine their model and making it more marketable and valuable to prospective franchisee candidates. Sometimes they think that they can make more money selling $40,000 franchises than they can selling their products and services. These "take the money and run" franchisors are seldom concerned about franchisee support, long-term franchisee financial health, or building a sustainable brand.

- **Bad or no market intelligence.** They overestimate the demand for their business and underestimate their cost and barriers of entry. These brand founders often think to themselves, "I did well. I put my kids through college and built wealth and cash flow. I'm no Ivy League MBA or Zuckerberg wunderkind, but I believe I can teach anyone to do what I do." Coming to the table with an "If I did it, anyone can do it" perspective, they automatically assume their business could and should be a franchise. They enter franchising with unrealistic expectations and completely underestimate the time, money, effort, complexity, and sophistication it takes to build a profitable and sustainable franchise brand. Simply put, Early Stage franchisors often falsely assume that since their concept plays well in small venues, they're naturally ready for a larger stage.

Franchising appears to be stacked with franchise attorneys and franchise consultants who easily convince small business owners their business is highly franchiseable and perhaps the next big thing. Then they charge professional fees of $150,000 to $250,000 or more to develop their systems and package a franchise for sale.

Statistically, Early Stage franchisors more often than not fall into one or more of the following predictable traps, preventing a successful franchisor launch:

- **No proof of concept/They come out too early.** Their brand is underdeveloped and their processes and systems are unrefined, leading to inconsistent, unpredictable, and unacceptable franchisee results. While the systems may work well for ownership and company managers, they may not be granular enough for new entrepreneurs who have no experience in the industry. These system flaws extend the franchisees' learning curve, burning precious cash. Many brands become franchisors after they successfully operate one unit or territory, meaning they have zero proof of scale, ability to penetrate new markets, or replicability.

- **They overestimate the demand for their franchise.** The fish don't jump in the boat as promised by the professionals who set them up as a franchisor. The unplanned shortfall of franchise fee revenue knocks the brand off their strategic plan, leaving people wandering in the desert, wondering what do I do next? They may have recruited 4–10 franchisees, and don't have the cash flow, desire, or expertise to support them properly to ensure franchisees' success. Furthermore, the franchisor may be so overzealous about their own brand they turned a blind eye to the capitalization and transferable background and skills of the new franchisees. They have a franchise to sell, and they sell to anyone who wants to buy regardless of fit, not necessarily because they are intentionally doing something wrong. They may just want to know they can do it.

- **They underestimate the amount of time it takes to get established.** Several years in, they feel like they're running in quicksand, questioning what happened. Remember, one recent study showed less than 5% of franchisors get to 100 units or territories in less than 10 years.

- **They are undercapitalized.** They were told it takes $150,000–$250,000 to get started, but later find out they will need to invest an additional $1 million–$2 million before they achieve royalty self-sufficiency and organizational stability. They're undercapitalized and simply bootstrap it. They need franchise fee revenue to pay the rent and keep the lights on. Often the franchisor siphons from profitable company store operations, putting the once healthy company operations at risk also.

- **They reject sound, practical advice from professionals.** They believe they know better. On one hand, they espouse to franchise candidates the value of experience and the risk of doing it all yourself. On the other hand, they reject investing in real-world franchising experience, choosing to go it alone.

- **They receive bad advice or a poor work product from franchise attorneys and franchise consultants.** This adds to both franchisees' and franchisors' risk and reduces their chances for success.

- **They recruit anyone who will buy their franchise.** They don't critically think through what it takes to be successful pioneering franchisees, don't have the discipline to walk away from unqualified candidates, or simply grab the cash because they are undercapitalized.

- **Leadership wears too many hats.** They operate as a part-time franchisor and part-time unit-level operator, leaving no time to do either particularly well. Key employees often don't have mastery-level expertise in the multiple tasks they're responsible for, increasing brand risk.

- **Their brand positioning may be too unrefined.** The brand promise may be too vague or confusing to attract new customers for the consumer-facing model and new franchise candidates for the business model. This confuses customers and may reduce customer trial and frequency, lengthening franchisees' ramp up and increasing cash needs and risk.

- **The new market penetration strategy may be undeveloped and ineffective.** The brand is an unknown entity outside local markets, which requires franchisees to invest more time and energy in marketing than perhaps they budgeted for. Often franchisors tell candidates they have to do community marketing, which can be code for "We don't have a proven marketing system nor the money to create it, so we throw marketing spaghetti against the wall and hope something sticks."

- **The revenue model may be incomplete.** The franchisor may not have mastered their complete revenue model, lacking systems, operations, marketing, and support to simultaneously increase and optimize customers' dollars-per-transaction, customer frequency, and customer retention.

- **The business may be behind the technology curve.** The business may not be fully leveraging the latest and best technology effectively for their customer-facing and franchisor-related business systems.

- **Nobody on the leadership team has ever done this before.** Ownership and leadership may be solely composed of product and service technicians and small business owners who have never scaled a franchisor across the United States. Growing a sizable business is theory for them. They don't know what to expect and won't see nuanced breakdowns as they are happening.

- **Personal agendas trump strategy.** Due to rapid acceleration, what was a reasonably flat organization where everyone is a colleague starts to form organizational hierarchies, creating a power grab among immature and inexperienced middle management. They fail to realize that success is a buffet and as the brand matures, everyone wins. Instead, they relate to the brand's newfound success and opportunities as a zero-sum game where there are winners and losers within their ranks and their access to advancement is by stepping over colleagues. If these attitudes aren't effectively dealt with, a toxic culture where personal agendas reign supreme will cement, trumping brand values.

Emerging Brands

Smart, capitalized, and aggressive Early Adopter investor types should target Emerging brands for investment. Among more cautious franchise candidates, the thought process is, "I don't want to be a pioneer. They get arrows in the back. I also don't want the franchisor to experiment with my time and money." They equate a franchisor's Early Stage with unmitigated risk and generally I would agree. In their world, once a franchisor has it all figured out (which often means 20 or more units), they have an opportunity to step up and cherry-pick the most lucrative markets.

Once a franchisor successfully navigates through the Early Stage, they will start feeling more momentum. In the Early Stage, a franchisor feels growth like pushing a boulder up a hill. As they successfully move through their Emerging stage, it feels like the boulder has crested the hill and is now starting to roll down on its own power, which introduces a whole new set of operational issues.

While a franchisor may have mastered what it takes to successfully onboard up to six franchisees per year, they are suddenly faced with a new problem: How do we successfully onboard 12–20 new franchisees per year (or more)?

Growth fuels brand awareness, driving year-over-year revenues to historical highs. Added units provide the franchisor with greater purchasing power, driving costs down and creating more resilience and liquidity. Growth also helps the franchisor build its brand as an employer of choice, adding more responsible and talented workers on both the franchisee and franchisor levels. The franchisor continues to refine its model, shortening the time to break even, value-engineering the investment level downward and negotiating better financing programs for startups and expansions.

Simply put, everything appears to be working better all at the same time. It's right about this time that franchisors begin to believe they now possess what it takes to build a large Regional or National brand. *The reality is that they have only enough steam to carry them to the next growth stage.* As the FPG Franchise Brand Growth Curve suggests, they will eventually experience decreasing marginal returns as they approach the next stage. At this point, successful brands reinvent their organization again to capitalize on the opportunities presented to successful Regional brands.

Emerging Growth Best Practices

Earlier I presented data explaining that only about half of Emerging brands crack the code, find their way past 100 units or territories, and graduate to Regional brand status. Those who do so share many of these characteristics:

- **Have tight operations training and support.** Franchisors successfully design their training systems to ensure franchisees rapidly achieve competency in the necessary areas to profitably meet and exceed their customers' expectations. In addition, their training has proven scalable, meaning the franchisor has successfully increased its new training class sizes to handle more growth without diminishing results. New franchisees often receive higher-quality training than the pioneering franchisees, compressing their learning curve and more quickly accelerating past break-even. The franchisor's training and field support teams are in sync and make successful handoffs as franchisees drive through their learning curve, shifting their focus beyond learning the business to maximizing opportunity and profitability.
- **Have adequate capital structure.** The franchisor has the necessary funds to hire staff as needed, fund initiatives, and fix broken, unscalable, or antiqued processes and systems that

201

may have worked in the past but aren't appropriate going forward. Many franchisors take 10 years or more to get to this stage of growth and haven't experienced much of a payback despite their efforts. Now the chain is heating up and money is starting to flow in at exponential rates. Some franchisors want to grab cash and take some chips off the table. However, this is the stage where franchisors often need to invest another $500,000 to $1 million–plus in infrastructure and brand and system refinements to maximize the opportunity and set the stage for the next level of growth.

- **Create a learning organization.** The franchisor's team and existing franchisees battle-test systems, improve tactics, measure KPIs (Key Performance Indicators), and engage in continual improvement. They identify problem areas before they are strained. They acquire the domain-area expertise through smart hiring decisions, outsourcing, or vendor relationships to ensure scalability while protecting key elements of the system and brand. Often franchisees identify and resolve systemic operational problems prior to the franchisor understanding the full scope of a problem. Franchisees push their insights up and smart franchisor incorporate these insights or techniques into system-wide operational best practices.

- **Identify and eliminate brand disconnects.** Marketing elements, customer experience, and complete brand experience are all finely polished and what you would expect to find at a large National brand. Franchisees understand the brand and what makes it work, and are committed to skillfully executing their business consistent with the leadership's brand strategy.

- **Encourage collaborative leadership.** Franchisee-franchisor relationships have evolved past casual interpersonal relationships associated with Early Stage into more and more commercially minded relationships. As the chain accelerates, leadership creates more professional boundaries. Early Stage franchisees begin to experience how growth is changing their relationship, and often they don't like it. Smart franchisors educate franchisees in advance how the culture will evolve and prepare them for change. Its critical franchisors minimize employee turnover at this stage as the growth demands the franchisor retain and build on employees' and leader's domain area expertise.

- **Protect the corporate culture.** Often to stay ahead of the growth curve, franchisors need to hire leaders and employees from other National franchise chains. Although their role demands that employees and leaders build the plane while they're flying it, the franchisor needs to pay careful attention to protecting existing corporate culture rather than importing and inadvertently blending cultures from other chains, creating some loss of corporate identity. Often the chain will charge one person with being the culture czar or bring in outside assistance to monitor and manage the culture, making sure organizational values remain intact and impact and influence the new leader's or employee's decision-making.

- **Stay in communication.** During this stage, franchisors run at 100 miles per hour, with team members often not knowing what each other are doing. Successful franchisors resist the natural urge to silo and make sure teams are communicating cross functionally. Franchisors throw away their M&M's (meetings and more meetings) in favor of smarter and more nimble communications and meeting protocols that ensure communication is on a need-to-know basis, eliminating hundreds of daily email cc's. Meetings become more streamlined and focused.

- **Have scalable supply lines.** Vendors scale supply lines and make strategic investments into the franchisor, franchisees, or their own infrastructure to get products to market faster and cheaper to help the franchisor maintain its competitive advantage and add more value for both franchisees and consumers.

- **Engage in systemic thinking.** Franchisors get off the one-off, break-fix merry-go-round of solving franchisees' operational issues. Instead, they objectively ask questions, like, "Is this a franchisee error or a system shortfall?" "What is it about our operating systems or training that is contributing to multiple franchisees breaking down in the same place or complaining about the same issue?" Rather than spending most of their time and energy fixing one problem at a time, they take some time to study how the overall system may have created a series of individual breakdowns. Then they make the necessary patches, fixes, and upgrades and communicate it to the chain, top-grading and institutionalizing new operating procedures and techniques.

- **Incorporate masterful marketing.** Franchisors begin to move from community marketing tactics to advertising co-ops in some markets, requiring a different level of marketing sophistication and greater coordination among franchisees. Franchisors and franchisees work together to leverage their numbers by pooling advertising resources to build name recognition in these developing markets, creating same-store sales increases and building name recognition in unserved neighboring communities, thus paving the way for easier penetration.

- **Hone their competitive advantages.** Copycat concepts start emerging, picking at the franchisors' value proposition in existing markets and new markets. Successful franchisors anticipate competitor knock-offs and have been investing time, money, and energy fine-tuning and perfecting their value proposition, leapfrogging the competition by creating a unique, profitable, valuable, and defensible customer offering. One of the strategies they need to master is successfully penetrating new markets in which copycat concepts beat them to market.

- **Increase organizational capacity.** While it takes the personality, initiative, and drive of a founder/CEO to power a franchisor past Early Stage into Emerging stage, sheer force of personality no longer works to drive small chains to become large Regional or National brands. The same micromanaging and "jack of all trades and master of none" organization that worked fine in the Early Stage becomes a barrier to continued growth. The chain needs professional management and domain area experts in areas like adult education and digital marketing. The run-and-gun founder entrepreneur has transformed into a CEO who manages through objectives, strategies, and tactics and runs a quality organization – or the founder has brought in someone who does.

- **Value expertise.** Franchisors create key strategic vendor relationships with suppliers and domain-area experts like supply chain, IT, and executive training and development. These experts are charged with identifying franchisor blind spots and increasing their field of vision, and identifying and eliminating potential problems before they occur, keeping the franchisor in growth mode.

Emerging Growth Risk Factors

Current market data shows that only 18% of total existing franchisors make it past the Emerging stage into Regional brand status of 101–500 units or operating territories. Here are some of the risk factors:

- **Overstretched operations and support.** Franchisors don't design their support systems to scale. New franchisees received highly personalized attention and support in the Early Stage.

Franchisors don't staff to provide the next wave of franchisees with the same level of support, often elongating new franchisee ramp-up and hurting unit-level economics. Staff often pull double duty, taking on roles within the organization beyond their pay grade or in areas where they have little experience.

- **Undercapitalization.** Franchisors often take more than 10 years to graduate from Early Stage to Emerging and cannot staff up as necessary. They wait for added royalty and franchise fee revenue, staffing as cash allows rather than as growth demands. Cash-strapped franchisors can't fund necessary initiatives or fix systems buckling under the pressure of growth. They postpone certain fixes, hoping problems don't escalate and become unfixable downstream. The franchisor has difficulty securing expansion capital for themselves and may resist taking on private equity or expensive mezzanine financing.

- **The Peter Principle.** As the theory states, employees and managers are promoted based on their performance in their current role, rather than how well they are suited for their intended role. As franchisors struggle to stay organized, employees are often promoted past their point of competence, leading to downstream organizational breakdowns.

- **Brand disconnects.** As the brand continues to grow, new and existing customers raise their level of expectations. They demand a more polished brand, efficient systems, and a more unified and cohesive customer experience. This means greater investments from both the franchisor and franchisees, often before they have reaped a strong return on existing investments. Since it may take a brand 10 years or more to graduate to this stage, the original concept and Early Stage franchisees may have outdated branding and systems, making the brand look fractured and obsolete.

- **Leadership.** Franchisors often have highly personal and informal interpersonal relationships with franchisees in the Early Stage. As the chain accelerates and expands, leadership needs to create more professional boundaries and rely on the feedback and performance of middle management. Early Stage franchisees begin to experience how growth is changing from an informal "call-me-on-my-cell-whenever-you-need-me" relationship with leadership to lower-level points of contact in middle management, thus losing their seat at leadership's table. Many decide to exit at this stage, thinking, "The culture changed. This isn't the system I bought into."

- **Corporate culture.** Struggling to keep up with growth, franchisors begin hiring leaders and employees from other franchise chains. Because the role demands that employees and leaders build the plane while they're flying it, they never learn or acclimate to their new franchisor's culture. Instead, they solve problems, manage, and lead the way they did in their previous corporate culture. This often creates a breakdown with franchisees and with valued existing employees, creating franchisee confusion and dissatisfaction and franchisor key employee turnover at a time when the brand is counting on its experienced employees to step up and take on more.

- **Lack of communication.** Franchisors run at 100 miles per hour, often not knowing what each team member is doing. This lack of communication can create relationship fractures and isolated work silos that often don't integrate well into the franchisor's overall brand strategy.

- **Supply lines.** Some vendors may be having a hard time keeping up. Other vendors start raising their prices, thinking it is an opportune time to start reaping the benefit of the brand's success. Some suppliers may have a hard time getting products to

Understanding Where Franchisors Are in Their Lifecycle

new markets, putting a burden on new market franchisees, often charging transportation costs that weren't planned for, driving up COGS, increasing time to break even, and increasing risk.

- **Lack of systems thinking.** Franchisors work on the franchisees' symptoms but ignore the systemic breakdowns that created the symptoms in the first place. Often, they blame their problems on poor franchisee attitudes and execution before they look at the quality and scalability of their systems or the skills and experience of their employees.

- **Marketing.** Franchisors begin to move from community marketing tactics to advertising co-ops in some markets, requiring a different level of marketing sophistication and greater coordination among franchisees. Franchisors may pull the trigger on additional marketing co-op fees guaranteed to them under the terms of the franchise agreement. Franchisees may push back, not seeing the value.

- **Increased competition.** Copycat concepts start emerging, threatening the franchisor's value proposition in existing markets and making it more difficult and costly to enter new markets. These copycat concepts evolve by watching the market leaders and designing business models that appear to fix the problems that hamper the market leaders, making it more difficult than before to penetrate new markets.

- **The founder's trap.** It takes the personality, initiative, and drive of a founder/CEO to power a franchisor past Early Stage into Emerging stage where the chain gathers momentum. It's toward the end of the Early Stage where the sheer force of personality no longer works. The founder needs to elevate to CEO and build an organization that drives results. The micromanaging that worked in the Early Stage becomes a barrier to continued growth in the Emerging stage. If the founder can't elevate into a CEO who manages through objectives, strategies, and tactics and runs a quality organization, then the franchisor will begin burning out its valued employees and have difficulty attracting new talent. The market will only give the organization what the organization has the will and skills to handle. Additionally, many entrepreneurs start a business because they don't function well inside of corporate environments. As the chain grows, these entrepreneurs find themselves having to create the same corporate structures they swore they'd never be a part of again. This "I must become what I despise" mentality creates organizational stress, resistance, and conflict.

Regional Brands

Regional brands are defined as those that have successfully expanded beyond their core markets, established multiple beachheads in previous virgin territory, and achieved the same level of success in new markets as in their core markets. Regional brands can best be described as multiple city, multiple state brands, crossing multiple geographical boundaries. In other words, the brand answers "Yes" to the old vaudeville question "Will it play in Peoria?" These franchisors have proven they have high-value products and services, a replicable market penetration strategy, and demonstrated success accelerating new franchisees through their learning curve into high levels of competency within a shortened time frame. Simply put, their model is successful, replicable, and scalable beyond core markets.

> Note that *Regional brand* does not confine itself to geography like Northeast or California; it means the brand is well established in multiple markets, but not in every region.

The franchisor's leadership team has transitioned the company from an informal entrepreneurial run-and-gun culture, to a more professionally managed organization with goals, objectives, financial plans, and budgets.

If the brand remains current and the team is built right, the organization will continue to scale rapidly until unit-level economics weaken, systems become strained, or the executives and employees become stretched beyond capabilities.

The market soon ensures franchisors will eventually constrict to receive only the growth they can prove to handle. Out of the current crop of franchisors, the data I presented shows only 18% have successfully crossed over into Regional (13%) or National brand (5%) status. Keep in mind most franchisors were already 20 years old when they crossed over into Regional or National status, competing in a time where there was less competition from franchise concepts, less government regulation, and fewer barriers to growth. Given today's more restrictive and competitive environment, had they started within the last 10 years, some of these chains would have been stymied in the Early Stage and Emerging stages.

Brands and leadership that successfully navigate the Regional brand inflection point without detonating one of the landmines listed later in this chapter often experience smooth sailing to critical mass, which is often 500 to 3,000 or more locations or operating territories, solidifying their position as a formidable, category-leading and possibly category-killing National brand, barring no geographic psychographic differences.

For instance, Philadelphia concepts such as Rita's Italian Ice and Philadelphia Pretzel Factory have cult followings in Philadelphia-influenced markets throughout the region, but have trouble re-creating all the elements that cultivated into their Regional cult status in new markets unrelated to Philly, where consumers might think, "So what? It's just a pretzel," or "It's just water and sugar." They don't have the stories about the uncles who showed up each Sunday to watch the Eagles games toting a bag of hot pretzels and cheese dip, or loading up the station wagon with the kids in back and driving to Rita's on a hot summer day. It's not embedded in the history or the culture of the region. It's the same with pizza. While there is nothing wrong with Domino's or Little Caesars, these brands don't play as well where Neapolitan-style pizza was originally invented, like the tristate area of New York, New Jersey, and Connecticut. Being from the pizza capital of the world – New Haven, Connecticut – I believe there is a special place in hell for any brand that adds ham and pineapple to a pizza.

Regional Brand Best Practices

The natural progression of a well-run Regional brand is toward growth. Customers, staff, vendors, franchisees, and other brand stakeholders act in a concerted effort to ensure the brand thrives. Seemingly everyone wants the brand to win, and so it does. Customers eagerly wait for the brand to open within their respective communities. Growth is natural and unforced. The chain enters into a predictable and natural growth rhythm.

Companies who cross the inflection point have many of the following elements in common, working in synergy to give the brand strong tailwinds, propelling it toward National and Iconic brand status:

- **Strong organic growth.** Existing franchisees are expanding and often represent 50% or more of the brand's new unit growth every year. Existing franchisees are easier to support, creating higher franchisor margins on recurring revenue dollars. If the franchisor were to stop investing in new franchisee recruitment, the chain would still achieve critical mass through the expansion efforts of existing franchisees.

211

- **Mass marketing expertise.** The brand pools advertising dollars and develops high functioning and strongly supported regional advertising co-ops which buy mass marketing opportunities (paid search, social media, digital media, cable, radio, etc.) that build brand awareness and move the sales needle by increasing customer trial and frequency. Increased awareness translates into pent-up customer demand in unserved markets, creating easier and less costly new market penetration.

- **Strategic lending relationships.** Based on the franchisees' track record for loan repayment, banks give favorable terms and easy access to funds to franchisees. This makes capital easier to access for new startups, expansion for existing franchisees, resales, remodels, fleet leasing, and other needs.

- **First consideration for available real estate.** Based on franchisees' positive track record within the real estate community, the brand becomes a desired tenant and earns first consideration for high-value real estate.

- **Strategic vendor relationships and preferred pricing.** Franchisees receive price, terms, delivery, and other key advantages vendors offer other national chains and market leaders as suppliers aggressively bid on their business.

- **Results rather than politics.** The franchisor's executive leadership and employees see opportunities and upward mobility for all. Managers and leaders don't typically invest in creating political capital to increase influence or power base, jockeying for position because the rising tide raises all ships. Key employees experience profit sharing or equity opportunities and start thinking like CEOs and owners.

- **The brand has a life of its own.** The brand has created its own identity, often grander than founders and leadership originally imagined. Customers, vendors, employees, and franchisees all build relationships and develop an affinity for the brand on their own terms. Customer brand fans seemingly make it their mission to drive brand awareness and customer trial through their own networks and communities. Every marketing piece, customer touch point, and brand experience seemingly echoes the brand's identity and reinforces its value proposition.

- **Contributions come from everywhere.** The brand occurs seemingly as a "brand of destiny." People and resources show up in unpredictable ways to make significant contributions, addressing needs and solving problems the brand may not have been previously aware they had.

- **The brand is universal.** Customers in almost every geography can identify and relate to the brand's value proposition and see high value in what the brand offers.

- **New customers are waiting.** The brand's reputation precedes itself. Franchisees walk into new markets with strong brand equity and pent up demand, often where customers have already tried the products and services in other markets and gotten hooked.

- **Systems are scalable.** The brand is limited only by franchisees' management capacity. The unit level returns are strong enough for the franchisees to build internal infrastructure to support unit level operations.

- **High barriers to entry and defensible position in the marketplace.** Franchisees are unique, valuable to their customers, and difficult to copy. This creates a long-term sustainable advantage in the marketplace. The brand is not under any significant threat of competitors stealing market share or commoditizing the marketplace.

- **Fish jump in the boat.** The word is out that the brand has created a unique and valuable investment opportunity, and smart and aggressive franchise candidates want in. Because franchisees continue to expand, opportunities are scarce, creating a strong secondary market for franchise resales, and high premiums and demand for open development territories. Franchise candidates move quickly through the recruitment process, fearing loss of opportunity.

Franchise Sales Organizations (FSOs) are often brilliant at creating higher demand than results would indicate the brand deserves in the marketplace. Beware of brands that have few units, little track record, and seemingly all of a sudden territories are being scooped up like a massive land grab. If it looks too good to be true, then my nearly 40 years in franchising would indicate it probably is. A brand should look and feel like it is growing naturally and is organically consistent by delivering franchisees solid results, rather than through hype and oily salesmanship.

Regional Brand Risk Factors

Regional brands often find themselves in no-man's-land. If they aren't a category leading brand, they don't have the budgets to compete yet with the larger National chains. Yet they are large enough that they can no longer fly under the radar screen. Unless they have high barriers to entry or a defensible position in the marketplace, copycat concepts will emerge in their open markets, making it more difficult and costly for them to penetrate these markets. If they have a signature product, often the larger brands will introduce a similar product to steal market share and to make it difficult for the brand to expand.

- **The brand, products, or services become dated or irrelevant.** Brands who successfully cross over into Regional brand status generally have been in business for more than 10 years and often more than 20, meaning the brand, product, or entire business format may need either a refresh or total brand overhaul.

- **Operations and support are overstretched.** Regional brands often need the same domain area experts as National brands but struggle to recruit the same level of talent. Senior executives of National brands would consider working with a Regional brand as perhaps going backwards in their career. Often Regional franchisors find themselves reliant on high-potential but unproven director-level talent looking to jump to the next level, creating brand risk. Often, talent from growing Regional brands get scooped up by National brands who pay more and can offer more upward mobility.

- **Increased competition.** More sophisticated copycat concepts entrench in the franchisor's untapped markets, making it more difficult and costly to enter new markets. If the Regional brand does occupy the first mover position, smart Emerging copycat concepts will study the shortcomings and fatal flaws and then launch with a more modern concept incorporating strategic fixes into their brand and operating systems.

- **Mass exit of mature franchisees.** Many long-time franchisees have seen the brand evolve significantly, and they often need to make significant investments to stay relevant. For instance, the franchisor may have changed their current look and offering, market expectations may have shifted, and competition may have changed the game. Rather than make these investments, many mature franchisees look to cash out. The chain loses hundreds of years of irreplaceable institutional knowledge in the process. Resales of these existing locations often cannibalize growth. Franchise candidates who would have entered new markets choose instead to buy locations from mature franchisees exiting the brand.

- **Brand disconnects.** As the brand continues to grow and enter new markets, customers are treated with the latest and greatest version of the brand. Often the franchisor's core market becomes plagued with outdated versions of the brand and product and service offerings, confusing and dissatisfying customers who have become accustomed to something newer or different. Huddle House, a diner concept, once suffered an inconsistent brand image because of outdated locations before new leadership successfully engineered a turnaround and brand resurgence through an aggressive remodeling incentive and financing programs. I often see disconnects with brands that have "and more" or "Not just" and "Plus," in their trade names, like *Not Just Cupcakes* (made-up name), which begs the question. "What else do you sell . . . tropical fish?"

- **The franchisor ownership cashes out and new owners don't understand the franchisee-franchisor relationships.** Private equity (PE) has been entering franchising at unprecedented rates, paying enticingly high multiples of earnings and creating a significant payday for ownership. Changes of ownership create changes in leadership, culture, and priorities. Private equity sometimes underestimates the necessity of generating franchisee buy-in and adopts a highly centralized command-and-control leadership style, pushing down on the organization to drive their agenda. This creates franchisee and franchisor friction that may not have previously existed. The heavy thumb of the leadership team may also create senior leadership turnover as these professionals would be in high demand from other Emerging, Regional, and National chains. Turnover creates consternation and disruption among franchisees and middle management. If ownership is looking to sell, they may be running lean in order to maximize EBITDA and resale value, leaving new ownership to make these investments. However, PE franchising platform players have evolved and in my opinion are professionalizing franchising at levels franchising has not experienced in the past.

- **Franchisee advertising co-ops mismanaged.** In earlier stages, franchisees are accustomed to managing local budgets and doing their own thing in a vacuum. As brands grow, franchisors often pull the trigger on clauses in franchise agreements that can force advertising co-ops to form without the buy-in of franchisees – effectively taxing franchisees with an additional royalty they may have not budgeted for, creating an immediate loss of significant net income and disrupting their operations. Often franchisors pull the trigger too early, hoping to create brand awareness for easier penetration into unserved markets, but add little benefit to many franchisees who may not be expanding in the near term. Franchisees do not see a return on this investment. Since advertising royalties are often a percentage of sales, larger and higher volume franchisees see their operations disproportionately damaged, as their margins are artificially squeezed, driving EBITDA down, and destroying enterprise value.

- **Decentralization and siloing.** Often franchisors open regional offices and push power and control of budgets and tactical execution down to managers of local regions. These director-level or regional VPs may not have the executive leadership pedigree of those who manage them. This results in on the job leadership training at the franchisees' expense. Often these new leaders, who no longer physically report to the corporate office, start forming regional cultures, such as command-and-control or local "dictatorships," creating regionally fractured franchisee-franchisor relationships and corresponding franchisee resistance and operational breakdowns. Conversely, franchisors can assign regional leaders' responsibilities but provide no budget or authority to carry out initiatives. This "responsibility with no authority" no-win situation will disempower key leaders, eventually creating turnover in the senior ranks and disruption to franchisees.

- **Misreading the tea leaves.** Officers may not understand the lag and lead indicators of brand performance, and effectiveness is measured almost entirely by revenues and profitability, with little effort put into measuring and improving the workability of franchisee-franchisor relationships. These relationships drive execution and future revenues.

- **Strained supply lines.** Some vendors may be having a hard time keeping up with supply lines and may reduce the number of deliveries or increase prices to outlier markets. Other vendors start raising their prices to cash in on growth, trying to find the right equilibrium price where they can maximize profitability yet the risk of switching vendors is too high. Others don't service new markets, which means franchisees pay higher shipping costs, reducing franchisee margins in new markets. Keep in mind, this may occur at the same time as when unit sales may be softer due to lack of brand awareness franchisees experience in new markets. Strained supply lines extend the timeline of franchisees break-even, deplete their capital, and add unmitigated risk to their investments.

- **It doesn't play in Peoria.** Franchisors and new franchisees overestimate their brand's universality and demand in new markets. They may also underestimate the effect of changes in seasonality, local economic conditions, the strength of local or regional competitors, and changes in customer preferences or expectations by geography.

- **Departments silo, and the brand becomes fragmented.** At this stage, franchisors hire domain-area experts and reduce the brand down into functional areas like marketing, training, operations, and finance. These departments have a tendency to silo and put out their version of the brand best practices relative to that function. Often these pieces aren't well integrated into the brand as a whole, creating a loss of brand synergy, identity, and brand magic – the intangible overall customer experience. Simply put, there are too many fingers on the brand with competing agendas, creating a brand built on the force of individual will, rather than letting the brand be what customers want and what the brand is supposed to be in its purest form.

- **Trappings of wealth.** Especially where there is original ownership, the brand is generating outstanding returns, so ownership may rest easy, thinking, "We made it," and become complacent and risk averse. Leadership and shareholders, who often up to this point have not experienced the returns they expected, start taking significant cash out of the company to make up for their longer-than-expected return horizon. Combined with an increase in ownership's desire to monetize their investment and a possible decrease in their desire for reinvestment, this adds risk to the long-term viability of the chain. Sometimes leadership and ownership sacrifices so much for so long that they overcompensate when they start winning and lose balance.

- **Stepping stones.** Franchisors' new leadership hires may use the brand as a short-term stint to pad their resume while planning for what's next. High-growth Regional franchisors cannot afford the disruption of leadership turnover.

National Brands

Brands with over 500 operating units and territories or more will have vast geographic coverage through most areas of the United States. Often their franchise development challenge is to backfill underserved existing markets rather than penetrating new. The brand is built. The franchisor's consumer value proposition is defined, as are the markets they serve. The corporate culture is instilled. The organizational structure is built. Strategy and budget are set. The brand is profitable.

> Out of the current crop of franchisors, only 5% can be classified as "National," which represents under 40% of the number of brands classified as "Regional," meaning historically most Regional brands remain Regional brands.

Since most franchisors operate in sectors with long product and service lifecycles such as residential services, food, auto care, and business services, large National brands will stay dominant if they continue to execute the basics well. Smart brands will have created a signature product or service that defines the category, cements value, and keeps the brand top of mind with their target and existing customers.

For brands that take the time to refine the brand, perfect systems, drive unit-level economics, and build out their infrastructure, it's now windfall time. Most franchisors become royalty self-sufficient, meaning they can fund payroll and initiatives and retire debt service entirely through royalty and other recurring revenues. As chains move into the National stage, it is not uncommon to see 50% of incremental royalty streams or more flow through to the bottom line. In addition, chains experience a premium valuation by equity firms or other potential acquirers.

Brands that maintain their market dominance and elevate to Iconic brand status share similar characteristics.

National Brand Best Practices

- **Organic growth.** Existing franchisees should continue to represent 50% or more of new unit growth and territory expansions. Existing franchisees are easier to support, creating higher franchisor margins on recurring revenue dollars. Many franchisors do away with the franchisee recruitment team at this point and focus on existing franchisee organic growth and supporting existing franchisees, which act as brand consolidators, exiting underperforming franchisees and fixing underperforming operations.

- **Mass marketing expertise.** Franchisors need to demonstrate consistent victories developing marketing campaigns, mass marketing, and social platforms, which drive sales and protect existing customer relationships. Emerging and Regional brands can't compete on marketing spend, which creates high barriers to entry for these otherwise competitive brands.

- **Strategic lending relationships.** Based on the franchisees' track record for loan repayment, the banks give favorable terms and easy access to funds.

- **First consideration for available real estate.** Based on franchisees' positive track record within the real estate community, the brand becomes a desired tenant and earns first consideration for high-value real estate.

- **Preferred vendor pricing.** Franchisees receive price, terms, delivery, and other key advantages that vendors offer other National chains and market leaders. They also may get added-value services, such as free assembly or stocking of merchandise.

They may get proprietary products or promotional materials, such as movie promos or other sponsorships. They also may get apps or other labor-saving devices to make it easier for franchisees to do business with vendors and provide a competitive advantage in the marketplace.

- **Brand champions proliferate.** The brand has developed an identity, often grander than the franchisor and franchisees could have originally anticipated. Customers develop a love, respect, and personal relationship with the brand. Customers relate to the brand as "my place" or "my brand," and make it a point to introduce the product or service to their world.

- **High emotional engagement.** Customers, suppliers, franchisees, employees of the franchisor, and other brand stakeholders want the brand to win. Therefore, they add value to the brand in their own way, from customer YouTube and Yelp testimonials to employee testimonials on GlassDoor.com.

- **The brand goes international.** International customers who become familiar with the brand in the United States anxiously wait for the brand to become established in their country of origin.

- **High barriers to entry or defensible brand position.** The brand offers its customers something unique, of high perceived and real value, and difficult to copy. This creates a long-term sustainable advantage in the marketplace.

- **Employer of choice.** High-quality leaders, domain-area experts, upwardly mobile management, and responsible employees seek employment opportunities on every level.

National Brand Risk Factors

- **The brand, products, or services become dated or irrelevant.** Suppliers, merchandisers, and the franchisor may become complacent due to a current dominant marketplace position. Risk aversion may be institutionalized, creating a formidable barrier to creativity, innovation, and new investments into product or service enhancements or extensions. Smaller, more aggressive chains will study the model, look for flaws, and attack the brand position from where the brand appears to be vulnerable. That's why smart National chains constantly move the brand from where they are now to where they want to be in the future. Competitors plan and attack the brand from where they have been in the past. Smart brands are moving targets.

- **Leadership becomes too enmeshed in the past.** Dominant National brands sometimes invest too much time and energy looking at competitive threats and fixing perceived weaknesses from the past. These brands seem to think and act from historical trends and make moves that impact the business for only one year out. They do not allocate enough time, capital, and resources to evolve and enhance their model based on what it needs to maintain a brand leadership position in the future, thus future-proofing the model.

- **Increased startup competition.** More sophisticated copycat concepts that design systems around the brand's perceived fatal flaws will emerge. For example, at one time Quiznos tried to exploit Subway's limited menu of hot subs, by promoting toasted subs. They aggressively grew their number of stores using this platform. Subway responded with a breakthrough piece of equipment that toasted subs faster than Quiznos "pizza slice" conveyor belt oven. Quiznos seemed oblivious to the fact that anyone at any time can toast a sandwich, and "toasted subs" was never a defensible position in the marketplace. Furthermore, Subway aggressively rolled out a $5 sub line, introducing a price point Quiznos could not profitably match, because Quiznos marked up franchisees' supplies above market rate to create an additional profit center for the brand at the expense of franchisees. While this price-leadership position may have hurt Subway in the long term, it proved enough to marginalize a rapidly growing competitor, sending it into a tailspin, which in my opinion they have not recovered from. This opened the door to stronger chains like Jersey Mike's and Firehouse Subs to establish a beachhead and gain national traction.

- **Mature franchisees are no longer invested in growth.** Many mature franchisees in the National stage often need to make significant investments to stay relevant. Rather than make these investments to modernize the aging businesses, they elect to milk the business for as long as they can prior to selling. These franchisees often have made a significant return on their investment and now apply a minimal level of effort to achieve their minimal acceptable level of performance. When these franchisees exit, they take valuable industry domain area expertise with them. Others pass the business to family members who may not have learned the business from the trenches like the first generation of ownership and therefore can't fully appreciate what it takes to win. The second generation may not have the drive to do what needs to be done to keep the brand relevant. I've heard that this issue plagues the McDonald's franchisee community, which may be on its second, third, and perhaps fourth generation of leaders.

- **Brand disconnects.** As chains run out of new territories to open, often brand leadership is pushed to drive year-over-year same store sales to improve the franchisor's revenue line. Leadership may start introducing questionable product extensions or new services that look like new incremental revenue opportunities to franchisor leadership but add complexity, expense, and create operational breakdowns for franchisees and are confusing to existing customers, such as one failing steak and cheese sub chain that introduced frozen yogurt as a staple item, and Wendy's salad bar.

- **Cycles of being bought and flipped by private equity.** Private equity (PE) has been increasingly investing in franchising by adding enticingly high multiples of earnings. Changes of ownership create changes in leadership, culture, and priorities that include how to flip the chain within five to seven years for twice what they paid.

Some PE firms don't understand the business of franchising. They do know, however, that they can drive revenues by increasing royalty revenue collected. They also know they can contain costs by reducing employees and services. Since the goal of some PE firms is to sell the chain at the highest possible multiple rather than build a long-term sustainable brand, they often make a series of short-term decisions that can have damaging long-term consequences. Kahala Brands, a food franchise platform, buys and holds damaged brands that have been kicked around the marketplace, like Blimpie, Pinkberry, and Planet Smoothie. Some franchisors start introducing ancillary nickel-and-dime fees such as technology fees tied to sales, or accounting fees, and negotiate rebates from suppliers tied to franchisees' purchases. Franchisees tend to see rebate revenue streams as hidden royalties (because these fees are not often fully disclosed), which creates franchisee-franchisor distrust, which in turn leads to breakdowns.

Often with change in ownership comes a change in leadership. Turnover may cause concern with franchisees, especially turnover of long-term employees who possess high domain-area competency and value both brand history and quality franchisee-franchisor relationships.

225

In addition, PE firms often negotiate heavily leveraged deals. The increased debt load means lower immediate earnings and less reinvestment capital to drive the brand forward.

- **Franchisee brand complacency.** Franchisees often become reliant on large media spend and no longer invest time building relationships with local institutions and community influencers and thought leaders. This leaves the door open for other competitors to come in and create a large local social platform.

- **Institutionalized thinking.** Many franchisors have turned over leadership to professional management rather than entrepreneurs, thus losing their entrepreneurial edge. Many in professional management have never owned a business before and may not value the day-to-day contributions franchisees make to the business. They may insulate themselves with middle management and make decisions from the ivory tower without a thorough understanding of the impact of their decisions on franchisees.

- **False sense of security.** Leadership may be trading off past successes, thinking these translate into future victories.

- **Large-scale franchisee consolidators emerge** and sometimes challenge franchisors' leadership and authority, pushing personal rather than brand agendas and thus creating dissension and division among franchisees and franchisors.

Turnaround Brands

Any brand that does not successfully navigate each growth stage will eventually become a Turnaround brand. On a day-to-day, moment-by-moment basis, brands strengthen or weaken with every action, conversation, decision, and allocation of resources.

The fall always starts with a lack of attention to the current reality of the brand. Simply put, the brand bought into false assumptions about who they are and what they possess. Then they made a series of bad decisions and resource allocations based on what they believed posed the greatest opportunities for the brand. I see this very frequently with Early Stage and Emerging brands that come out too early. Ego-driven owners want to believe they are on to something special and they encounter an unethical franchise consultant or attorney who butters them up, saying, "We studied your concept and feel you have something unique. For only $150,000 to $250,000, we will help you go to market and get rich." My fellow Connecticut native P. T. Barnum once said, "There's a sucker born every minute." I don't know if that's true, but each year there are 250–350 new concepts entering franchising with about the same number exiting, meaning the only ones who made money were the attorneys and franchising consultants who did the initial paperwork.

Turnaround brands can become so in any stage, for many of the reasons I have described. These brands almost uniformly follow the same patterns.

- **The franchisor pretends their business model is better than it is and ignores all evidence to the contrary.** For instance, they often shift the blame to franchisees, thinking, "Franchisees are not successful because they don't follow the system," without ever asking, "How did we fail so bad by bringing underperforming franchisees into the system?" and "What is it about our training and system that the majority of franchisees can't follow it and feel the need to change it?"

- **The franchisor makes several of the classic mistakes chronicled in each stage of the FPG Franchise Brand Growth Curve.**

- **The franchisor continues down the same path until breakdowns are apparent and can no longer be ignored or denied.**

Understanding Where Franchisors Are in Their Lifecycle

- **There is often a massive lag between poor decision-making and the discernable impact of those decisions on results** (as long as three years), leading to incorrect problem identification and therefore poor turnaround planning and decision-making.

- **The franchisor pivots, but often too late to capitalize on an opportunity or to save the brand and make a healthy turnaround.** The brand can linger indefinitely in Turnaround until franchisees start closing and fail to pay royalties.

> Due to a lack of experience and resources, many Early Stage and Emerging brands do not survive or get stuck in a turnaround.

Some may survive due to the strength of the corporately owned outlets or territory and a few solidly performing franchisees. Often these chains consolidate and retract to the point where a turnaround is not possible, given the franchisor's limited resources and improbability of attracting financing or other sources of capital. Franchisees suffer and fail at an accelerated rate, defaulting on loans and earning a black mark from creditors, making it harder for new and existing franchisees to purchase underperforming units or territories.

Because the franchisor diversifies its revenue across a base of multiple franchisees, some franchisee failure, while unfortunate, is acceptable to the franchisor as the franchisee's share of lost royalty income won't materially impact the franchisor's bottom line. Too often the franchisor pivots too late to help struggling and failing franchisees survive. It's often only when franchisee failure becomes an epidemic that franchisors stop blaming franchisees and start looking at the system that recruits, trains, supports, and resources franchisees, and the flaws that lead them into failure.

Unlike Early Stage and Emerging franchise brands, Regional and National brands will have at one time had a track record of success and a customer base large enough to elevate the brand to its larger brand status. Often these brands aren't so far gone that a turnaround isn't possible. They also have the size and potential cash flow to attract PE and other investors who specialize in Turnaround brands and recognize the potential upside when the brand resurges. These brands also generally possess many mature franchisees with operational competency and domain experience to create a turnaround. From Turnaround to Resurgent brand is often a long, arduous, and expensive undertaking of three to five years, and often requires more talent and resources than the brand at that time possesses.

Turnaround Brand Best Practices

Brands that successfully engage in an effective three- to five-year turnaround and begin to resurge often have many of the following characteristics in common.

- **They gather the necessary data** to objectively measure and assess their problems, gaining perspectives from staff, customers, suppliers, lenders, and franchisees.

- **They correctly identify primary root problems,** which in turn spins off more downstream problems. So they have correctly identified the cause rather than confusing the cause with symptoms or impact of the cause.

- **They identify the key areas, brand attributes, strategic relationships, and staff that are working well,** need not change, or are essential parts of a turnaround. These are protected at high cost.

- **They hire third parties** to help craft a turnaround plan, knowing the same team and perspective that created the downturn is unlikely to create an upturn. These third-party consultants offer brutally honest and accurate assessments and tactical turnaround plans within their areas of expertise.

- **They communicate the plan** and key performance benchmarks to all stakeholders such as staff, suppliers, lenders, shareholders, and franchisees as well as what the chain needs from each stakeholder. Stakeholders buy in and now become part of the solution rather than part of the problem. The franchisor, franchisees, and suppliers begin the process of reestablishing trusted relationships.

- **They skillfully execute the plan and create a breakthrough.** The brand resurges and enters the Resurgent phase of their lifecycle.

Turnaround Brand Risk Factors

Regardless of the brand or stage in the FPG Franchise Brand Growth Curve, Turnaround brands often make one or more of the following mistakes, which prolong the turnaround and can even kill the brand.

- **They blame franchisees** for the franchisor's poorly or inconsistently performing business model. If the franchisor assumes no responsibility for designing the systems that manifest in problematic franchisees, then they have no responsibility in crafting a solution.

- **They look for a million-dollar idea** or a Hail Mary pass to rescue the brand instead of going back to basic business fundamentals and creating a new, unique, profitable, and sustainable niche. For instance, Batteries Plus now sells hard-to-find light bulbs and fixes phone and tablet screens, because their core business of stocking hard-to-find batteries and selling them at a premium did not create enough value for franchisees across the brand.

- **They diversify their product and service offerings,** often out of their sweet spot, creating brand confusion and more operating and supply line problems.

- **They don't sign key members of the turnaround team to employment contracts,** risking turnover of key staff.

- **They don't cement support** for their turnaround strategy with franchisees or key strategic suppliers. They leverage the control they possess from the franchise agreement rather than harnessing the power of emotional buy-in from franchisees. Eventually, more often than not, this will create franchisee resistance and stall or thwart a turnaround.

- **They pivot one to two years too late,** extending the time a brand languishes in the Turnaround stage.

- **They put pressure on franchisee recruitment to do bad deals** in order to fund new initiatives, perpetuating the negative cycle while pretending to turn it around.

- **They put on a happy face** and engage in positive thinking to convince franchisees, franchise candidates, suppliers, and themselves that negative trends and operational issues are a speed bump rather than a negative trajectory and offer no strategic change of direction.

- **Leadership loses priority** and starts investing time and resources in pet projects or urgent pain points instead of masterminding a brand turnaround. Franchisors engage in a never-ending cycle of one-off, fix-it now decisions, and brand strategy goes out the window.

- **Brand ownership becomes too possessive** and fails to sell the brand to a more qualified team that has the knowledge and financial resources to create an effective turnaround.

- **Brand ownership overestimates the value of their company** based on what they think the business was worth when they appeared to be winning, walking away from PE and other firms with the capital and experience to turn things around.

- **Fearing a loss of control,** brand ownership would rather possess 100% of a declining, hemorrhaging brand than a minority stake in a high-value, Resurgent brand. Wendy's resisted this impulse when it sold Arby's to Roark Capital in 2011 for $430 million, which included a $130 million cash payout by Roark and assumption of $190 million in debt, according to the *Wall Street Journal.* At the time, Wendy's also kept an 18.5% minority ownership in Arby's, valued then at $30 million. Arby's resurgence made that 18.5% ownership worth $775 million by the end of 2017, according to Stifel Nicolaus analyst Chris O'Cull. I designed Arby's franchise opportunity website around that time, and got to see firsthand what a brilliant brand turnaround looked like under the leadership of CEO Paul Brown, now CEO of Inspire Brands, and marketing guru Rob Lynch, then CMO of Arby's, and now CEO of Papa Johns.

Resurgent Brands

Brands upgrade to Resurgent brand status when they are successfully executing a turnaround strategy that reengages customers, suppliers, and, most importantly, franchisees. These once wayward brands gain traction through some combination of modernizing, upgrading, reinventing, recapitalizing, top-grading leadership, or simply getting back to their original roots.

Resurgent Brand Best Practices

- **They stay the course.** They skillfully execute the strategic plan in a highly disciplined manner without significant deviation.

- **They regularly communicate** with brand stakeholders and report results against key benchmarks with full transparency. They communicate what is and isn't working well, backed by data. The case for any adjustments or pivots must be supported by best available data.

- **They celebrate little victories** to keep all stakeholders informed and engaged.

- **They stay nimble,** quickly adjusting tactics as necessary to hit key benchmarks.

- **They protect their team.** Leadership rewards their impact players and minimizes key staff turnover.

- **They show patience.** Leadership knows they didn't become a Turnaround brand overnight and they don't expect an overnight turnaround either. They know it takes time and effort to engage all stakeholders and re-create market forces to restart the flywheel.

Resurgent Brand Risk Factors

- **Franchisees lose confidence** in the turnaround strategy and go into survival mode, stop reinvesting, and start doing their own thing, creating brand confusion.

- **The franchisee-franchisor relationships become strained.**

- **Other brands poach Resurgent brand's impact players.** The brand loses their institutional knowledge and skillful execution, possibly halting the brand's resurgence.

- **Brand leadership deviates from the plan** before the plan is fully implemented.

- **Brand ownership or shareholders lose confidence** and stop funding initiatives and engage in layoffs and severe cost-cutting measures.

Sandler, a sales training specialty franchise, is experiencing such a resurgence. As part of the turnaround, my company is assisting Sandler with recruiting new franchisees. The Sandler model prior to COVID-19 was a face-to-face model, where franchisees conducted live training events at Sandler training centers around the country or at the client's premises. COVID-19 wiped out the live, face-to-face meetings and events, destroying a highly profitable business over-night and threatening the livelihood of Sandler franchisees and staff. Sandler pivoted lightning fast, rolling out a virtual training model delivered through a learning management system (LMS).

Arby's at one time wallowed in obscurity, lacking a definable brand identity. Under Paul Brown's leadership Arby's staked a claim in the deli segment, using their drive-thru locations as a distinct competitive advantage over chains like Subway and Jersey Mike's, which mostly operate in storefront locations without a drive-thru. They implemented a witty "We've got the meats" campaign akin to the old Wendy's "Where's the beef?" and highly intelligent viral social media posts, such as a running war with Jon Stewart from *The Daily Show* to boost name recognition and gain a whole new generation of consumers.

Summary

I did my best to give you a robust insider's look into franchising in as few words as possible. If you invested in a paper copy of this work, I hope you have added enough yellow highlights and dog-eared pages to almost ruin the book. Armed with this knowledge, it's now time to explore brands and find your best options.

Part 2

How Do You Find the Right Franchise?

I designed Part 1 to give you a behind-the-scenes look at franchising, which should impact which brands you choose and hopefully was worth the price of this book. Now it's time to start looking at which brand is your best fit.

This part provides you with the necessary insights about what to look for and expect during each stage of the buyer journey.

If you follow the steps closely, you should be able to identify a responsible franchisor whose actions show that they exist to make you successful and ask that you exist to add more value to customers than you extract from them in price.

You should also be able to spot and avoid irresponsible and unethical franchisors who exist to take your money and pump up their enterprise value and cash flow through franchise fees and royalty collections but don't honor or respect your time, money, and capital.

Chapter 10

Identifying Potential Franchise Options

Most franchise candidates begin their search and identify potential franchise options business the following five ways:

- They start with brands they know and love.
- They know someone who owns a franchise of a particular brand or has done well within a particular category of business.
- They visit a franchise portal (such as FranchiseGator, Franchise.com, or Entrepreneur.com).
- They research and learn about brands, industries, and categories on search engines, news, publications, podcasts, or other content streams.
- They work with a franchise broker (also known as a consultant).

There are pluses and minuses for each source of information, as discussed in this chapter.

The Brands You Know and Love

I wholeheartedly applaud looking at brands you already understand and shop regularly. However, you may run the risk of not looking deep enough into the mechanics of the business to determine fit. I see this often with franchise candidates who regularly eat at certain restaurants. They see the parking lot packed, the meal is presented well (there is an old saying, "First you eat with your eyes, then with your mouth"), the service is pleasant, and the overall customer experience brings you joy. But perhaps they don't have restaurant operations experience and only evaluate the business from what experienced restaurateurs call "the front of the house," meaning from in front of the counter where the customer enjoyment and business owner's emotional payout occurs. Food service is one of those unique businesses where owners receive constant and immediate customer feedback. But if they have never, as those same experienced restaurateurs say, "put on an apron," then they really don't know (more food service expressions) "how the sausage gets made." Sometimes food service isn't what franchisees new to the industry think it is, leading to a mismatch and a bad investment.

Sometimes a business is exactly what it looks like. For instance, Wild Birds Unlimited is a specialty retailer of bird enthusiast products and feed. It's a business for bird enthusiasts, also known as ornithophiles, to buy so they can be around other ornithophiles and talk about ornithophilic stuff like *The Birdman of Alcatraz*. Their franchises go "cheep" and you can fund it with "seed" capital or take money out of the "stork" market. The head of franchising is a friend of mine. I once suggested he add the following qualifying question to his recruitment process: "Have you ever faked your own death, laid perfectly still on the ground, for the pure joy of watching vultures circle above you?"

You Know Someone Who Succeeded in a Particular Brand or Business

Again, this is a good data point and a good place to start. But left unexplored, you never get to why they succeeded. Using the same logic, I should become an actuary. My brother Jamie and his wife, Courtney, do actuarial work and they live a great life. But do I have what it takes to be an actuary? Am I willing to do what it takes? Would I enjoy the day-to-day responsibilities of being an actuary? Those are better questions to ask.

Also, by the same logic, you may dismiss solid business models where someone you know struggled or failed. On face value, that doesn't make that brand, business, or industry a poor universal choice. Again, it comes back to answering these questions:

- What does it take to win?
- Do you have what it takes?
- Are you willing to do what it takes to fill in the gaps?
- Would you enjoy the day-to-day responsibilities?

Start by looking at what you already know is a good way to shave perhaps a year or more off your learning curve, which can dramatically reduce your capital needs, which in turn reduces your risk.

Franchise Portals

Franchise portals such as FranchiseGator and Franchising.com should play an important role in your preliminary investigation for a startup franchise, but they never really fulfill what franchise candidates need these portals to be. The portals are designed with the franchisor in mind, not the franchise candidate using the service and driving the traffic. I've had many conversations with GMs of franchise portals and they see the franchisor as their customer, and not the franchise candidate. Therefore, many monetize your contact information by selling it to as many franchisors and franchise brokers as possible on a cost-per-lead basis. I am not alleging that they illegally sell your name against your will. It does mean they are in the business of capturing your contact information and selling your data. They are not in the business to educate you on your best franchise options, helping you to maximize your rewards or mitigate your risk.

Unlike Realtor.com or Zillow, franchising does not have franchise information portals that offer a transparent deep dive, offering you the information you want to know rather than summary data and hype. Portals are a good source of finding brands you would not necessarily find on your own. Therefore, they serve a role at the top of your research funnel where you are exploring your options, but they don't provide enough meaningful data to help you eliminate choices and get to a short list of your best options. Treat portals the same way you treat free used car magazines you pick up on your way out of the grocery store, where every car is the bargain of the century and no one with bad credit is turned away.

Use portals with discretion. Consider the content they publish as a data point and not the gospel truth. Know that a request for more information is taken as a request for conversation and franchisors will be in contact with you to understand where you are relative to their brand. I recommend answering the emails or texts with your level of interest rather than ghosting, which will translate into more emails and more texts.

> For franchise resales or existing businesses, websites such as BizBuySell.com are a good source for exploring existing franchise operations that are actively listed for sale.

Brands in the News

Publications such as *Franchise Times, Entrepreneur, Franchising World*, and a host of podcasts can help you get under the hood of generally faster-growing or more interesting brands. These publications and podcasts have a tendency at times to favor franchisors who excel at selling franchises, but not necessarily franchisors who excel at making franchisees wealthy. Many of the podcasts are hosted by franchise brokers who have a vested interest in selling you a franchise. The publications rely on franchisor advertising to survive, which means don't expect old-fashioned journalistic integrity. You may only be seeing the shiny side of the penny. That isn't to say they are doing anything bad or illegal because with many brands there is a shiny side to the penny. It does mean not to expect the full story. In other words, they will flush out the opportunity side of the ledger without identifying all of the corresponding risks. I recommend listening to podcasts hosting brand CEOs. At the end, ask yourself these questions:

- Do I trust them?
- Can they articulate their vision well and am I in alignment with that vision?
- Are they doing what it takes to make brand unique, profitable, defensible, and sustainable for the long haul?

The entire brand ecosystem in a franchise organization depends on these.

Franchise Brokers

Franchise brokers – also known as consultants, advisors, coaches, or a host of other names – are basically business brokers. Their fees are paid by the franchisor out of the franchise fees you pay when you join the brand. They have large inventories of franchisors at their disposal and a good broker will possess good working knowledge of many brands and should be able to share keen insights and a backstory. Experienced brokers will often have personal relationships with brand leadership and understand the personalities involved as well as what it takes to win as a franchisee. An experienced broker will profile you based on your work history, transferable skills, available market, risk tolerance, and capital you have to invest and an intelligent recommendation of several brands you should consider based on who you are and what you are looking to achieve.

If you find a good broker with integrity, they will help you maximize your opportunities and minimize your risk. My wife is a franchise consultant, so I'm not down on franchise brokers as a rule. However, the broker channel is set up to create mischief, so individual brokers have to possess a personal integrity level that transcends their current playing field to offer you real value. Therefore, I recommend only certain brokers, but not the entire channel. Here's why.

According to FranConnect Franchise Sales Index and Franchise Performance Group estimates, brokers represent 10%–15% of the number of new franchisees who enter franchising, so perhaps 2,000 franchisees per year. Since there are zero barriers to entry and anyone can hang a shingle and be a franchise broker, there are thousands of franchise brokers specifically looking for you. There is simply not enough of you to go around, creating franchise broker desperation to do a deal. Desperate people often do desperate things, which may not be in your best interest.

For instance, brokers will claim that if you work with a broker or not, it will not cost you more money in franchise fees to join a particular chain. While this is technically true, it isn't completely true. Franchisors raise their initial franchise fees, often $25,000 to $30,000 or more, to pay the broker $25,000–$100,000 commissions they pay brokers to find you. Before you investigate the brand, the brand already increased their cost to you usually without adding any value or services to mitigate your risk. The broker commission is often pure unmitigated risk already tacked on to your investment. Now that does not mean brands who do business with brokers are doing anything wrong. It also does not mean these brands are poor investments. It also does not mean every broker is sleazy and sees you as a transactional meal ticket. It does mean beware and walk cautiously.

Some broker chains work behind the scenes to put intense pressure on brands to accept you as a franchisee even if you are not a good fit. A franchise broker named Mick once sent me a franchise candidate who inherited $150,000 from a dead relative. He had no meaningful business experience and his last job was waxing bowling alley lanes for slightly above minimum wage. The broker tried to place him in a business I was representing that required executive-level business experience to succeed. I told Mick he didn't have the requisite experience and would certainly fail so I couldn't in good conscience continue. I didn't want to hurt the candidate's confidence by telling him he was unqualified, knowing full well he could be successful in an entry-level owner-operated business such as power washing or carpet cleaning, which this broker would also represent. Taken aback that I would question his expert judgment, he chirped, "Well I thought you guys had a training program!" To which I responded, "We do. But we aren't the Wharton School of Business. He needs executive experience. He has entry-level experience so show him an entry-level franchise." Rather than doing what was in the best interest of his client and alter his recommendation, Mick did an end-around, went to the CEO, tried to ram his unqualified candidate through, and at the same time tried to have me fired.

A second sleazy broker trick is to try to get you to invest in multiple territories or locations before you succeed in one. Beware of franchisors who promote a land grab, as the data would show exponentially more times than not, franchise candidates fall behind on their development schedules and lose these incremental territory investments. The franchise salesperson and the franchise brokers know this yet have no accountability. They carve out territories they think you will buy rather than what you can realistically develop according to their demanded timelines, simply cash their inflated checks, and move on to the next sucker. You can measure how many undeveloped territories a franchisor has sold in Item 20 of the

Identifying Potential Franchise Options

Franchise Disclosure Document (FDD). I discuss this in greater detail in a section about how to read the FDD (see Chapter 11).

If you like a brand, unless you have already developed a multi-territory or multi-location business, start small. Don't be intimidated by other franchise candidates who blow their cash scooping up huge tracts of green grass and blue sky. It's important to conserve your cash as much as possible, because if a franchisee struggles, rather than having additional working capital to invest to secure their investment, their cash is out of circulation, increasing their risk. I find that smart, cautious franchisees can also grow through strategic acquisition, taking out franchisees who bit off more than they can chew. Be smart. Wait. Start small and get to know your business before you decide to go big. By the time you do decide to expand, you may have acquisition opportunities you cannot anticipate right now as well as opportunities to develop new territories. You may even be able to negotiate a better deal because the franchisor will not be saddled with franchise broker commissions years after you open.

Franchise Opportunity Shows and Events

In my opinion these shows are antiquated and not worth the price of admission. They attract new brands who don't know these shows are a failed strategy to attract someone like you. And what is your opinion of a brand that feels like they have to lure you into their booth by handing out Hershey's Kisses or squishy stress balls?

The Last Word on Franchise Opportunity Sources

Franchising represents over 4,000 to 7,000 brands (depending on the source), generating an aggregate of over $800 billion in sales, and yet in many ways franchising is still the Wild West. Franchising is not adequately taught in business schools, doesn't possess comprehensive third-party rating systems such as Consumer Reports or JD Powers, and doesn't have a significant amount of advocacy or oversight like the Bureau of Consumer Protection and the Food and Drug Administration or any meaningful protection against bad players. Franchising doesn't generally offer unbiased sources of information to help you find the right business and make the right choice for yourself and your family. You have to aggregate information where you can and conduct your own thorough self-directed research. These sources of information, while imperfect, will most likely house multiple concepts that meet your needs and will help you achieve your objectives.

Self-Directed Research

Once you select the franchises you want to investigate, you may want to engage the franchisor right away or begin some self-directed research. There is no right or wrong answer here. In this section, I assume you will start with self-directed research and then choose to engage the franchisor.

Here are sources of self-directed research:

- **Facebook, Instagram, and other social media streams.** Read the customer comments closely. Are there raving reviews and brand fans extolling the virtues of the brand, product, or service? Make allowances for fake accounts and trolls. Let's face it – the world is full of people living in their parents' finished basement with nothing better to do.

- **Yelp, Google, and other reviews.** What are customers saying about the products and services or the brand? For bad reviews, is the brand on it, trying to salvage the customer or is the comment hanging out there unattended, destroying brand reputation?

- **Your own customer experience.** Make a road trip and shop the brand if possible. If you have already shopped the brand, do it again but view it differently. Slow down. Watch the operation from beginning to end. Look at the presentation. Watch the employees carefully. If it's a brick-and-mortar operation, study all four corners. Check your gut. What experience are you having?

The founder and CEO of an Emerging Growth artisan donut shop reached out to me looking for help, and I found they had a franchised location about 15 miles from where I live. I walked in and immediately felt comfortable and at home. The place was impeccably clean and well designed and presented. Because these donuts are over-the-top gigantic, a huge part of the overall customer experience is to salivate like Pavlov's dog while staring at the product behind a glass case and asking questions about all the decadent toppings and fillings, anticipating a tremendous sugar rush. Most likely, customers will only eat one or risk going into cardiogenic shock, so they take their time and enjoy the process. The place reminded me of the neighborhood in New Haven where I grew up, with the old-fashioned Italian bakeries that used to line the streets, smelling like fresh-baked cookies. Employees wore spotless branded T-shirts and ear-to-ear grins, happy to be there even on an early Sunday morning. Why wouldn't they be? They weren't slaving over a hot fryer, getting splashed with hot oil. I sent pictures to the founder/CEO congratulating him on fielding quality franchisees who in turn built a fabulous business. On face value, I could see why this chain is successful. However, like any business, it's not for everyone. In the next chapter, I take you through a process of how to vet a franchise to make sure it's the right fit for you.

Chapter 11

The Franchise Buyer Journey

The typical franchise buyer journey occurs over six process steps or phases. The franchisor's process may not mirror the typical buyer journey, so I identify the steps I believe you should take in a linear order, after self-directed research when you are ready to engage with the brand. If you are looking to acquire an existing business, you will most likely engage in this process while working with a franchisor, but you will also have additional steps while working with a business broker or the franchisee seller.

These are the six steps:

Step 1: Initial interview

Step 2: Qualification (financial/skills/experience) and prequalification for financing

Step 3: Reviewing the Franchise Disclosure Document (FDD) and franchise agreements

Step 4: Due diligence (franchisee validation, financial modeling, and applying for financing)

Step 5: Discovery Day (virtual or face-to-face)

Step 6: The decision

Step 1: The Initial Interview

Step 1 is an initial interview and often a presentation of the franchise concept, usually conducted by telephone or video with a representative of the franchisor whose job it is to recruit you.

The Two Franchising Philosophies of Franchisors

When you engage with a franchisor, you will be talking to people who employ one of two possible philosophies or approaches to their job – a sales philosophy or an executive recruitment philosophy. It's important to know who you're talking to.

The first is a sales philosophy. They believe their job is to sell you a franchise. Therefore, whether or not you like them as people, they may prove to be a danger to you. They pay less attention to whether you have the requisite background, skills, or necessary capital for you to succeed in the business, minus obvious disqualifiers or basic minimums. They want to know if you are a "closable deal" and meet their minimum financial requirements.

They often gloss over or ignore evidence that you lack the transferable background, skills, and experience that would put your investment at risk. They won't ask the necessary questions or invest the time to do a deep dive to get to know you as a person and a professional. They won't put in the work or effort to see how closely you match the franchisor's profile of a successful franchisee or communicate areas of possible concern.

FPG has been mystery shopping brands for CEOs for 20 years. In 20 years and counting, FPG mystery shoppers have never been adequately interviewed for a franchise. Not one time. We've only been asked self-serving questions, such as:

- "Why are you looking for a business?" (To determine your hot buttons and motivations)

- "What does your family/spouse think about you opening a new business?" (To determine downstream resistance)

- "Why haven't you started a business like this before?" (To determine what's stopped you in the past so they can craft answers to your future objections)

- "How much money do you have?" (To determine if you meet financial minimums, but not what is optimal)

- "What market are you looking at?" (To determine territory or site availability)

Not one time have our mystery shoppers been asked relevant work-related questions, such as:

- "What do you consider to be your greatest skills?"

- "What do you consider to be skill sets you need to improve?"

- "What types of job functions do you know you like to do or want to see more of?"

- "What types of job functions do you dislike and aren't suited for?"

- "Knowing what you know now about this business, what do you think it takes to succeed as a franchisee?"

- "What do you think it would be like for you to manage employees like ours?"

- "What do you think it would be like for you to serve customers like ours?"

- "From your perspective, why do you think this franchise is a fit for you?"

If the franchisor was going to hire a manager to run a corporately owned territory rather than recruit a franchisee to run the same business, there is no doubt in my mind the manager candidate would be vetted more thoroughly than the franchise candidate.

> Franchisors who believe franchisee recruitment is a sales role will hire salespeople to pitch you a business, increasing your risk.

The second philosophy is one of executive recruitment or talent acquisition. They, like you, want to determine if you will be successful as a franchisee of the brand they represent. They will ask you probing questions like the ones I listed. To reinforce observations, they may also run behavior profiles to help predict your skills and aptitudes relative to what is necessary as a franchisee. They may run values assessments to determine culture fit, or how closely your value system matches the stated organizational values. These professionals may also come from a sales background, but generally employ a consultative approach, knowing that candidates don't want their business per se, but are looking to employ time, money, and energy to produce a desired outcome, which requires some understanding. They are there to help you and at the same time safeguard the brand. All things equal, these are the franchisors you want to do business with. Generally speaking, this caring philosophy is overarching and determines how the franchisor interacts with franchisees.

The Franchise Sales Organization (FSO)

The person running point when you start your conversation is sometimes not an employee of the franchisor, which can also create more mischief. This person can be an employee of a cottage industry of franchisor service providers called Franchise Sales Organizations (FSOs). I own an FSO, so obviously I am not opposed to the franchisor employing FSOs. I am, however, vehemently opposed to the way many FSOs conduct themselves in the marketplace.

Many FSOs charge a retainer and are awarded a commission if you join the chain. This compensation structure on face value is not bad, because it rewards performance. However, how the philosophy by which the recruiter approaches their role will determine whether you increase or decrease your risk as a franchisee within that system.

As their name suggests, FSOs are often sales organizations, so they often approach their role as salespeople would. You aren't a person; you are a transaction. They don't determine fit; they determine how likely you are to buy.

For this very reason, I won't call the service we provide franchisors an "FSO," although categorically this is correct. Because we employ a recruitment philosophy, I call us an "outsourced franchisee recruitment solution." We see it as our role to understand and predict which candidates offer the brand the highest probability of success. Therefore we have the discipline and the integrity to walk away from franchise candidates whom we predict are at higher risk or don't fit the corporate culture. Why? Because we are also entrepreneurs, we have great respect for what you bring to the table and a genuine concern for your financial and personal well-being as well as protecting the integrity of the brand.

During a training session I led for franchisee recruitment professionals, a woman asked me, "What should I do if I have two candidates looking at the same territory?"

I answered, "I would share with each party that there was interest in the same territory, and our policy is to award the franchise to the first qualified candidates who commits to the brand."

Another gentleman blurted out, "So you would do a classic take-away," which is salesperson's speak for a manipulative technique to fake taking something away from the buyer as a way to coerce them into buying sooner than they would prefer. In other words, he heard me the way a salesperson listens.

I corrected him. "Absolutely not. That's critical information each buyer needs to know to make an educated decision, because sometimes entrepreneurs have to make decisions with imperfect information and imperfect timing. I would rather a qualified candidate tell me no than be blindsided by me telling them no."

> You can determine whether you're being sold or recruited by the questions your primary point of contact asks. You should have an experience of being thoroughly interviewed, qualified, and screened, as if you are a key leadership hire.

In my opinion each franchisee is occupying a key leadership position as the chosen market leader ensuring that the brand is built within their territory. There is only one way to build a powerful national brand in franchising – one franchisee, one territory, one neighborhood at a time.

The Interview

Often the first interview is 45–90 minutes, a give-and-take of information. This is a "getting to know each other" step, where you help the franchise representative understand who you are, what makes you successful, and what you are looking to accomplish. The franchise representative in turn helps you understand who the franchisor is, what makes the franchise opportunity unique, and who makes a successful franchisee. You both begin the process of determining whether your skills and aptitudes match the skills and aptitudes required to succeed within the franchise. It is designed to give you a quick gut read about whether the franchisor's KASH model of success (discussed in Chapter 4) is in alignment with your personal KASH model and your objectives can be met with a high degree of probability. When done correctly, you should experience an honest and robust give-and-take of information you can trust. When done incorrectly, you will experience being pitched. That doesn't necessarily mean this is a bad opportunity for you. It does, however, usually mean the brand doesn't pay careful attention about who joins their chain, which can create organizational chaos downstream.

Smart franchisors will offer you collateral information about the brand and what it takes to win as a franchisee. They want you to go into business with your eyes open and with carefully managed expectations.

Step 2: Qualification

The overall objective of Step 2 is to determine whether there is a fit from the franchisor's perspective. If you create an open and honest dialogue with the franchisor, they will probably see the potential fit before you do because they have an insider's perspective on what it takes to win. If for whatever reason you don't possess the necessary KASH or capital (from the franchisor's perspective), you want to find out now, before you have invested significant time and money into the investigation process. If from the franchisor's perspective you do have the proper capital and KASH, you still need to verify the details and performance levels of the other franchisees to see whether there is a fit from your perspective.

Most franchisors will have you submit a financial statement at this time. They may not have you submit a resume and give you a behavior or skills assessment or a profile, which may predict your level of success. That isn't necessarily bad on face value, but again it doesn't show the level of concern about who joins their franchisee community as other brands who do. Take the initiative to submit a resume even if you're not asked and offer the franchisor an inventory of your skills akin to the worksheet I offer in Chapter 4 (the section entitled "Determining Your Starting KASH Balance"). Ask the franchisor pointed questions they should be asking you, such as "I have never sold your product (or service) before and don't have outbound sales experience; how does that add to my risk?" You may have the franchisor representative roleplay a sales call so you know what one feels like. You may ask them if you can fly or drive to a franchisee's market to shadow them on a sales call. A reputable franchisor will encourage this. A disreputable franchisor will try to sell you on the idea that such diligence is unnecessary or will blow off your concern or, worse, gaslight and manipulate you by saying something like, "Sounds to me like you lack confidence. Are you sure this business is for you because we have several other candidates vying for the same territory?"

Early in my career, Mobil recruited me for a senior franchisee recruitment job at their beautiful new franchisee recruitment and training center, complete with an indoor fully functional gas station and convenience store, even with its own striped parking lot and pumps. During an all-day series of face-to-face interviews at their ivory tower corporate office, a Mobil-proud senior manager in HR said to me, "Tell me why you are excited to join Mobil." My honest answer was "I am still investigating. Most of my career has been with small entrepreneurial companies so I don't know how I would fit into a Fortune 500 corporate culture and that's what I am here to find out." His face immediately changed, and I didn't get offered the job. As it turns out, I am an entrepreneur, I don't do office politics, I often take a contrarian position, and I freely speak my mind. That's why these same executives continue to hire me as an outside consultant yet would never hire me as an employee. And I don't blame them.

So I encourage you to be brutally honest and vulnerable during your interviews and investigation process. Ask tough questions. The right entrepreneurial environment values straight shooters.

They should also offer you some information about the historical unit-level economics of the business to help you quickly determine if the business meets your minimum return expectations.

The franchisor may try to shortcut your investigation process by encouraging you to read their Franchise Disclosure Document (FDD) and talk to successful franchisees. I encourage you not to proceed until you can answer these questions:

- What makes this business unique, profitable, valuable to the customer, and sustainable for the long haul?

- Can I see myself running a business like this? Can I see myself working with the employees and serving these customers?

- What does it take to win as a franchisee?

- What are the requisite skills, education, and background of a successful franchisee? Do I appear to match the profile of a successful franchisee?

- How do successful franchisees spend their day? Can I see myself doing this?

- How does this business scale?

- What is the investment? What may be financed? Does this investment match my risk profile?

It is about this stage that you will be asked to fill out a personal financial statement.

At this early stage, many franchisors accept a financial summary statement like this and won't make the request for asset verification. They simply want to see a financial line of sight to qualify you for startup costs, working capital, or a path to financing. I encourage you to submit a financial summary and be transparent with information. Unless instructed otherwise, don't provide social security numbers or banking account information. Some franchisor representatives don't understand finance, and they may try to pull credit in a way that dings your credit at a time you want your credit score as high as possible.

I recommend you do a *soft credit pull* (which does not impact credit) by visiting one of the credit bureaus such as Equifax, Experian, and TransUnion, and then send the franchisor a screen shot from their computer showing their score. Again, anything over 660 is good for SBA-backed loans.

Fun fact about credit scores. Earlier I told you my brother does actuarial work for insurance companies. He told me insurance companies try to create predictive indexes to assess risk, to better predict which people are most likely to create traffic accidents or other mischief that insurance carriers would have the burden of paying out. He said that regardless of the algorithm and complexity of the custom predictive indexes insurance companies create, the best predictor of insurance risk is a simple credit score. A good score (anything in the 700-plus range) is an indicator of good character, personal responsibility, conscientious driving, someone unlikely to commit crime, and I therefore assume more likely to succeed than someone with bad credit.

Financing Options

This section explains how most people finance businesses. These aren't mutually exclusive; some franchise candidates combine two options, such as a HELOC and an SBA loan. I prioritized this list according to what is typically the lowest-cost and easiest-to-access financing sources.

- Home equity line of credit (HELOC)
- 401(k) rollover/self-directed IRA

- SBA
- Friends and family
- Partnerships

The following sections look at the advantages of each.

HELOC (Home Equity Line of Credit) or Home Refinance

Advantages:

- Low interest rate.
- Highly flexible. Interest only if necessary. No set repayment schedule.
- Low documentation. You don't need to write a robust business plan or disclose where the funds will be utilized.
- Conserve your cash and liquid assets. Helps your business be more resilient. No prepayment penalties.

Important considerations:

- You can borrow a total of up to 80% and sometimes 90% loan-to-value (LTV). To determine LTV, multiply the value of your home by 80% and then deduct your current outstanding balance of your mortgage(s). Certain states may not allow second mortgages. Real estate appraisals are required.
- You need to demonstrate your ability to repay loans through your existing sources of income prior to approval. Projected income generated from your new business will not be considered. A general rule of thumb to determine your ability to pay is to multiply your current household income by three. That will give you a conservative estimate as to what total mortgage

a bank may approve you for. So the ultimate math will look something like the example shown in this table.

Household Income	$150,000
3x Household Income	$450,000
Current Home Value	$500,000
80% Home Value	$400,000
Outstanding Mortgage	$150,000
Estimated Financing Available	$250,000

It's important to remember to apply for this financing before you leave your job and start a business.

401(k) Rollover/Self-Directed IRA

Advantages:

- Allows you to start your business using qualified 401(k) and IRA funds with no declared income or 10% penalty.
- Low documentation. You don't have to write a robust business plan or participate in elaborate loan closing.
- Conserve your cash and liquid assets.
- Pay yourself the interest, not the bank.

Considerations:

- Many people consider their retirement plans a "nest egg." You need to start looking at your business as your nest egg.
- Determine if the combination of the interest you save and income you make as a franchisee will beat what you will predict the stock market will give you.

SBA Loan

To qualify for a SBA-backed small business loan (see SBA.gov), you must meet the following criteria.

- 660 credit score or above
- No criminal convictions
- No bankruptcies for at least seven years

Advantages:

- Government-backed loan; eliminates bank's risk
- 20%–30% Cash injection; conserve your cash
- Reasonable cost of money; typically 2.5–3.0 points over prime
- No prepayment penalties
- 7–10 year payback
- Scalable (You can access additional capital with less collateral to open more units once you have a track record of success.)

Considerations:

- Longer process than others; often 90 days or more
- High documentation; often requires 60–90 days to gather and complete necessary paperwork
- Balance of the loan often requires 100% collateral. If most of your collateral is in home equity, you should consider HELOC before SBA.
- Work experience is an important consideration for attaining a loan.

Friends and Family

Advantages:

- They know you.
- Typically flexible on repayment terms because of your previous relationship.
- May bring certain areas of expertise into your business.
- Loans may not require collateral.

Considerations:

- If business performance is not what is predicted, it may impact important relationships moving forward.
- If friends and family are seeking equity in the business, see "Partnerships."

Partnerships

Advantages:

- Synergy – partners should have complementary skill sets and add value to each other.
- There is greater leadership and management capacity, and ability to grow faster together than apart.
- There are more eyes on the business.
- Individual partners may have more time flexibility.

Considerations:

- Partners divide the rewards and equity. This may be the most expensive source of financing.

- Business relationships are different from family and friendship relationships.
- Partners need to have discussions about who is responsible for what, who is investing what, and how partners divide income, shares, and benefits.
- It's hard to dissolve without impacting the business.

> Franchisors should have banks and vendors they can recommend to help you finance your business.

Once you complete the qualification and business overview step of your investigation process, a franchisor may not offer you official approval for a franchise because it's still early in the mutual investigation. However, any skilled franchisor representative who isn't supremely confident you will be approved when the time comes will either end your investigation process or stall it in order to communicate what you are missing and give you the opportunity to provide it. For instance, you may be missing basic computer skills, which may disqualify you as a franchisee. A skilled, high-integrity franchisor may ask you to take some computer classes and invite you back into the process once you offer some proof of completion (such as a certificate).

Determine Your Next Steps

At this stage in the franchise investment process, the franchisor gives off one of two experiences:

- You will have an experience that the franchisor is making a genuine effort to get to know you. You will feel like they are listening for what you want your life to look like, and if they can't produce your desired results, you would expect them to tell you.

- You will experience "being sleazed." You will have heard from the franchisor, "Not everyone will be awarded a franchise," or "You better keep the process moving forward because we have other candidates looking at the same area." In sales, they call this "doing a take-away." The franchisor representative is merely testing you to see whether you are a viable buyer or if you are wasting their time.

At the end of the mutual qualification step, make an evaluation about whether you want to take the next step in the process. Don't concern yourself yet with having to someday write the franchisor a big check. That day isn't today. Skilled franchisors are not going to put any pressure on you at this point to make any decisions other than deciding if you want to move forward in their investigation process and gather more information. Some franchise sales representatives may ask you questions such as "If you had to make a decision right now, what would it be?" Answer however you choose to answer.

If the franchise recruiter seems overly anxious, it could mean they are simply happy to have you in their pipeline. Only about 5% of people who request information about a franchise actually take the step to submit their financial qualifications. Although submitting financial qualifications only takes minutes and obligates you to nothing, franchisors recognize it is a big emotional step for you to take. They pay attention to people like you. In the eyes of the franchisor, you have elevated yourself from the 99% who don't do anything to the 5% who have taken at least one bold step of committed action and have the potential of being a franchisee in their system.

Step 3: Reviewing the FDD

During Step 3, you conduct a business review of the terms and conditions of the FDD (Franchise Disclosure Document) and make sure you and the franchisor are in material agreement on all major points. The FDD is a document the Federal Trade Commission (FTC) mandates each franchisor to offer franchise candidates. This section explains each item of the FDD, what each item means, and the types of information you should or should not find there. Some states may require additional disclosure information in the FDD than the FTC does. However, often state-by-state changes are nonexistent or are so minor they aren't worth discussion.

There are two ways to look at an FDD. The first is through the eyes of a businessperson. From a business perspective, does the FDD make sense? Can you live with the terms and commitments of the agreement? I don't recommend investing in a franchise attorney at this point, because FDDs are written in plain English and should be pretty easy to understand. Having read hundreds of them, I will walk you through the FDD, saving you time and money. Afterwards, you can bring the FDD to an attorney, who will review it from a legal perspective. Once you have established the franchise fits and you are close to making a decision, it will be time to conduct a legal review and uncover any legal risks that may exist. Again, in Step 3 of your investigation, I assert that conducting a legal review may be premature and an unnecessary expense.

While the FDD defines the legal obligations between you and the franchisor, the true relationship between franchisees and solid and reputable franchisors transcends the obligations outlined in the FDD and franchise agreements. These are deeply committed personal relationships. When franchisees and franchisors pull out the franchise agreement to define their relationship, it is because the personal relationship has been damaged and trust has been violated. You will be able to measure how often this sacred trust has been violated as open and closed lawsuits are disclosed here. I discuss this as I detail each section.

Although it may not be described in these words in the FDD, the real working relationship between the franchisee and the franchisor is a social contract, not a legal one.

In the social contract, the franchisor agrees:

- To do whatever it takes (within reason) to give franchisees the tools, help, and support necessary to win
- To maintain the integrity of the brand

You agree:

- To master the franchisor's business model
- To deliver products and services to your customers to the best of your ability, consistent with the spirit and intent of the franchisor
- To maintain the integrity of the brand

Franchisees' profitability is the lifeblood of any franchise organization. If franchisees are not profitable, the franchise system eventually collapses like a house of cards. There is no way to build a successful franchise system other than by building on the successes of profitable franchisees.

However, no franchisor is going to expressly state in a franchise agreement that it is their responsibility to make you successful. They develop tools and systems for you to use. You make yourself successful using the franchisor's tools and systems. They are going to place the responsibility squarely on your shoulders and the FDD will reflect this.

All FDDs follow the same format, mandated by federal and state regulators. They all consist of 23 items, plus franchise agreements, and any exhibits and appendices or any additional licenses a franchisee has to sign, such as a software license.

This section reviews the first 23 items. Before you sign a franchise agreement, you should hire an attorney specializing in franchising, which is not the expertise of every contract lawyer.

You should also have an accountant review your financial projections and the franchisor's three years of audited financials if you do not have the background or sophistication to do it yourself. A franchisor's financial statement is too complex to discuss here. Have their finances reviewed by a professional before you invest to determine the franchisor's long-term viability. Pay attention to such things as cash reserves, EBITDA, and short-term and long-term debt.

Item 1: The Franchisor, Its Predecessors, and Affiliates

This item gives you a brief history of the franchisor, how it came to be, and what business they are in.

What to look out for:

- If a franchisor has fewer than seven years of operating corporate units or territories business model, this dramatically increases your risk. They may be testing their model with your money. However, if its key executives have substantial experience in similar businesses, your risk may be lessened.

- If the franchisor has not successfully opened multiple locations or territories, they have no proof of replicability and scalability, which again increases your risk. However, if they are proven multi-unit operators of similar brands in similar industries, your risk lessens.

Item 2: Corporate Officers and Business Experience

This section offers you background on officers and decision-makers. What to look out for:

- Do the officers have franchise experience? Have they grown other franchise chains before? If so, how successful are these past chains currently? Did these executives move onto another challenge after giving the chain stability or jump ship after they ran aground? Franchising is often described as a closed society. Many franchise professionals bounce around from company to company because companies look for experienced franchise executives. Keep in mind "experience" doesn't always mean "competent." Check leadership profiles on LinkedIn. Do you see a track record of long-term sustainability or job hoppers?

- Since many franchisors are family run, many family members are named officers, not because of merit, but because of their last name. Are they qualified to hold those positions?

If this is a team who has never scaled a successful and sustainable brand, this increases your risk. If the brand is small, unit-level economics are strong, and the leadership understands franchising and has a demonstrated track record of growing meaningful brands, this increases your chances of success.

Item 3: Litigation

Pay attention to this section. Franchisors need to disclose in this section which people (identified in Item 2) have pending civil, criminal, or other actions alleging violations of franchising, antitrust, securities law, and unfair or deceptive trade practices. They have to disclose a full 10-year history of such activity. Be mindful that we live in a highly litigious society, so some legal disputes are normal and acceptable.

I once took a small poll of franchise attorneys and experts that showed 50% of those polled thought it was acceptable if 1% or less of their franchisees engaged in some form of litigation. For instance, if a franchisor has 200 active franchisees, it would be normal to see two cases of litigation (past or pending). Another group of franchise attorneys and experts stated that you should look more at the nature and severity of the litigation rather than the percentage. Either way, litigation is an indicator of a breakdown in the franchisee-franchisor relationship. Even if the franchisor is winning these cases, use caution. Remember, the agreement is designed so they win. It doesn't mean the franchisor is innocent.

Item 4: Bankruptcy

Affiliates, predecessors, partners, and officers must disclose, over a 10-year period, any personal bankruptcies and bankruptcies of companies that they owned or were officers in or if they declared bankruptcy within 12 months after their tenure as an officer. While bankruptcies are more common and less stigmatized now than in the past, still pay attention. In a bankruptcy, someone who is supposed to be getting paid isn't. While the people declaring bankruptcy may have followed the proper legal processes to discharge their payment obligations to pay their creditors, you have to make a determination as to whether they have discharged their moral obligation to honor their commitments. Why is this important? Franchisors typically promise you little in their written franchise agreement. The success of a franchisee-franchisor relationship transcends any legal obligations that exist. It is built on a foundation of morality, integrity, ethics, and trust. Bankruptcy is a legal maneuver to cancel personal and corporate commitments and obligations. What is legal isn't always moral. If they used the legal system to cancel their commitments to others in the past, it is possible they will do the same to you in the future.

Even if no moral issue exists, bankruptcy is usually a clear sign of business failure. Again, the past, left unchecked, has a way of repeating itself. Find out what the officers or people involved learned from their bankruptcy. Unless they have taken steps to put measures in place to prohibit this from ever happening again, take caution.

> COVID-19 threw a monkey wrench in many businesses, outside the businesses' control. It's important to see how the franchisor responded to existential organizational threats to their business. Many executives shined, pivoted fast, put the brand on their backs, and marched downfield. Others were slow to respond, leaving franchisees wallowing and directionless.

Item 5: Initial Franchise Fee

This section is to include all the fees and payments to the franchisor to open the business. If the franchise fee is not uniform, such as in larger or smaller territory fees, the franchisor needs to disclose how these fees are determined. Most franchisors charge $35,000–$50,000 for franchise fees for single-unit territories (which may not provide a protected territory). Many franchisors will discount franchise fees if franchisees invest in three units (or territories) or more upfront.

Beware of franchisors who take large franchise fees (over $50,000) upfront. Franchisors who do this understand they are priced higher than what most franchisors charge. Sometimes franchisors will charge a higher franchise fee if their business model produces exceptionally high financial returns. Some charge high fees in order to pay a franchise broker $25,000 or more to find you, meaning they charge you to pay their broker, increasing your risk with zero benefit to you. Here's another kicker – because franchise fees are supposed to be uniform to all buyers, if the franchisor works with franchise brokers

The Ultimate Guide to Responsible Franchising

yet you learned about the brand on Google or Facebook, you get no discount.

Item 6: Other Fees

Franchisors must disclose all recurring fees or payments that franchisees pay the franchisor and affiliates. They must also disclose how they compute those fees.

Those fees are typically:

- **Royalties.** Royalties are the lifeblood of any franchise organization. Royalty rates fluctuate depending on the size, nature of the business, level of ongoing support, and financial returns. Most franchisors in the service, retail, and food sectors charge 4%–8%. However, there are currently over 70 different industries represented in franchising and different industries have different norms.

- **Marketing (brand) fees.** Many franchisors charge a marketing or brand fee of 1%–2% of sales, which should be considered a second royalty. Some franchisors use these fees to offset the salaries of their marketing department and offer little measurable value to the franchisees. Others develop marketing content, websites, applications, and other valuable tools that would be cost prohibitive for you as a single franchisee to produce on their own. Some franchisors will stipulate a minimum level of local advertising expenditure such as Google Ads. They maintain the right to audit your marketing spend but generally do not collect such fees.

- **National (or regional) ad co-ops.** The vast majority of franchisors in the United States have fewer than 100 units, and it can take 600 units or more (depending on the type of business) to have the critical mass necessary to be able to afford national advertising and serve the customers it will reach. Some national ad funds may not be able to effectively market the brand. Keep in mind these fees are above and beyond the national marketing or brand royalty. If the franchise you are looking to join has the necessary critical mass within the United States or within a region to benefit from mass media (radio and television advertising) or aggressive social media spends, these funds can offer franchisees substantial value. Where no such critical mass exists, these funds may offer little value beyond ego gratification to the franchisees and could be considered a second royalty. How much a franchisor charges and where these funds are allocated speaks volumes about the competency and integrity level of the franchisor. Skilled, high-integrity franchisors will want you to spend your advertising dollars where they are best spent to drive brand awareness and customer trial, regardless of whether it is on the local, regional, or national level. If they can create leverage by co-oping the advertising expenditures of their franchisees on a regional or national level in order to create substantial buying power, it is in everyone's best interest that they do so. And responsible franchisors will. Look closely at how this money is collected and where this money is spent. Also look at whether the franchisees have any say through committees, task forces, or advisory boards.

- **Technology fees.** The right tech stack helps franchisees manage their business properly and efficiently. Franchisors will often leverage existing technologies, threaded together to create their stack. Some franchisors elect to develop custom programs to suit their needs and the needs of their franchisees. If franchisors have custom applications, that means they have to hire programmers and other tech specialists to manage, adapt, enhance, and debug their stack. This always complicates the franchisor model, so generally I am not a fan. These fees are pushed to the franchisees, which drives their costs up, which I am not opposed to as long as the benefits exceed these incremental investments. Many franchisors charge technology royalties, meaning the higher a franchisees' sales, the more they pay for technology, penalizing performance. Since most tech companies charge the franchisor on a per-user basis, tech fees are usually flat to the franchisor. I like to see tech fees passed along as is to franchisees. Unless the franchisor incurs costs outside of typical vendor relations and feedback loop, I don't like to see the tech stack as a profit center for the franchisor.

- **Transfer fees.** Franchisors will charge you a nominal fee (generally less than the franchise fee) to train and develop the purchaser of your business. This is of great benefit to franchisees because once they sell their business, the franchisor will help with the training, development, and transition of new ownership. The seller is then free to focus on what is next. This fee usually only triggers with a change of ownership.

- **Renewal fees.** At the end of the term of your franchise agreement, franchisors charge a nominal fee to renew the agreement for another term. A typical franchise has a 10-year agreement and a 10-year renewal option. Renewal fees are typically less than the cost of a new franchise, to encourage renewals.

Beware of what contingent liabilities you possess, if any, if unfortunately your business does not succeed. You may be personally guaranteeing 10 years or more of minimum fees regardless of whether you are still in business. I know a franchisor who charges damages to further penalize failing franchisees for going out of business and tarnishing the brand as if the franchisor has no responsibility for their franchisees' failures. I call this the "kick franchisees when they are down" clause. You see this primarily with franchises that have a minimum royalty clause. It may not be expressly written that minimum royalties continue post termination. However, more likely than not, you will be personally liable for your financial obligations to the franchisor, which is not unreasonable. There have been cases where franchisees signed a corporate guarantee, and as soon as they were open, they de-identified their business, operated with the franchisor's know-how, and failed to pay the franchisor royalties. So bad faith can go in two directions. You should only sign an agreement where you have no additional liabilities except perhaps a noncompete and a confidentiality clause that says you agree not to share trade secrets.

There was a residential home services franchisor who used to waive these fees as long as the existing franchisee would sign a non-disparagement agreement, meaning they can't badmouth the brand. So when franchise candidates reach out asking about the brand, they either refuse those calls or make up stories in order not to violate the non-disparagement agreement, but putting the new franchise candidates' investment potentially at risk. There is a FTC guideline that says franchisors cannot engage in steering, which means prohibiting franchise candidates from equal access to all franchisees for feedback. While this may not be steering according to the FTC guidelines, it basically accomplishes steering by tying past franchisees hands with a gag order. Ask the franchisor if such non-disparagement agreements exist, because the FTC does not currently require franchisors to disclose such agreements.

Item 7: The Initial Investment

Your total investment is broken down into categories such as franchise fee, equipment, leasehold improvements, inventory, grand opening advertising, pre-opening expenses (such as travel and lodging for training), and working capital. You get to see where your money goes. You also get to see when the cash gets dispersed. In a typical franchise (aside from the franchise fee and some proprietary products), most of this money will go to outside vendors and contractors and these expenditures do not represent a profit center to the franchisor.

Most skilled and high integrity franchisors will do whatever it takes to help keep your front-end investment as low as possible so as not to deplete your cash and to increase your chances of survival.

The one cost franchisors have a tendency to underestimate is the working capital. *Working capital* is the cash you need to inject into the business to cover operating costs until the revenues generated can cover all your costs and you reach your break-even point. The Federal Trade Commission only requires franchisors to disclose *three months* of working capital. Since many businesses do not break even until after 6–12 months (some even longer), this number can be misleading and perhaps patently false while still being legal. Make sure you know how long it takes to break even so you possess enough working capital.

DO NOT TRUST THE WORKING CAPITAL NUMBER IN ITEM 7. The correct working capital is the cash you need to invest until your business produces positive cash flow. Any additional capital you need to live on during the launch would be in addition to that.

The correct working capital number is personal to you. It includes how much cash you need to float your business until the business achieves break-even, meaning revenues exceed expenses. You need to include any debt service and income you must derive from the business to meet your household expenses. This will not be disclosed in your FDD and you need to do the math.

Therefore, the initial investment listed in the FDD is not the full tally of your total risk. You may be personally liable for royalties, rent, and other liabilities that exist above and beyond your initial investment. Know your risk. Franchisors often present this table as if this is your total risk, which is seldom the case.

Item 8: Restrictions on Sources of Products and Services

Franchisors must disclose your obligations to purchase products and services from the franchisor, affiliates, or approved suppliers.

It is reasonable for a franchisor to mandate who a franchisee purchases from to maintain consistency and quality. However, talk to other franchisees to make sure these products are reasonably priced with reasonable terms and can't be purchased elsewhere for a lower price. Some franchisors will generate revenue from your purchases in the form of rebates from the supplier. They will negotiate an attractive national price and then keep a percentage of the savings for themselves. While not entirely bad, negotiating best prices is a service skilled franchisors offer franchisees as part of the value of their royalties. These franchisors will often pass the entire cost savings along to the franchisees. A rebate may be justified in lieu of lower royalties. There are companies who have no royalties and depend on profits from franchisees' direct purchases or rebates from other suppliers for their revenues.

Many years ago, Quiznos mandated that franchisees purchased their food from Quiznos at what the franchisees claimed was an unreasonably high markup. Franchisees posted on social media how they could purchase items cheaper at local discount retailers than they could from national suppliers, placing the franchisees in jeopardy because customers' price sensitivity and stiff price competition would not allow the franchisees to pass these added expenses their competitors did not have on to Quiznos customers. Franchisees were often faced with bad choices: honoring the franchise agreement, buying from approved suppliers and losing money, or going rogue and buying the same supplies locally cheaper to protect their investments and keep their businesses afloat.

If you take a step back, you can see the different ways unskilled or low-integrity franchisors can put their hand in franchisees' pockets without knowing exactly how much is being taken. Those ways include:

- Marketing funds
- Technology fees
- Rebates to the franchisor from franchisees' purchases

High-integrity and highly skilled franchisors will fully disclose and want you to know what your investment is now and in the future without hidden or hard-to-calculate fees or surcharges. They will take their money in royalty payments or in other disclosed ways. For those high-integrity franchisors who sell proprietary products and services, they will take reasonable markups and offer you reasonable terms. They will disclose exactly what those markups are.

Item 9: Franchisee's Obligations

You will receive a detailed list of everything you will be held responsible for, including (but not limited to) such things as:

- Purchases
- Initial and ongoing training
- Compliance standards
- Restrictions
- Warranties
- Quotas or minimum performance levels
- Fees
- Insurance

- Advertising minimums
- Staffing requirements
- Submitting to inspections and audits
- Record keeping
- Dispute resolution

Since this is a legal document, this section can be dense. It can also appear very threatening. Don't be spooked by the language. The franchisors are protecting the interests and investments of the franchisor and other franchisees. They make sure their agreements have plenty of teeth in case they are forced to protect the brand. You want to do business with a franchisor who has a solid reputation with its franchisees for win-win problem-solving, which you can measure if you return to Item 3, which details litigation.

Item 10: Financing

Franchisors who offer franchisees direct financing will disclose the terms and conditions here. However, most franchisors will direct you to outside lenders and leasing companies and do not finance franchisees themselves.

Any franchisor you select should have a good track record of SBA loan repayment.

Item 11: Franchisor's Obligations

The franchisor must disclose the services they will perform prior to your business opening, such as:

- Training (location, duration, and subject matter)
- Site selection assistance/lease negotiation
- Construction assistance and design assistance

- Advertising
- Permitting
- Software support

Here is where you often run into "legalese." You will read paragraphs that state such things as, "Although not obligated, from time to time and at their own discretion, the franchisor may do [this and that]."

Most reputable franchisors promise little in the way of support in their FDD as a legal maneuver to avoid responsibility in the case of a rogue lawsuit by a franchisee. I don't like it, but I get it and don't on face value disagree with their need to do that to protect other franchisees' investments. When it's time to talk to franchisees in the system, detail what a franchisor actually does above and beyond what a franchisor is legally obligated to do. This is one instance where corporate policies often exceed promises.

Item 12: Territory

If the franchisor offers protected territories or territory restrictions, how they determine territory descriptions and what those restrictions are will be spelled out here. Your actual territory description will appear in your franchise agreement.

We hear sad stories in the media about struggling franchisees from prominent fast-food chains like Subway who feel they are too close together and competing for the same customers selling the same product under the same brand. This is why I believe having protected territory is such an important issue. The franchisor should know where the bulk of your customers are coming from and protect your interests. For instance, if you own a quick-service restaurant, most of your business will come from within an 8–10 minute drive time from your location. Therefore, franchisors should keep their restaurants at least a 15-minute drive time away from each other.

I do believe some territory overlap is prudent to dissuade the competition from staking a claim and camping out at your borders. Franchisees often come from the mentality of "Sure, I want to grow the chain, but not in my backyard." They feel threatened by another franchisee coming into their geographic area, even in a noncontiguous trade area, thinking, "This new franchisee will restrict my ability to grow in the future." Franchisors, on the other hand, want to keep the territories small in an effort to gain critical mass, dominate the market, and outpace their competition. Because of this dynamic, franchises many times will not achieve the same critical mass other centralized chains such as Starbucks has achieved. That is why Starbucks chose company-owned stores over franchised. Threats from franchisee litigation would have doomed the "Starbucks on every corner" strategy.

Some franchisors reserve the right to open company outlets within your territory, operating under the same brand name or perhaps under a different brand name. Their thinking is if you are not upholding the standards of the brand, then they can open up in your territory and protect their interests. However this also gives them the legal right to steal your brand equity if you are a top performer. Few franchisors would ever consider doing this but may still reserve the right. Most agreements give franchisors plenty of other protections, making such clauses unnecessary.

I will go out on a limb here and say if these clauses exist, regardless of the brand, this is a deal killer because you cannot mitigate your risk. A franchisor can legally drive your business into the ground evoking this clause, and you can do nothing about it. Feel free to tell them I said so!

Item 13: Trademarks

Franchisors must disclose which trademarks, service marks, names, logos, and symbols they use to identify the franchise business. They must disclose if these are registered with a United States Patent and Trademark Office, the corresponding dates of registration, and proper identification numbers. If franchisees will not have such protection, the franchisor must disclose this lack of protection. If a franchisor cannot protect its trademarks, it is entirely possible you can build your brand and have a competitor coming into the same market and advertise to your customers, using your name, logo, or slogans. Any franchisor that cannot protect its brand is not a franchisor you want to sink your money into.

Item 14: Patents, Copyrights, and Proprietary Information

If a franchisor owns patents or copyrights, they must be disclosed here. Franchisors will often make general references to their proprietary business systems and trade secrets in this section. If a franchisor doesn't own patents or copyrights, depending on the industry, it might be okay. For instance, a residential cleaning franchise such as Molly Maids or The Maids may use the same vacuum cleaners as other competitors, but the power of their franchise system is not dependent on proprietary technology of their vacuums. Their genius is in how they find, manage, and retain good help, satisfy existing customers, and market for new customers. Other chains, like Lawn Doctor, a large national lawn service business, have proprietary equipment and chemicals that give them a competitive advantage in the marketplace and add value to their system. Most franchisors do not have patents, and most do not need to in order to be competitive.

Item 15: Obligation to Participate in the Actual Operation of the Franchise Business

If a franchisor is going to require you to work full time in the business, it will be disclosed here. Many franchisors require you to work full time in the business, putting forth your best efforts in the early stages so your business makes it and your investment is protected. Other franchisors, such as Sport Clips and Great Clips, national hair care franchises, may want you to keep your job or other business interests so you can plow all your cash flow back into their business in order to accelerate your growth.

Many franchisors are now promoting their businesses as "semi-absentee," meaning they claim you can start the business on a part-time basis and build a robust cash-flowing business on the backs of loyal and responsible employees. I see this quite a bit with service franchisors, particularly in the residential home services space or businesses promoted by franchise brokers who get paid if you buy a franchise, regardless of whether you succeed. An honest and reputable franchise broker will act consistent with your best interest, but many will not. If you find such a franchisor or broker who is touting the value of absentee or semi-absentee ownership, this claim may be exaggerated, so be skeptical and exercise caution. For most businesses, I find the owner's effort more in year one, not less. It's hard and time consuming to successfully launch a business. I see the promise of semi-absentee largely as an empty promise. Ask seasoned franchisees the likelihood you can succeed starting the business on a part-time basis or launching successfully leveraged employees.

Item 16: Restrictions on What a Franchisee May Sell

Franchisors must describe your obligations to sell only goods and services they approve. They must also disclose any restrictions they will impose on the customers you can sell to. For the most part, this is entirely reasonable. At one time if you were a Dairy Queen franchisee, you could sell anything including egg rolls. You can see how this could create brand confusion. Warren Buffet bought the chain and standardized the menu. I think egg rolls got yanked.

Item 17: Renewal, Termination, Transfer, and Dispute Resolution

Franchisors will present a table identifying the following:

- The length of term of the franchise.

- Renewal or extension terms.

- Requirements for a franchisee to renew or extend.

- How a franchisee can terminate their agreement. Many franchisors do not give franchisees the right to terminate their agreement. They expect them to sell the franchise to a new owner in order to protect their royalty stream. This is normal and acceptable. This also prevents a successful franchisee from suddenly taking down the franchisor's brand and putting up their own brand and forgoing royalty payments.

- How the franchisor can terminate their agreement without cause. Pay particular attention to this section. Most franchisors do not reserve any right to terminate your agreement without cause. It is not normal, nor is it generally acceptable for a franchisor to reserve this right.

- How the franchisor can terminate their agreement with cause. For instance, a franchisee may be selling unauthorized, inferior products to their customers. A franchisor may default on them as a result. As long as the products are removed from the store within an agreed time frame, the franchisee will be marked back in compliance. If they refuse, they run the risk of having their agreement terminated.

- "Non-curable" franchisee defaults, meaning a franchisee has no opportunity to correct a problem and it is grounds for immediate termination of their franchise agreement. For instance, a franchisee may be convicted of a felony, which may allow a franchisor to immediately terminate their franchise agreement. As long as a guilty verdict is reached, a franchisor may reserve the right to protect their brand and move swiftly by terminating the agreement without further hearing. This is normal and reasonable to protect the integrity of the brand and the interests of franchisees.

- Franchisee's obligations upon nonrenewal or termination. If a franchisee elects not to continue in their business or is terminated, they may have certain obligations, such as taking signs down and turning in their confidential operations manual and proprietary marketing materials, and paying outstanding balances.

- Assignment of contract by franchisor. Franchisors will typically reserve the right to sell their own business and assign their obligations to the acquiring party. This is normal and acceptable.

- How to transfer your business. Franchisors will discuss acceptable methods of selling your business to a third party. They will typically reserve the right to approve who you are selling to and require the new buyer to go through their training programs. Most franchisors will charge you a transfer fee to cover their expenses to train and support the new owner. Some franchisors will reserve a first right of refusal to purchase your business. In other words, you may receive an offer from someone who wishes to purchase your business for $100,000 cash. A franchisor may reserve a window of opportunity to purchase your business for the same $100,000 cash. If a franchise candidate offers you some obscene amount of money that the financial statements cannot support, the franchisor may step in and kill the deal to avoid a future failure.

- What will occur if you die or become disabled and incapable of running the business. Franchisors will typically give your heirs or estate six months or so to sell the business to a new owner.

- Noncompete clauses during the term of the franchise agreement and after the agreement expires, is terminated, or you sell your franchise. It's important to know that the laws of your state supersede the terms of your franchise agreement. Some states don't enforce noncompetes.

- Modification of your agreement. This agreement details the steps you and the franchisor must take if you both agree to modify your franchise agreement in any way.

- Dispute resolution. Some franchisors will restrict how you resolve disputes. For instance, many franchisors require you to waive trial by jury and resolve your conflicts by binding arbitration. Some franchisors even require that you present your case first to a panel of fellow franchisees and key employees of the franchisor. In case of legal action, many franchisors require you to resolve your dispute in the state they are located in and under the jurisdiction of their state laws. Usually this means travel expenses and additional attorney fees on your part, raising your motivation level to try to resolve these issues outside of costly court battles. This is normal and typical.

Item 18: Public Figures

Franchisors need to disclose any financial arrangements they have with public figures in the use of their franchise name or symbols. Franchisors using public figures in this capacity run a high risk. For instance, at one time Kenny Roger's Roasters was a very popular and high-growth quick-service chicken chain. Then Kenny Rogers got caught up in a highly publicized phone sex scandal, which tarnished his image and that of the franchise brand. Sales suffered.

I was standing next to a Subway multi-unit franchisee the moment Jared Fogle's allegations of child pornography and sex trafficking hit the news. According to Technomic, sales fell by more than 3% and the following year for the first time in history Subway closed more stores than it opened.

I recommend you carefully consider the risks of doing business with any franchisors who are attached to high-profile people, such as sports figures, politicians, or celebrities. In the short run, a sports figure or celebrity social capital can be highly beneficial to the brand because endorsements work. In the long run, dirt can come out that can tarnish the brand by association. The media tends to build celebrities up and then rip them down.

Item 19: Financial Performance Representations (FPRs)

If a franchisor makes a FPR, it must be in this section. Some franchisors fear the legal risk and simply don't do it. Others have weak unit-level economics and therefore aren't transparent with results. However, more and more franchisors are honoring the requests of franchise candidates who want this information disclosed.

The accepted legal standard is that this information must be historical data (actual results) and representative of the brand. In other words, the results disclosed must be historical and still attainable by franchise candidates investigating the brand.

FPRs can take many forms. Franchisors may elect to disclose some or all of the following:

- Average sales
- Average sales by thirds or quartiles, to give you an understanding of high versus low volumes
- Geographic results where some markets outperform others
- Ramp ups: what are typical sales for year one, year two, year three, and so on
- Some franchisors will disclose P&Ls of franchisees or of corporate locations

I applaud franchisors who disclose as much as possible without manipulating the data, respecting the franchise candidates' time, money, and energy and doing as much as the law allows to help candidates ensure fit and mitigate risk.

Some disreputable franchisors will tell you they don't offer any FPG information because the FTC prohibits it. This is completely false. They choose not to disclose such information for generally one of two reasons:

- They don't collect and monitor the data. Do you really want to do business with a franchisor who doesn't know how their franchisees are performing?

- The numbers are poor and they choose not to disclose. Do you want to do business with an unprofitable franchisor?

Neither look is good.

Item 20: Outlets and Franchisee Information

Here you will find an updated owners list, giving you the street addresses of the franchise locations, as well as the franchisees' names and phone numbers for you to contact. You will also receive a three-year trendline of how many franchisees opened, terminated, were acquired by the franchisor, closed, or ceased operations, and the net number of units or territories that remained open.

If a franchisor has a high failure rate, listen to the reasons why. If you hear them put the responsibility squarely on the franchisees by making comments like "Well, if the franchisees had followed the system, they wouldn't have failed," keep probing. Isn't the franchisor responsible for bringing the franchisees into the system? Isn't the franchisor responsible for training and developing franchisees on their systems and holding them accountable for executing their business strategy? Doesn't the franchisor share equally in the responsibility of franchisees' failure?

Ask follow-up questions like, "What is it about your recruiting methods that you are bringing in the wrong people?" and "What is it about your operating system that so many franchisees are refusing to or unable to execute it properly?" If you see franchisors absolving themselves of responsibility for their franchisees' poor performance, then chances are if you struggle, they won't know how to help you, either. Inexperienced or unsophisticated franchisors look at franchisees' failures as just that – franchisees' failures. They look at franchisees' victories as the system working. They take ownership of the victories and absolve themselves of responsibility for their losses. Consider eliminating them from consideration.

Top quality, responsible franchisors see the franchise network as one body consisting of the franchisor, franchisees, and perhaps even suppliers. If one member suffers, than the body suffers. If one member wins, the body rejoices. Franchisee victories are their victories and franchisee failures are their failures. If a franchisee is struggling, they will look at potential system failures as well as look into why the individual franchisee is suffering. They will ask, "What (if anything) in our system allowed for this event to occur?"

As it relates to franchisees selling their franchises, it is normal and predictable for a mature franchisor (10 years as a franchisor or more) to have upwards of 10% of their franchises for sale. Many franchisees keep their business roughly 7–10 years. To put this in perspective, according to a March 1, 2023, article in *RedFin*, the average American sells their house every 12 years and the US Bureau of Labor Statistics show people keep jobs on average for four years. As you call franchisees, if you get a sense more than 10% of franchisees are selling, this may not be an indicator of a problem. However, if you see a three-year spike, probe for reasons why franchisees are exiting. Something may not be working within the system, and disgruntled franchisees want out.

Look also closely at Projected Openings, particularly information about franchise agreements signed but not opened (called SNO). This is a recent epidemic where overzealous franchisors upsell unwitting franchise candidates to take on more territories than they can realistically open at time frames that simply don't work. If you are being pressured by franchisors to make a land grab, pay attention to this section. Don't tie up your funds trying to open several unprofitable territories at the same time, which sucks your cash and jeopardizes your investment.

Item 21: Financial Statements

Franchisors must disclose audited financial statements in accordance with generally accepted accounting principles, and balance sheets. If you do not know how to read a financial statement, bring this section to an accountant for review. Pay particular attention to items such as:

- Cash on hand. The lower the cash balance, the more temptation a franchisor has to sell you a franchise and build their cash reserves.

- Long-term debt. Make sure the franchisor isn't so heavily financed they can't reinvest back into their system.

- Cash flow. Make sure the franchisor is cash flow positive, or in the case of a new franchisor, is on track to become cash flow positive shortly. You want to see more cash flow tied to royalties than to franchise fee revenue, otherwise franchisors have intense pressure to close deals to keep their lights on, meaning unqualified or unskilled franchisees may make it into the system, potentially tarnishing the brand.

- Balance sheet. Make sure the franchisor has assets in the company and has something at stake. Some franchisors show statements with fewer assets or net worth than the investment level they require franchisees to make. This is upside down. Franchisors should have as much or more at stake than franchisees.

When it's time, bring the three years of audited financials to an accountant to analyze the financial health of the franchisor.

Many franchisors are privately held companies and franchise under a shell corporation to limit their liability and therefore keep assets out of their company, which may explain some poor financial statements.

Item 22: Contracts

Franchisors will provide copies of all documents you are required to sign in this section, including the franchise agreements, lease or financing agreements, and so on. The terms of the franchise agreement should accurately reflect what is stated in the FDD.

The franchise agreements and other contracts and licenses should all be cataloged in this section and the full agreements will generally appear as an appendix.

Item 23: Receipt

This is a document you sign that states you acknowledge receiving the FDD, which the franchisor is required to provide you by law. Signing this document simply offers the franchisor some protection that they provided you with the FDD, but obligates you to do nothing.

Read your FDD, keeping these points in mind. Highlight anything in the FDD that appears off, that you are uncomfortable with, or that you simply cannot agree to. Make an appointment to review these with the franchise recruiter.

If you hire an attorney, make sure you are hiring an experienced career franchise attorney to review these documents. Franchising is a highly nuanced business. I've seen franchise candidates unnecessarily run up thousands of dollars in legal fees on attorney comments that an experienced franchise attorney would never have made because they have an understanding of how franchising works and what is and isn't normal.

Step 4: Due Diligence (Franchisee Validation, Financial Modeling, Applying for Financing)

The purpose of Step 4 is to interview franchisees, gather data, compare the information you receive from franchisees with what you received from the franchisor, and determine whether you will produce your desired results with a high degree of probability. This is a period of intense data gathering and heavy analysis. This is where you test the veracity of the franchisor's systems and determine whether the franchisor is skilled. If the franchise appears to produce your desired lifestyle with a high degree of probability, it is time to make some investments in professional advice. You need to have a franchise attorney review your FDD and an accountant review your business plan.

Franchisee Validation Best Practices

Franchisee validation is a series of conversations with franchisees designed to ultimately help you make a final determination about how to produce the desired results you seek as a franchisee. This guide will assist you in getting the most out of this step. As a general rule, you will find franchisees to be open, honest, and willing to answer all types of questions, including the most important questions about unit-level economics, that is, making money.

Consider that franchisees may have many franchise candidates calling them all the time. They are not paid to field calls, nor are they obligated to do so. They donate their time to franchise candidates in the same way others donate money to charity. And like money, their time is finite and valuable. Respect their time by doing the following:

- Prepare your questions in advance.
- Limit your conversation with a franchisee to 15 minutes.
- Spread your questions out over multiple franchisees.
- Request an appointment after finding out the best time for them to speak. Just because you reach them by telephone or they are on premise when you stop in, that doesn't mean it's a good time for them to speak with you.
- Be flexible. Some franchisees may want to speak with you during off-peak business times.
- Be inquisitive and willing to be educated. Validation calls are not to disprove the concept, but to get insights on what works to create top performance, and common mistakes to avoid.
- Thank them for their time. They may invite you to call again as needed.

If you have basic questions about the brand, it's best to reserve those questions to ask your franchise recruiter. Ask franchisees questions about their experience as a franchisee. Don't be afraid to ask questions about sales, margins, profitability, and how this business ramps up. While some may hesitate to tell you what their specific individual stores are doing, they can tell you chain averages, regional averages, and what you can expect to achieve as a franchisee.

There isn't any magic number of franchisees you should call. Most franchise candidates call between three and eight franchisees before they have heard enough consistent and predictable information. Franchise candidates with a higher risk tolerance seem to call fewer, and more cautious franchise candidates will call more. It's important that you hear some consistency of information and manage your expectations accordingly.

It is a good idea to get a well-rounded view of the business at each stage of the business lifecycle – The Launch, Grind, Winning, and The Zone (see Chapter 5). If you are talking with a franchisee who has been in business less than two years, they are often in The Grind, so their feedback might be biased because they are working hard to get established but often haven't seen the full impact of their efforts yet, which can at times be frustrating for them. However, they can be a great source of information on what to expect and how to approach the early parts of building your business, as well as what activities to focus on and skills to build.

Franchisees in the Winning stage can verify consistent numbers, success metrics, and financial returns, and how these are generated. These owners can also share insights on the best operational and management approaches to keep the business moving forward and generating profit.

Make note of where each franchisee is in their learning curve and balance their feedback accordingly. Whenever possible, I suggest you speak to owners with a similar background or career history as you. In business similar people often produce similar results.

If you are looking at a brick-and-mortar business, location is often a large factor in determining the brand potential. The skills and effort that franchisees bring to the table determine how much of this potential becomes realized, but all the effort in the world can't drive "A" results from a "C" location.

Here are sample questions to ask franchisees. These are intended to help you draw an accurate picture of the franchise opportunity:

- How long have you been a franchisee?
- What first attracted you to the brand?
- How do you rate the effectiveness of the franchisor's training and support?
- What does it take to win as a franchisee?
- What are the greatest challenges franchisees face?
- How does the franchisor help franchisees overcome these challenges?
- How do you differentiate from your competition?
- How would you describe your relationship with the franchisor?
- How would you rate the value of the ongoing training and development you are receiving from the franchisor?
- Before debt service, how long does it take to achieve break-even?
- What are customers saying about your business?
- How available is the franchisor's support team to answer your questions and offer assistance?
- Knowing what you now know, if you could do it all over again, would you invest in the franchise again? Why or why not?

Financial Modeling

It's important you get a full understanding of how the model makes money, ramps up, and scales. Much has already been written about how to read a P&L and build financial models, so I won't address those topics in detail here. If you don't have an understanding of how to create a proforma or read a P&L, hire an accountant at this stage and get their assistance in helping you build out a model and make projections.

When building financial models, make sure you know the following before you invest:

- **How does the business ramp up?** What is the revenue model? How do sales predictably grow as the business ages?

- **What is the cash flow?** Cash flow refers to the difference between the money that comes into the business and the money that goes out. Cash flow is different from net income. You determine profit by deducting all cash and noncash expenses such as depreciation and amortization and taxes. A business is cash flow positive after it achieves its break-even point.

- **What is the break-even point and when will the business achieve break-even?** Break-even occurs when revenues exceed expenses, which is the point at which the business is self-sustaining. This does not mean you are achieving your financial objectives, but generally determines the point the business will survive.

- **What are the margins?** This is the difference between the price at which a product or service is sold and the related costs associated with delivering the product or service to the customer. Margins, generally speaking, only include variable costs, such as labor directly attributed to producing and delivering the product or service as well as the costs of goods sold. Fixed costs such as financing and rent are not factored into determining margins.

- **What are the fixed expenses?** These are expenses that you will incur even if you don't generate a dollar in sales, which include such things as rent, vehicle leases, and other recurring expenses. The higher your fixed expenses, the higher your break-even point.

- **What is the projected exit evaluation?** Most small businesses currently sell for about two to four times their "Seller Discretionary Income," also known as SDI. You determine SDI by adding back nonrecurring expenses to new ownership, such as aggressive personal write-offs, and nontransferable financing and loans. Assuming a new owner could take the entire benefit of the business in one lump sum, what would that amount be? Let's assume that lump sum would be $150K to an owner-operator, the value of the business would predictably be $300K to $600K, depending on a number of factors. Compare the exit evaluation to the startup costs, and the cash-flowing business should be worth more than what it costs to start, thus building your equity.

Generally speaking, a good business ramps up quickly, surpasses break-even quickly (so it's cash flow positive), has high margins and low fixed expenses, and builds equity.

High startup costs and high fixed expenses are not necessarily a negative, although these would increase your risk. High startup and fixed expenses can also create high barriers to entry, which may keep some competition out. Remember, earlier in this book I talked about how a business needs to be unique, valuable to the customer, profitable to the owner, and defensible in the marketplace.

Applying for Financing

When obtaining financing you need to consider the following:

- What is the least expensive expansion capital available to me?
- What is the easiest to attain financing available?

- What financing strategy will tie up the least of my liquid assets to keep me resilient in the case of an emergency or slow ramp up?

The most common methods franchisees use to finance their franchise are covered in detail in a previous section under Step 2, "Financing Options." Don't select a financing option without first running it by the franchisor. Certain franchisors already have one or more of these financing relationships for you to leverage. Consider consulting an accountant to help you build a business plan.

Step 5: Discovery Day (Face-to-Face or Virtual)

Many franchisors hold all-day face-to-face business meetings known as "Discovery Day" or "Meet the Team Day." Many franchisors have abandoned this practice due to lingering concerns they or their franchise candidates have over COVID-19 or other contagious diseases. As a general rule, don't do business with a franchisor whose leadership you have not met. While you may not get facetime with the CEO of larger brands like McDonald's, do your best to gain access to leaders who have the power to add to or diminish the value of your investment so you can ask them tough questions. You are entrusting your dreams and capital to the care of the franchisor leadership. Decisions made on the executive level may significantly impact whether you are positioned to hit your personal objectives. If possible, go to their corporate offices, meet the decision-makers, shake their hands, look them dead in the eye, and ask them tough questions. You have already evaluated the business model against its ability to produce your desired results. Now it's time to complete your evaluation of the competency level of the franchisor's leadership in the business of franchising.

Discovery Day Preparation

Your preferred outcome for attending Discovery Day is to answer the following questions wholly and completely:

- Can I achieve my personal objectives with a high degree of probability as a franchisee of this system?
- Do my skills, background, and experience match the profile of a successful franchisee?
- Is the franchisor leadership skilled in the business of franchising and positioned to build a unique, profitable, sustainable, defensible, and valuable brand?

Right now you should be saying to yourself all of the following:

- "I can see myself managing this business. While I have more investigation to do, the opportunity appears to meet my objectives."
- "I understand what it takes to win as a franchisee and believe I have what it takes."
- "I understand the brand's corporate culture and believe I am a culture fit.
- I know how I will finance my business if I choose to go forward. I've reached out to the lending institution and started the loan approval process."
- "I understand the *franchisor's* unit-level economics and ramp up. I see how my financial objectives can be met."

If this is not where you are, you may be too early in the process to attend Discovery Day. Pick up the phone and call your franchisee recruiter and let them know what's missing. To further prepare, follow these tips:

- Get plenty of rest the night before. Be alert. This will be a fast-paced exchange of information.

- Take excellent notes.

- Work with your franchisee recruiter to make a list of questions to gather the missing pieces of information you need to decide if the opportunity is right for you. Your franchisee recruiter will help you organize your questions and make sure they are directed to the correct person on the leadership team.

- Ask for the agenda and executive bios in advance. Know who you will be talking to and prepare questions accordingly. Don't be afraid to ask the same questions to different leaders to see if they give you similar responses.

Post–Discovery Day Follow-up Activities

After Discovery Day, take a day to review your notes to make sure all your questions were answered and what new questions have arisen, if any. If you don't have an appointment scheduled to review the day with your franchisee recruiter, contact them to set up a meeting to get your new round of questions answered and to provide feedback on the day.

If you are attending a virtual or face-to-face Discovery Day after you have completed most or all of your diligence and franchisee validation calls, the franchisor will start encouraging you to wind down your investigation and make an investment decision. Many franchisors will communicate after these meetings whether you have their final approval to join the franchise. Most of the time this decision is a rubber stamp, as they would not commit all the executive time if they didn't value you as a franchise candidate.

Step 6: The Yes/No Decision

It is time to make up your mind about whether you are prepared to move forward with the brand you are investigating.

I've prepared a detailed decision-making checklist to help you think through any overpowering fears or emotions to help you isolate the data and make the most rational decision you can.

If this is your first business, you will be excited, but you may also be terrified. I was 25 years old when I purchased my first franchise and started my first business. I flew to Florida to sign my franchise agreement face-to-face. After I signed my name and presented the franchisor with my cashier's check, I politely excused myself, made my way to the men's room, and projectile vomited into the toilet like Linda Blair in the movie *The Exorcist*. Some people get excited. Others react like I did. I've spent about 25 years of my almost 40-year career self-employed. It worked out for me and, purely statistically speaking, if you pick the right opportunity it will work out for you.

Psychologists have a term called *confirmation bias*, which describes the human tendency to favor data that supports their opinions and desires and dismiss data that contradicts it. Confirmation bias plays a large contributing factor to the final outcome of the franchise investigation process.

Back in the mid-'80s, I recruited franchisees for Subway when Subway was a 400-unit multi-Regional chain, with restaurants open in only about 20 states. Franchise candidates used to dismiss the Subway opportunity by telling me such things as "Why did they name the chain 'Subway?' Have you ever ridden a New York City subway? There is graffiti, junk on the floor, gum on the chairs . . . no one will eat in a Subway!" I also remember at that time, Tennessee and Alabama were virgin territories with no Subway restaurants open. I was engaged in conversations with an Alabama Subway franchise candidate who dismissed the opportunity while telling me unequivocally, "Subway is Yankee food, boy. We don't eat Yankee food in Alabama." At the time he was right. They didn't. Confirmation bias.

You have to ask yourself how well this brand holds up to scrutiny. I threw much at you throughout this chapter. Chapter 12 summarizes this information in the form of a decision-making checklist.

Your Final Decision Checklist

This chapter summarizes a list of questions primarily into "yes" or "no" responses to force you to choose to better understand your risk. I understand that most of these questions could be answered on a spectrum, but at this stage of your investigation, I want to cut through the noise and mind clutter to help you identify where the brand is competent and where your risks will predictably come from so you can do your best to head them off. *Special thanks to my colleague Alicia Miller for compiling this list.*

Questions About the Brand

- Will this brand be successful over the long term?
- Does this brand have the potential to become iconic?
- Does this brand have the potential to scale to Regional leadership status? National? International?
- Does the brand have a clear identity, make a clear brand promise, and offer real and perceived value to customers that exceeds price?
- What are the brand risks or threats (competition, technology, emerging products, regulatory, other)? Does the franchisor have a reasonable and workable strategy to mitigate these risks?

- Is this franchise system organized to maximize the opportunity and fulfill the brand promise?

- What is the consumer value proposition? Is the value proposition unique, profitable, and defensible?

- What is the brand reputation (online reviews, social media platforms, net promoter scores, consumer ratings, and so on)?

Questions About Fit

- Is this brand the best use of my time, capital, and best efforts compared to other available investment options?

- Can my objectives be met with a high degree of probability?

- Is this brand the best fit for my skills? Do I match the profile of a successful franchisee?

- What are my personal risks?

  - What is the total investment, including working capital, to achieve break-even?

  - What cash do I need to set aside to pay my personal expenses until the business can support me?

  - What contingent financial obligations exist (such as real estate leases, SBA loans, equipment leases, and so on)?

  - Do the financial returns justify the risk and the investment?

  - Do I accept the risk?

- What are the key deal terms in the franchise agreement?

  - What am I obligating myself to?

  - Am I willing to do what I am obligated to do?

Questions About the Franchise Opportunity

- Once my business is built, what will it predictably be worth? How does this compare to the startup costs?

- How long will it take to achieve my personal financial goals? Is this acceptable to me?

- What is the revenue and profitability trajectory of the franchisee community?

- Are existing franchisees expanding and taking on more units or territories?

- How many closures has the franchisor experienced? Are underperforming franchisees operating above what it takes to survive or are they in danger of closing? What will the impact be on the brand and other franchisees?

- How many franchisees up for renewal actually renewed their franchise agreement? How many are up for renewal and how many are expected to renew?

Questions About the Franchisor

- Is the leadership team skilled in operating both the consumer-facing model and the franchising model?

- How well is the franchisor capitalized? (If necessary, hire an accountant to review three years of audited financial statements.) Do they have the resources to achieve their objectives?

- What is the franchisor's cash flow and earnings trajectory? Is the franchisor profitable now and predictably into the future?

- What if any pending and past litigation exist that can threaten the brand?

- Where is the franchisor on the franchisor lifecycle (Early Stage, Emerging Growth, and so on)? How well are they positioned to move through the next inflection point?

- What is the corporate culture of the franchisor? Do I fit?

- How is the quality of the franchisee-franchisor relationships?

- When asked, "Knowing what you know now, would you make the same decision again?" would more than 80% of franchisees say yes?

- What are the key vendor relationships and supply chain? Are the terms reasonable and is supply dependable?

- Do franchisees receive the necessary training and support to rapidly move them through the learning curve, past break-even, and into profitability?

- Is the size of the organization large enough to support the service needs of the franchisees?

- Are the systems up to date?

- Is the technology stack up to date and the data secure?

- Would franchisees say the value of the training, tools, support, and brand equity is equal to or greater than I would be contributing in royalties?

Questions About the Industry

- What is the trajectory of the industry? Is the industry growing above the rate of inflation?

- How does the industry segment? What are the submarkets within the broader market?

- Which segment does this brand currently occupy?

- Does the brand possess a unique and defensible position in the marketplace?

- What is the size of the available market and estimated brand's market share?

- Who are the competitors? How well is this brand positioned against competition?

What Can I Count on Myself For?

After asking yourself these questions and examining your responses, what final decision do you come up with?

As long as the opportunity appears solid and the franchisor appears skilled in both the consumer-facing model and the franchising model, there might only be one more question to ask yourself.

Are you the type of person who can be counted on to get the job done, even when you don't know how at the time? Are you resourceful and impactful? In the face of imperfect information and tight resources and deadlines, do you find a way to produce acceptable results?

Do you work just as well with no supervision as with constant supervision? Do you need micromanagement to stay focused and produce your best?

In the end you can only count on the franchisor to create opportunity. You must count on yourself to actualize the brand's potential.

In my experience, the best predictor of future success is past performance. Winners find a way to win. If you have not been successful in your past career, you can't count on the business to make you successful. On the contrary, *you* make the business successful. If you have a spotty career or entrepreneurial track record, you may need to do more introspection by identifying skill deficits and investing time, money, and energy in addressing your weaknesses before you put significant capital at risk.

If you are a first-time businessperson with a successful career trajectory, on one hand it should be comforting to know that you possess the tools it takes to win as an entrepreneur. On the other hand, it may also be terrifying. You just might be out of excuses.

Conclusion

In 1985 I was 21 years old and fresh out of college when I took my first job in franchising. At the time I had no idea what franchising was or how it worked. I recruited new franchisees and penetrated new markets for Subway, who at the time had about 400 restaurants open in about 20 or so states. I used to ask all franchise candidates the same question: "Why are you looking at Subway?"

I expected to hear things like, "It's a safe investment, everyone has to eat," or "It's a noncooking restaurant and easy to manage," or "It's a small restaurant with low overhead costs," which of course came up in conversation, but it was almost never the primary driver.

People used to pour their hearts out to me. I would hear stories about firings and layoffs, economic uncertainty for families, careers that were stagnating or stopped, and dreams that were left unfulfilled. Within a few months I came to the conclusion that people really didn't want the business at all; it was a means to achieve an end. They wanted extraordinary lives and careers. They wanted to make a difference for themselves, their families, and their communities, and they were willing to put some or all of their finances at risk to do so. They were brave, if not heroic.

I remember thinking as a marketer, is there a greater product to represent than someone's dreams back to them as a reality if we do business together? I knew at that time that this was all I was ever going to do. Fast-forward almost 40 years, and this is almost all I have ever done.

I want to tell you two stories that changed the trajectory of my career and that hopefully will add value to you.

The first was 9/11. At the time I lived in northwestern Connecticut in the Berkshires, about 100 miles from Ground Zero. Just as there were rumors circulating about additional bombers in the air possibly hitting other future targets, we had rumors in Connecticut of terrorists spotted poisoning our water supply. It was three o'clock in the morning of September 12, and I was sitting alone in my kitchen, sipping coffee, wondering if I should wake up my wife and three kids, pile them in the minivan, and drive to safety in Montreal, about five hours away.

Then all of a sudden I heard a booming male voice, clear as a bell, powerful enough to bounce off the walls. It seemed to come from everywhere at once, rather than a singular direction. I immediately recognized it as the Voice of God, audibly speaking just as in the Old Testament. God spoke only two words: "Get writing!" That's it. Despite the clarity of the command, I still had no idea what He meant because I had never written anything.

I remember thinking, "I live in the Berkshires! Get a writer! They're a dime a dozen around here." Pulitzer Prize–winning novelist Philp Roth lived a few miles away from me off a lonely dirt road. I was thinking God should wake him up and sit him at his laptop. After a short period of resisting, I tried to do what God demanded of me, and I began writing.

Since that time, including this title, I've written five books on franchising, a fictional novella, and I've written or contributed to about 100 articles on entrepreneurship and franchising for such publications as the *Wall Street Journal, USA Today, Fortune* magazine, *Entrepreneur,* and many more. This was never my goal or the direction I wanted to go with my career.

The second God encounter was a little more than 20 years ago. I had written what at the time were two training programs for franchisors, considered the gold standard in my field. I was sitting in my office full of ego, thinking about the early success I was having as a trainer and consultant.

Then God made Himself known again. This time it wasn't audible. It was like a body of knowledge was jammed into my chest with the force of a blow. Because the knowledge wasn't verbal, I will frame it in words the best I can.

God communicated, "This isn't your intellectual property, It's Mine. Take these ideas and publish them." I was shocked. I remember thinking, "Well I guess I am out of business. Who hires trainers and consultants with no proprietary intellectual property and methodology?" So I chunked down my manuals into long articles and published them. Keep in mind, this was before content creators and social media strategies existed, and platforms like LinkedIn were relatively new. Shockingly, not only was I not out of business, but work came pouring in at unprecedented levels. These articles seemed to give a voice to franchising leaders who couldn't fully express what they believed. I still get work from articles I wrote decades ago.

So why am I telling you this?

There's an old saying, "There are no atheists in foxholes." I find this to be similarly true for entrepreneurs. For first-time businesspeople, starting your business will alter you at the core, and most likely alter your family trajectory for generations. I've witnessed a pattern of entrepreneurs producing more entrepreneurs.

Second, whatever business you start will most likely feel bigger than you. Sometimes your business turns out to be a vehicle to explore what or who is bigger than you.

If you are an entrepreneur or an entrepreneur-in-the-making, then business will be your chosen form of self-expression. In the introduction, I presented myself as a failed artist and here in the conclusion I shared how I've morphed into a writer. Whether as an artist or an author, to succeed you have to have something to say to people who want to hear it, otherwise you might as well be screaming into an echo chamber. If you don't have an audience, you can't monetize.

Business is no different. Consider that your products and services represent you. Your employees represent you. Your brand should stand for what you stand for. In many ways, you are your business, so your business should give you a voice.

The 7 Habits of Highly Effective People by Steven Covey is often heralded as one of the most influential business books of all time. But I think Covey made a greater contribution that few talk about. He wrote a follow-up book called *The 8th Habit,* which is to find your authentic leadership voice and inspire others to find theirs. Covey agrees that, in the end, business is about self-expression, a catalyst in an overall process of you becoming more like you.

Artists tell an old story about a conversation Michelangelo had with an admirer of a sculpture he made of an angel. The admirer asked, "How can you make such a beautiful angel out of a block of marble?"

Michelangelo replied, "The angel was always there. I just removed what wasn't."

My hope is this book helps you find your authentic entrepreneurial voice, resulting in you being more like you and creating a business that makes thunder.

Acknowledgments

I want to acknowledge all the good folks at Wiley who brought this work to life. In particular, I would like to thank Zachary Schisgal and Amanda Pyne (who reached out to me with the book idea), Sangeetha Suresh (managing editor), and editor Kezia Endsley, who edited my words to make me sound all kinds of smart.

I would like to acknowledge all my clients, past and present, who allowed me to study their brands and ways of doing business to help me create clarity about what does and doesn't work for franchisors, franchisees, franchise candidates, and the brand as a whole.

I want to acknowledge all franchising professionals who take an emotionally invested stand for the financial success and well-being of the franchisees they are responsible for. I hope this work can provide you with a detailed guide to assist you in cultivating a corporate culture that acknowledges, honors, and celebrates the investment, risk, and everyday efforts of individual franchisees.

My sincere hope is that this book clearly articulates the thoughts and beliefs of all franchising stakeholders who take a positive stand for responsible and ethical franchising.

About the Author

Joe Mathews has been in franchising sales and leadership roles since his first days out of college in 1985. He was among the first 40 employees at the corporate office at Subway, at a time when they had only 400 locations. In 2002, Mathews founded Franchise Performance Group to provide a full-service, outsourced franchise development solution for franchisors. Since then he has worked with 150 different brands, including Mobil, Dunkin' Donuts, Midas, Arby's, Marco's Pizza, Mountain Mike's Pizza, Stratus Building Solutions, College Hunks, and other National, Regional, and Emerging Growth brands.

Mathews has written five books on franchising: Amazon.com bestseller *Street Smart Franchising* (Entrepreneur Press) and self-published industry trade publications *The Franchise Sales Tipping Point, Developing Peak Performing Franchisees, How to Create a Franchise Sales Breakthrough, Guaranteed*, and *The Future of Franchising*.

He has also written or been featured in almost 100 articles and podcasts on franchising, including *USA Today, Fortune, Businessweek, Working Woman, Wall Street Journal*, and *Entrepreneur*. Joe was the creator and instructor of two classes for the Institute of Certified Franchise Executives (ICFE) and wrote the ICFE study guide section on franchise sales and lead generation.

Mathews resides on a small barrier island in North Florida with his wife and fellow franchising professional, Tara Merchant, where every Friday night is pizza and date night.

He currently has two hobbies: entrepreneurship and pickleball. He's only good enough to get paid at one of those.

Index

317

319

Index

Initiative, destruction, 157
Inner critic, attention, 28
Innovation, 157, 164–165
Interest rates, high level, 176

J
Job security, security, 175

K
Knowledge
  building, focus, 88
  gaps, 88
  KASH element, 72–73
Knowledge, Attitude, Skills,
    Habits (KASH), 98
  acquisition, 102
  franchisee acquisition, 105
  franchisor KASH distribution,
    86–92
  gap analysis, conducting,
    74–75
  possession, absence, 253
  starting balance,
    determination, 75–80,
    254
  success, formula/model,
    72–81, 85, 106, 252–253
Kroc, Ray, 117

L
Large-scale franchisee
    consolidators,
    emergence, 226
Late-stage Emerging Growth
    brands, classification,
    177–178
Launch (franchisee stage), 83,
    85–86, 93–97, 291

attitude, 94–95
habits, 96
knowledge, 94
skills, 95–96
success, strategies, 96–97
Leaders
  facilitator role, 155–156
  price leaders, 165–166
  service leaders, 166
Leadership
  collaborative leadership,
    encouragement, 202–203
  inexperience, 131
  KASH starting balance
    element, 77
  members, identification, 189
  mistakes, linear progression,
    141
  plan deviation, 233
  strategic plan, 193
  technology savviness, 193
  thought leadership brands,
    170
Learning
  curve, 96, 99–100, 102, 183
  organization, creation, 202
  process, 97, 104
Learning management system
    (LMS), usage, 234
Lifecycle, location
    (understanding), 183
Life disruptions, minimization,
    167–168
Lifestyle brands, 168
Litigation (FDD item), 266–267
Loan-to-value (LTV),
    determination, 257